AGENTS OF HOPE

Other Fortress Books
by Donald Capps

Deadly Sins and Saving Virtues (1987)

The Depleted Self:
Sin in a Narcissistic Age (1993)

Reframing: A New Method
in Pastoral Care (1990)
(1990 Academy of Parish Clergy Book Award)

AGENTS OF
HOPE

a pastoral psychology

Donald Capps

FORTRESS PRESS   MINNEAPOLIS

AGENTS OF HOPE
A Pastoral Psychology

This publication is designed to provide accurate and authoritative information in regard to the subject matter covered. It is sold with the understanding that the publisher is not engaged in rendering legal, accounting, or other professional services. If legal advice or other expert assistance is required, the services of a competent professional person should be sought. *From a Declaration of Principles jointly adopted by a Committee of the American Bar Association and a Committee of Publishers.*

"The Mean Words of Jesus" is from *Sleeping Preacher* by Julia Kasdorf, copyright © 1992 Julia Kasdorf. Reprinted by permission of University of Pittsburgh Press. The first ten lines from "Integrity" are reprinted from *The Fact of a Doorframe: Poems Selected and New, 1950–1984* by Adrienne Rich, copyright © 1984 Adrienne Rich, copyright © 1975, 1978 W. W. Norton & Company, Inc., copyright © 1981 Adrienne Rich. Reprinted by permission of Adrienne Rich and W. W. Norton & Company, Inc. "Suspended" is from *Evening Train* by Denise Levertov, copyright © 1992 Denise Levertov. Reprinted by permission of New Directions Publishing Corporation. "You are the future" is from *Twenty Poems from the Book of Hours* by Rainer Maria Rilke, trans. Joan M. Erikson (Taucross Farm Press, 1988). Reprinted by permission of Joan M. Erikson. Unpublished poem "Hope" by Joan M. Erikson is reprinted by permission of the author.

Scripture quotations unless otherwise noted are from the New Revised Standard Version Bible, copyright © 1989 by the Division of Christian Education of the National Council of the Churches of Christ in the United States.

Cover design: Brad Norr Design

Library of Congress Cataloging-in-Publication Data

Capps, Donald.
    Agents of hope : a pastoral psychology / Donald Capps.
      p. cm.
    Includes bibliographical references and index.
    ISBN 0-8006-2578-1 (alk. paper) :
    1. Hope—Religious aspects—Christianity. 2. Pastoral counseling.
    I. Title.
    BV4638.C267   1995
    253.5'2—dc20   94-31466
                                              CIP

Manufactured in U.S.A.   AF 1-2578

99   98   97   96   95   1   2   3   4   5   6   7   8   9   10

To the memory of Frank H. Hanson

"Through him we have obtained access to this grace in which we stand, and we rejoice in our hope of sharing the glory of God. More than that, we rejoice in our sufferings, knowing that suffering produces endurance, and endurance produces character, and character produces hope, and hope does not disappoint us . . ." (Rom. 5:2-5, RSV)

CONTENTS

Acknowledgments   *ix*

Introduction: Grounded in Hope   *1*

1. The Need for Hope: Three Pastoral Cases   *8*

2. The Origins of the Hopeful Self   *28*

3. The Experience of Hoping   *52*

4. A Woman Dares to Hope   *79*

5. The Three Major Threats to Hope   *98*

6. The Three Major Allies of Hope   *137*

7. Hope and the Reframing of Time   *163*

Index   177

ACKNOWLEDGMENTS

I am most indebted to pastors Victor Aloyo, Guy Drab, Gene Gall, and Emil Thomas for the case studies presented in this book. I also want to thank John Capps for typing the manuscript and preparing the index. Timothy G. Staveteig, acquisitions editor, Fortress Press, provided many helpful comments and suggestions. My special appreciation to Joan M. Erikson for permission to use her poem entitled "Hope" and her translation of a poem by Rainer Maria Rilke. I also wish to thank University of Pittsburgh Press for granting permission to use Julia Kasdorf's poem, "The Mean Words of Jesus," W. W. Norton Press for permission to use Adrienne Rich's poem, "Integrity," and New Directions Press for permission to use Denise Levertov's poem, "Suspended."

This book is dedicated to the memory of Frank H. Hanson, who was the first and for many years of my life the only pastor I knew. About midyear in our second year of confirmation under his tutelage, he told our class that if we worked diligently through our catechetical and Bible instruction we would have a month or so at the end of the year when he would teach us about astronomy, his favorite avocation. The class was insufficiently diligent, and he expressed his disappointment that there would be no astronomy lessons that year. Yet the memory of this "nonevent" has remained with me ever since, as he had communicated to us that learning doctrines and credal statements is fine as far as it goes, but there is also a large universe out there, and we should want to know of it and learn of our place within it. His hopes for our class had not been realized, but mine for the ministry, and my potential within it, had been awakened. As a line from William Stafford's poem "Vocation" puts it: "Your job is to find what the world is trying to be."[1]

1. William Stafford, *Stories That Could Be True: New and Collected Poems* (New York: Harper & Row, 1977), 107.

introduction

GROUNDED IN HOPE

My purpose in this book is to explore the role that pastors play as the agents of hope. In my view, what pastors have uniquely to give others is hope. Where other professionals may offer hope as a byproduct of what they do, the offer of hope is central to what pastors do. Oftentimes, it is all that they can offer. To be a pastor is to be a provider or agent of hope.

Although written for pastors, this is not a "how-to" book. I intend that this book help pastors become more effective and confident in their task of providing hope to others, and I therefore hope that it will be a practical book for them. But the problem with "how-to" books is that they give so much attention to strategies of overcoming certain problems that they neglect to give adequate attention to understanding these problems. Moreover, when readers of "how-to" books try to put what they have read into practice, they often discover that it doesn't work out the way the book says it should, mainly because the problems are more complex and intractable than the "how-to" book represents them to be.

The other side of the coin is that many pastors through years of experience are already proficient at what they do and are not in need of a "how-to" book. What they are looking for is confirmation that *what* they are doing is what they *ought* to be doing. This book is confirming in this sense, as it seeks to provide theoretical support for what many pastors already construe their ministries to be about, namely, the agency of hope.

This book is about the nature of hope: what it is, and how it influences our daily lives. It also addresses what it means to be without hope and explores what makes the difference between hope and hopelessness. It gives particular attention to the importance of maintaining

1

a hopeful attitude in life, and it identifies the factors that help us to maintain such an attitude and the factors that undermine it. With the insight thus provided into the nature of hope and what aids and threatens a hopeful attitude in life, readers should have no difficulty in discerning for themselves how they might be even more intentional in their ministry of hope. Recognizing that pastors are quite resourceful in this regard, and taking into account that each pastor's situation is unique, this book stops short of offering specific recommendations for instilling or inspiring hope in given circumstances. Books on circumstances that threaten hope—death, terminal illness, divorce, addictions, victimization—are readily available, and many books on these subjects have been written specifically for pastors.

Why is it important for pastors to have a sound understanding of the nature of hope and of its influence in our daily lives? One obvious answer, already mentioned, is so that pastors can help instill hope in other persons. Yet, an equally important answer, also already mentioned, is so that pastors will have a better sense of what makes them unique among professionals. In recent years, the line between pastoral ministry and the other "helping professions" has become rather blurred. Especially in the area of ministry of care, there is often not much that clearly distinguishes pastors from other professionals. Our predecessors in the field of pastoral care and counseling were concerned to secure a place for clergy among the helping professions (i.e., psychiatrists, social workers, psychotherapists, nurses, etc.), and they were largely successful. Chaplains are considered part of the health-delivery team in hospitals, and ministers, priests, and rabbis have ready access to their hospitalized parishioners. Pastoral counselors are also gaining the same accreditation as other helping professionals and are sometimes even better trained in psychotherapeutic methods.

Yet, as Paul W. Pruyser points out in *The Minister as Diagnostician,* the success of these initiatives has had predictable costs.[1] In gaining acceptance among the helping professions, pastors have also tended to lose their distinctiveness. In the case conferences that Pruyser witnessed as a clinical psychologist at the Menninger Foundation, ministers would often use psychiatric language in describing a patient or assessing a patient's problem. All the other helping professionals had their own language. The clergy were the only ones who borrowed the language and terminology of another. So Pruyser contends that ministers must recover their own unique language, and he made a specific

---

1. Paul W. Pruyser, *The Minister as Diagnostician* (Philadelphia: Westminster Press, 1976).

proposal toward accomplishing this, advocating the ministers' use of theological themes in "diagnosing" patients' problems from a religious perspective.

In the fifteen years since Pruyser issued this proposal there is not much evidence that the situation has changed. The distinctiveness of the ministry in relation to the helping professions is no less endangered now than fifteen years ago. Ministers are just as likely to view themselves as members of one of the helping professions, and they are just as likely to discuss personal problems in the language of one of the other helping professions.

I support Pruyser's view that ministers have a different language from that of other helping professionals, and they are therefore to be distinguished from these other professionals in the way they talk about life's problems. But language is rooted in our conceptions of the world, and I am contending in this book that the worldview that underlies the pastoral ministry is grounded in eternal hopefulness. To be a pastor means to be eternally hopeful. Other professionals may be hopeful by virtue of their own personal attitudes toward life or their own personal religious faith, but pastors are hopeful by virtue of their profession. One could say, to put it most starkly, that a pastor who is no longer eternally hopeful has ceased to be a pastor. I intend no personal indictment or judgment against such a pastor in this statement, for many pastors find themselves in situations or circumstances that are profoundly trying and in which such eternal hopefulness proves impossible for them to maintain. Yet, I believe that the basic and fundamental role of the clergy is to be providers or agents of hope, and it is terribly difficult, if not impossible, to be an agent of hope if one has oneself lost hope.

On the other hand, knowing that it is their task to be the agents of hope, pastors can be assured that they are unique among the helping professionals with whom they come into contact, often in mutually supportive ways, and this very uniqueness means that pastors need to have a working knowledge of hope and of the factors that enable us to maintain a hopeful attitude toward life. This book attempts to provide such understandings. The fact that pastors know that all they may have to offer *is* hope can make them feel vulnerable, even helpless. This book seeks to provide a better appreciation of the importance of what pastors have especially to offer and thus of the importance of their profession vis-à-vis other helping professionals.

In John Bunyan's classic work, *The Pilgrim's Progress,* the name of the friend who accompanied the hero Christian throughout most of his journey was Hopeful. As Christian entered the River Jordan to the Promised Land, the last stage of the journey, he felt himself sinking and cried out to Hopeful, "I sink in deep waters, the billows go over my head, and the waves go over me." Hopeful responded, "Be of good cheer, my brother, I feel the bottom, and it is good." But Christian continued to cry out to Hopeful, convinced that he would die in the river and never gain entrance to the gate of the city. As he sank deeper and deeper, it was all that Hopeful could do to keep his friend's head above water. When Hopeful comforted him, saying, "Brother, I see the gate, and men standing by to receive us," Christian replied that it was not himself but Hopeful for whom they were waiting. But Hopeful persisted, telling Christian that his troubles and distress were not a sign that God had forsaken him. He encouraged Christian to be of good cheer, for Jesus Christ is even now making him whole. With this, Christian broke out in a loud voice, exclaiming that he could see his Lord again and could hear him telling him, "When you pass through the waters, I will be with you; and through the rivers, they shall not overflow you." At that very moment, Christian found that the ground underneath him was solid, and as the river at this point was shallow, the crisis was over. Both men reached the other shore and were met by two Shining Ones who had been sent to minister to those who were soon to be welcomed into the house of salvation.[2]

Without Hopeful, Christian would surely have drowned. Without Hopeful's encouraging presence, he would have succumbed to despair. Hopeful then is a powerful image of the pastor, as the one who gives assurance that all will be well, that when others sink they will feel the solid ground beneath them, and that when their lives have fallen apart, the Christ is even then at work to make them whole. Hopeful is not the one who makes Christians whole—only Christ is able to do this— but is the one who holds his friend's head above water so that he can see his Christ and hear his promises. To be the agent of hope is what ministry is inherently and ultimately about. It is what makes the pastor unique among helping professionals. To put it quite bluntly, hope is the pastor's stock in trade.

A few words about the plan of this book are now in order. Chapter one focuses on three typical pastoral care cases that illustrate the importance of hope for the practice of ministry. Chapter two concerns the formation of a hopeful attitude toward life, tracing its origins to

2. John Bunyan, *The Pilgrim's Progress* (New York: Washington Square Press, 1957), 151–52.

infancy and early childhood. Chapter three develops a model of the experience of hope, focusing on the major elements of hoping and on the characteristics of a specific hope. In chapter four, the model is illustrated by another case study. Chapter five is concerned with the major threats of hope, including despair, apathy, and shame, and chapter six discusses the corresponding allies of hope, including trust, patience, and modesty. Chapter seven focuses on the reframing of time as an important contribution to an attitude of hope and considers two such reframings: the method of "future visioning," by which one takes a future perspective on a current problem, and the method of "revising the past," by which one gives the past a new meaning in light of present attitudes and intentions for the future. This chapter locates hope within an eschatological framework and demonstrates that the reframing of time is often key to forming and maintaining a hopeful attitude in the here-and-now.

This book was written shortly after I wrote *Reframing: A New Method in Pastoral Care,* a major part of which was devoted to the case of Job and his three counselors.[3] In the course of writing *Reframing,* I was impressed by the degree to which the book of Job centers on his struggle to find new grounds for hope, and by his counselors' failure to recognize that their efforts to reassure him actually contributed to his sense of hopelessness. The fact that I have identified patience as one of the three major allies of hope is due to my realization that the traditional attribution of patience to Job (James 5:11) is based on the perception that in spite of massive losses and grievous sufferings, Job never relinquished his determination to hope. What he did abandon, precisely in order to remain hopeful, was his religious orthodoxy.

While I have had interest in the subject of hope for many years, an interest first stimulated by Paul Pruyser's 1964 article on the phenomenology and dynamics of hoping and William Lynch's book *Images of Hope* published in 1965,[4] and sustained by my subsequent reading of Jürgen Moltmann's *The Theology of Hope* and my brother Walter's analyses of the tensions within the school of hope,[5] I doubt that I would

3. Donald Capps, *Reframing: A New Method in Pastoral Care* (Minneapolis: Fortress Press, 1990), chaps. 6–7.

4. Paul W. Pruyser, "Phenomenology and Dynamics of Hoping," *Journal for the Scientific Study of Religion* 3 (1964): 86–96; William F. Lynch, *Images of Hope: Imagination as Healer of the Hopeless* (New York: Mentor-Omega Books, 1965).

5. Jürgen Moltmann, *The Theology of Hope,* trans. James W. Leitch (New York: Harper & Row, 1967; Minneapolis: Fortress Press, 1993); Walter H. Capps, ed., *The Future of Hope* (Philadelphia: Fortress Press, 1970); idem, *Time Invades the Cathedral: Tensions in the School of Hope* (Philadelphia: Fortress Press, 1972); idem, *Hope Against Hope: Moltmann to Merton in One Decade* (Philadelphia: Fortress Press, 1976).

have written a book on hope were it not for the fact that Erik H. Erikson not only places hope at the very beginning of the human life cycle but also considers hope to be the very heart and soul of the religious view of life and world. Thus, this book is related to *Deadly Sins and Saving Virtues*,[6] for, whereas the earlier book centers on Erikson's schedule of virtues or essential human strengths as a whole, this one centers on the one that, by virtue of its association with the earliest stage of life, has primacy over all the others. Also, if Erikson is correct in viewing hope as the heart and soul of religion, it follows that whatever else religious professionals may be, they are the representatives of hope and witnesses to the hope that does not disappoint us.

If this book is related to *Deadly Sins and Saving Virtues* in terms of its subject matter, it is, however, closer to my *Pastoral Care and Hermeneutics* in its emphasis on the disclosive power of pastoral actions.[7] In this book, I discussed the disclosive features of pastoral actions in terms of "what *may* be happening" (i.e., what God is doing in and through "what *is* happening"). It is a natural step from this emphasis on the disclosive power of pastoral actions to our present exploration of the pastor as agent of hope, for human events are hopeful to the extent that they are potentially disclosive, reflected in the fact that those who appropriate them experience significant change (illumination, transformation, or conversion) in self-understanding.[8]

In *Time Invades the Cathedral,* Walter Capps suggested that one of the weaknesses of the "theology of hope" school associated with Jürgen Moltmann and Johannes Metz is that it failed, by and large, to address the question of the self. While its failure to do so is understandable given its concern to call attention "to the way in which preoccupation with matters of 'personal salvation' tends to conceal or mitigate the Christian's proper interest in caring for the world,"[9] Capps noted that "in an age of transition questions about the self emerge in an almost overwhelming way."[10] While I do not develop a systematic theory of the self in this book, I do give considerable attention to the role of the self in the experience of hoping. Informing this emphasis is the understanding of the self I have presented in *The Depleted Self.*[11] Thus

6. Donald Capps, *Deadly Sins and Saving Virtues* (Philadelphia: Fortress Press, 1987).

7. Donald Capps, *Pastoral Care and Hermeneutics* (Philadelphia: Fortress Press, 1984).

8. Ibid., chap. 5.

9. W. H. Capps, *Time Invades the Cathedral,* 134.

10. Ibid., 137.

11. Donald Capps, *The Depleted Self: Sin in a Narcissistic Age* (Minneapolis: Fortress Press, 1993).

I view this book as an attempt to do what the theologians of hope have been unable or unwilling to do, which is to view the matter of hope from the perspective of a Christian understanding of the self.

I invite the reader, then, to view this book as a sequel to my *The Depleted Self*, in which I explored the side of the narcissistic self that receives inadequate attention in the media and other forms of public discourse—not the self-aggrandizing, self-promoting, and self-vaulting side of narcissism, but its needy, hungry, empty, shameful, depleted underside. I tried, as best I could, to conclude that book on a strong note of hope, by focusing on the ministry of Jesus to certain depleted selves, including the woman who came to Jesus and anointed his feet with costly ointments, and the two mourners who stood under the cross—his friend and his mother—whom he bade to behold one another. In these and so many other episodes recounted in the Gospels, he gave individuals new grounds for hope and instilled in them a new sense—a new spirit—of hopefulness. In this book, *Agents of Hope,* I explore hope in a more systematic fashion, and write more explicitly and less allusively about the attitudinal or dispositional allies of hope: about trust and patience and modesty. I believe that Jesus, as revealed to us through the Gospels, exemplified these characteristics of hopefulness in his person and actions, and that the fundamental purpose of his ministry was to give persons reasons to be eternally hopeful. Persons came to him in their depleted condition, and they left with every reason in the world to be hopeful for the foreseeable—and unforeseeable—future.

one

THE NEED FOR HOPE

Three Pastoral Cases

When persons who are experiencing problems and difficulties seek assistance from a pastor, they are, in this very act, seeking hope. They may not have much confidence that the pastor can help them, but their act of reaching out, however hesitant or uncertain it may be, is an indication of their desire to hope, to find grounds for hoping rather than despairing. When the pastor initiates contact with a person who is in difficulty, the pastor, through this very gesture, offers hope. The pastor may be very cautious and tentative so as not to raise false hopes, and yet the very act of making contact indicates to the troubled person that there are grounds for hope, however hopeless the situation may seem to be.

In this chapter, I will review three typical pastoral care cases in which hope played a central role. In the first case, involving a teenage pregnancy, the pastor helped the young woman see that her situation, while very serious, was not hopeless, and therefore she should not make additional mistakes out of some misguided assumption that her life was already irrevocably damaged and beyond repair. In the second case, the pastor found himself feeling very frustrated because he could not seem to find a way to convey to a very sick woman his belief that her situation, while grave, was not as hopeless as she seemed to feel it was. In the third case, a young man was beginning to feel that his situation was hopeless because he didn't know how to stop engaging in self-destructive behavior. The pastor assured him that his situation was not hopeless, but left the clear impression that if something was not done soon his situation could indeed become a hopeless one. Thus, all three cases focus on the theme of hope and hopelessness, and all three pastors see their role as being an agent of hope. For these pastors, their ministry either succeeded or failed to the degree that

8

they were able to foster and nourish the hope that was already present and to instill hope where it seemed to be absent.

At the time this book was being conceived, these three cases played a significant role in sensitizing me to the importance that pastors assign to hope in their pastoral care and counseling endeavors. I regret that women pastors are not represented here, especially as I have every reason to believe that women and men are equally committed to engendering hope in the persons to whom they minister. These cases do, however, reflect ethnic diversity, as the three pastors are of African, European, and Hispanic descent.

"NO EMPTY HOPE"

Our first case is provided by the pastor of an African-American congregation in California. After a regular Wednesday night Bible class a teenage girl notified him that Wanda, a fifteen-year-old youth in the congregation, was pregnant. This news took him by surprise because Wanda had been president of the youth group and was very talented. He contacted her mother, Clara, by telephone to set up an appointment with Wanda and Clara. Clara was a divorcee and functioned as the single parent to Wanda and her three brothers, who were between the ages of ten and fourteen. The meeting was arranged to coincide with the regular choir rehearsal time and took place in the pastor's study. From his telephone conversation with Clara, he had learned that Wanda was going to have the child, "not an unusual decision for pregnant teens in our local community." After a few pleasantries, the pastor got down to business.

PASTOR: Well, I wanted to have a chance to talk to the both of you personally. I mainly wanted to raise more questions than anything. So if I sound like I'm interrogating you or giving you the third degree, raise your hand and I'll back off. Actually, I want to know a little bit more about what is going on in your lives right now and what kind of decisions and plans you are making for the future.

CLARA: Well, I'm glad that you are going to ask some questions because it may help us, you know, to work things out.

PASTOR: O.K. I want you to know that I admire your decision to keep this child, because I know that you are aware of the other options available. You obviously love this child and have the courage to take this baby as a responsibility. That really says a lot about you.

CLARA: You know, Reverend, I'm from the old school, and our parents told us that for every action there is a reaction and they told us that whatever action you take, you'd better be ready for the reaction. 'Cause you know as good as I do, you may get by, but you can't get away.

PASTOR: That's right.

CLARA: I raised five, four of them on my own. And you know my mother raised twenty. So I know God will make a way somehow.

PASTOR: God had to make a way with twenty! That's a whole nation in itself!

The pastor then turned his attention to Wanda, who had hardly spoken up to this point in the conversation.

PASTOR: So how have you been coming along, Wanda?

WANDA: I've been doing all right. I'm a little uncomfortable right now, but I'm all right.

PASTOR: You're how old now?

WANDA: Fifteen.

PASTOR: A junior?

WANDA: Yes.

PASTOR: You go to Tremont, right?

WANDA: Yes.

PASTOR: What's going to happen with your education now?

WANDA: Well, I'm planning to graduate on time next year. I'm going to go back to school this fall.

PASTOR: Is there a special program there for young mothers?

WANDA: Yes. I'm already signed up for next year and everything. I can have her right there at school with me.

PASTOR: Her? It's a girl? You know already?

WANDA: Yes. We had a sonogram, and she's a girl.

PASTOR: Tell me about the baby's father.

WANDA: He's very supportive. We love each other very much. He's working and is going to contribute to the baby and everything. We're going to classes together, and he is going to be there when the baby is born.

PASTOR: Does he attend church?

WANDA: Yes, he's a member of Solid Rock Missionary Baptist Church.

PASTOR: How do his parents respond to you two? Do you go to the same school?

WANDA: No, he's twenty-six. He has an apartment and supports himself. He has talked about getting married, but I am going to get my diploma before I do anything.

The pastor was surprised at the man's age, but tried to disguise his reaction. He then began to address Wanda in a very serious tone.

PASTOR: Now, let me share this with you, and I want you to listen very closely and consider this very carefully. I know that as a young person and as a Christian, you want to do things right and make things right. We could name some girls in this church that recently got married while in high school because they had a baby by a young man. But don't make that decision yet. It would be wise for you to continue with your education before looking at that aspect of life. This may be the right man for you to spend the rest of your life with, and it may not. But take all of the time in the world to make that decision, at least until you get out of school. I hope that you understand me. I'm sure that your mother has told you how great a responsibility having a child is. From now on, your life will never be the same. You are no longer a girl, you are a woman. Even though you still have a lot of youthful ways, you now have adult responsibilities. It is a blessing that you have a mother who can give you the kind of love and respect that you are now getting. But your life has changed now, and you can't go back. Now you don't have to hang your head low and say that this is the end of your life. You can still go on and make a great life for yourself. When I graduated from college, another woman graduated at twenty-one years of age who had an seven-year-old son. She is now a corporate lawyer. And you are a gifted and talented young lady. Think twice and three times before you get involved in marriage out of pressure to look good. Believe me, it will be hard enough for you with this child. Make sure that you don't have a bad marriage to go along with it.

Wanda did not respond to the pastor's words of advice, but Clara did, thanking him for telling Wanda these things because "that's just what I've been trying to tell her." She continued:

CLARA: Wanda has always been bright. That's why I think a lot of this has happened. She has been bored in school. And sometimes I think this is the worst thing that can happen to a child—to get bored, because the devil finds work for idle hands. But she can go on from here and make the best out of her life.

PASTOR: I just want you to know, Wanda, that I'm going to support you, and I want you to hold your head up and get on with your life. You have made a mistake. I wish to God that you were not so involved so early. But as my mother used to tell me, "If you make a mistake once, you're human; if you make that same mistake twice, you're a fool." But you certainly could have done worse. Your decision to go ahead and have this child was courageous and right, and I believe that God is going to bless you for having a child. You see, I don't believe that there is any such thing as an illegitimate child, for every child that is born through natural processes on this planet is legitimate. Well, I don't know—maybe a test-tube baby or a baby from a sperm bank is illegitimate. I don't know. But some of God's best people were born out of wedlock! Jesse Jackson, Willi Brandt of Germany—even Jesus was conceived out of wedlock. God can forgive you, but your child doesn't need God's forgiveness. She doesn't come from you—she comes through you—she comes from God.

Again, Wanda did not respond verbally, so the pastor, after a brief pause, continued.

PASTOR: Now, I need to mention another thing to you. I'm going to ask you to take a leave from singing in the youth choir, and I'll tell you why. It does not look right for you to be singing Zion songs as a young unmarried woman. It is discouraging and distracting to worshipers. It will also be protection for you, because people like to gossip, and I want to spare you from that. It is a common policy that I have that I utilize for all unwed expectant mothers, regardless of age. Also,

WANDA:

if you get any bad remark or statement from anyone in this church, I want you to tell me, O.K.?

O.K.

In his interpretation of the basic dynamics of this case report, the pastor said that his discussion with Wanda and her mother "heavily emphasized acceptance of her and her situation, and encouragement and exhortation to her to maintain her dignity in light of her pregnancy while remaining committed to reach for her personal potential as a child of God." He pointed out that Wanda's "sense of self was in danger of deterioration and decay because of the moral implications of her pregnancy," and that "through this pregnancy, her behavior has been made public, subjecting her to shame and embarrassment." He advised against a precipitous marriage, suspecting that it would be motivated by a desire to ease her shame and humiliation by "giving the child a name." On this point, he and Wanda's mother agreed. But there was some disagreement between them concerning Wanda's involvement in the youth choir. He suspected that Clara wanted Wanda to continue in order to keep her as involved in church as possible, but he felt that her singing in the choir might invite the "scorn and criticism" of some, whereas her "quiet attendance at worship in the pews would elicit support from many others." He felt that his approach on the matter of public criticism was balanced. Wanda was being dissuaded from singing in the choir, but he would support her unconditionally if negative remarks were made to her or overheard by her.

In his theological interpretation of this conversation with Wanda and Clara, the pastor made a direct allusion to hope. As he put it, "The practical belief that the Lord will 'make ways out of no way' was not a leap of faith for suffering people, but a necessity that evolved out of a history of pain. Therefore, the possibilities for Wanda to transcend her troubles, rising above them with her child to new heights, is not an empty hope, but a living reality in the lives of many of us." Here, the pastor appeared to be identifying two possible ways in which hope might be understood. In some circumstances, hope is "empty" because it appears to counsel resignation to a dead-end situation. On the other hand, hope may also be living and vital when it is based on the "practical belief" that the Lord will "make ways out of no way"—when, in other words, hope is associated with possibilities, not with resignation to a situation in which there is no way to turn, no way out, no means of escape. The second type of hope is the only real hope, and the pastor wanted Wanda to understand that his counsel was not intended to discourage her, but was actually based on a living and vital hope.

What we do not know from this case is whether Wanda's hopes for herself and the hopes that the pastor had for her were compatible. His image of hope for Wanda is the woman who graduated from college at twenty-one years of age with a seven-year-old son, and who subsequently became a corporate lawyer. Wanda's hopes appeared to be associated with the more immediate goal of completing her high school education and perhaps giving serious thought to marrying the father of her child in the meantime, because the two of them "love each other very much." While the pastor seemed to be looking further into the future than Wanda was, he emphasized his conviction that the possibility of a bright and open future for her depended on her not becoming discouraged now. The present time is a time for patience and endurance, not for despair or hopelessness. As he put it, "Now you don't have to hang your head low and say that this is the end of your life. You can still go on and make a great life for yourself."

He saw the situation then as one in which his role was that of agent of hope. It is no accident that an African-American minister would be especially conscious of the role that hope plays in human life, for, as he himself indicated, he identified with a "suffering people" for whom the hope that the Lord will "make ways out of no way" is not a leap of faith, but a necessity that evolved out of a history of pain. Hope is not resignation to an intolerable situation, but the anticipation that sooner or later one will find a way out.

So, this case draws our attention to the importance of hope in pastoral care ministry and points to the pastor's role as the agent of hope. Wanda will be involved with a variety of helping professionals during the course of her pregnancy and her subsequent efforts to continue her education, and these other professionals will certainly contribute to the maintenance of hope in her life. But this case illustrates that the central and primary task of the pastor is to be an agent of hope. Some may disagree with the stands that he took on certain moral issues (for example, his view that the only right thing for Wanda was to proceed with the birth of her child and then to care for the child herself). Some may also have questions about his counseling technique (for example, his decision to talk with Wanda and Clara together; his support for the decision even though it appeared to have been made largely by Clara and not necessarily by Wanda; his tendency to ignore Wanda's feelings, especially when he seemed to discount her expressions of love for the father of her child; or his inclination to preach at Wanda on an issue—her continuing education—on which there did not seem to be any obvious disagreement). Some may question his decision not to allow Wanda to continue to sing in the choir, possibly for the reasons that Clara apparently considered persuasive (that Wanda might become less involved in church at this critical time in her life), or possibly because he seemed to be bowing too much to social pressure. What about Mary, the mother of Jesus, that other unmarried and pregnant woman, whose "Zion song" is recorded in the Gospel of Luke?

Yet, on the major issue here—his role as the agent of hope—there is unlikely to be significant disagreement. This was clearly an appropriate role for him to assume, and it was a role that did not seem to require special reflection. It came naturally to him, and he did not even have to give a great deal of thought to it. He knew that it was his task to help Wanda and Clara to maintain hope under very adverse circumstances. Even some of the above criticisms of his counseling approach—such as his tendency to stress Wanda's continuing education when there did not seem to have been any controversy about this—can be viewed as a reflection of his desire to place his role as agent of hope above all else. Furthermore, his perception of his role as the agent of hope enabled him to speak freely, gave him a sense of knowing how to approach the problem, and enabled him to think in a coherent way and to move the session toward a sound and defensible conclusion. Knowing that his central task was to be an agent of hope among his people, this pastor knew what he was doing and why he was doing it.

"I GOTTA BE PATIENT"

Our next case is reported by a student chaplain who was assigned to the Urology floor of a hospital in a large city. The patient, a white woman about thirty years of age, had been hospitalized for more than two months and was described by the head nurse as being depressed. It was likely that this patient would continue to be hospitalized for some time to come. The student chaplain had visited her the previous week and observed on that visit that she had been more interested in watching television than conversing with him. On this occasion, she was watching television as he entered the room.

PASTOR: Hi, Mary. I'm Chaplain Reed. We met last week and I said I would come again.

MARY: Yes, I remember.

PASTOR: I see you're watching "MacMillan and Wife." I hope that I'm
            not disturbing your program.

MARY: No, it just started.

PASTOR: Good, I wanted to see how you are doing. How are you
            feeling today?

MARY: Not real good. I had to go back in for surgery on Monday.

PASTOR: Oh no! Why, what happened?

MARY: I had an infection from my previous surgery. They had to
            reopen it to clean it out.

PASTOR: I'm sorry. I didn't realize you would have to have more
            surgery.

MARY: Yeah. Well, I'm used to it.

PASTOR: This has happened before?

MARY: Yeah. I've had problems with infections for eleven years,
            but what can you do about it? It doesn't do any good to
            complain. I know that everyone is doing their best.

PASTOR: Still, it has to be awfully frustrating.

MARY: Sure, but what can you do? I just gotta be patient.

The student chaplain confessed to not knowing how to respond to
Mary's comment about patience. He was afraid to say something that
might reinforce her depression—such as "Yeah, what can you do?"—
but unsure, on the other hand, whether he should encourage her to
take a more assertive, less resigned attitude toward her situation. Instead, he brought up the matter of her family and its supportiveness
during her hospitalization.

PASTOR: I recall that you said your family was a couple of hours
            away, down by the shore?

MARY: Yeah, they come by pretty often.

PASTOR: You feel supported by your family.

MARY: Oh, yeah. They've been real supportive. I get a lot of support
            from my family. I have a cousin who's a minister too. She's
            a Methodist. She writes and sends me cards.

PASTOR: I imagine that you have people praying for you then.

MARY: Oh, sure. She prays for me, and my grandmother prays for
            me all the time. There are lots of people praying for me.

PASTOR: It sounds as if you come from a religious family.

MARY: Yeah. I've got an uncle who is a Baptist. When he prays, he just goes on and on. You know, his prayers are more like sermons. I don't like that. My cousin, when she prays, it's short and to the point. I like that a lot better. When we have Thanksgiving or Christmas dinner, we take turns each year to say the grace. We always dread it when it's my uncle's turn to pray. He just goes on and on while the food gets cold. Now, my cousin, she gets right to the point. I like that a lot better.

PASTOR: You really don't like long, drawn-out prayers.

MARY: No, not at all. I think they should be to the point and not drag on and on. But I know my uncle means well. It's just the way those Baptists are. My grandmother is a Baptist, too, so she prays all the time for me. She had her whole church pray for me. They even sent me a card.

PASTOR: How do you feel about that?

MARY: Pretty good. I'm going to send them a thank-you card.

PASTOR: You sound thankful for their prayers.

MARY: Sure.

PASTOR: Do you pray?

MARY: Sure. I believe in God. I don't really feel like I belong to any church. I don't go very often, but I believe in God and I pray. I figure that if you just try to be a good person and do what's right, help other people, you know, that's what counts. I'm not like my uncle and I'm not real regular about prayer like my grandmother, but I pray.

PASTOR: When you pray, what kinds of things do you find yourself praying for?

MARY: Mostly for other people. You know. I mostly pray for other people instead of myself.

PASTOR: You don't pray much for yourself.

MARY: No, I mostly pray for other people. I know that God didn't make me sick. I don't think God wants me stuck in the hospital. It's just my body. It's just the way things are. There are other people worse off than me, so I pray for them. If I'm meant to get better, I will, but there's nothing that I can do about it now except be patient. It isn't God's fault though. I know that.

PASTOR: Would it be all right with you if I prayed with you?

MARY: Sure, I don't mind.

PASTOR: Good, I would really like to pray with you. And although I know that you usually don't pray for yourself, I would like to pray for you, that God would help you to get well as quickly as possible. Is there anything else that you would like to remember in prayer?

MARY: Just my parents. You know. Just that they're O.K.

PASTOR: Good. Do you mind if I hold your hand while we pray? It's sort of a custom with me.

MARY: Sure, I like that.

PASTOR: I'll try to keep it short and to the point, the way you like it. . . . "Lord, it's hard to understand sometimes why things are the way they are. I wish that Mary wasn't sick here in this hospital. But we are grateful for the family and people who are so important to her and who have given such good support to her during this time and throughout her life. Thank you for the many people who pray for her. Thank you too for letting me have the opportunity to meet her and to be able to pray with her. Lord, Mary wants especially to remember her parents, to give thanks for them and to ask that you watch over them. I would like to add a special prayer for her. Lord, we ask that you send your Spirit of comfort and healing to her. We pray that your Spirit of wisdom might guide doctors and staff as they use the talents and gifts that you have given them in her behalf. May all these things work together for the good of Mary and her loved ones according to your promise, and so may your name be glorified. Thank you for hearing our prayer now in the name of your Son, our Lord Jesus. Amen." *(After a short pause)* I hope that wasn't too long.

MARY: No. Thank you.

PASTOR: I do hope that you'll be feeling better soon.

MARY: Yeah, well, when it happens it happens.

PASTOR: I'll be praying that it happens soon. I need to go now, but thank you for letting me visit with you.

MARY: I'm glad you came. You'll be coming back again?

PASTOR: Unless you get tired of seeing me.

MARY: No.

PASTOR: O.K. then, I'll see you next week. Take care.

MARY: All right, see you again.

In evaluating this pastoral visit, the student chaplain wondered whether Mary had given up hope. Granted, she was tired and not feeling well after her second surgery, and, because she did not as yet know whether the surgery would help her or not, she was understandably depressed. But, in his view, the depression had gone further, toward a kind of hopelessness or despair. As he put it, "Coupled with the sentiment that there is nothing that can be done, her God seems impotent to act in her behalf." Also, while she seemed to believe in the value of prayer for the sake of others, she did not pray in her own behalf: "Perhaps this may indicate that she does not believe that God is willing to listen to her cries in her own behalf. Perhaps it is because she may feel that she is not worthy of God's attention. Whatever the case, she seems to have surrendered and is just waiting for something or someone to solve the problem one way or another. Perhaps this is a kind of passive faith, but it seems that she has just given up on life and hope. She closes the door and just seems to absorb herself in television watching, and even that is without any real interest."

He went on to admit that he found himself "feeling very frustrated with this patient. I found it difficult to just think of her as depressed but became more aware of my own sense that she had become apathetic toward life and herself." Sensing her apathy, and hoping somehow to get beyond it, he found himself focusing on "her concept of prayer in an effort to restore a sense of empowerment and, hence, hope. In trying to explore her feelings about prayer, I had hoped that she might be more specific concerning the kinds of things that she prayed for or about. I just didn't know how to get beyond the very general answers that she gave without seeming too pushy or becoming manipulative."

In the prayer, he deliberately focused on the positive aspects of her situation, "but was painfully aware that she did not respond to anything said in the prayer." The only hopeful aspect of the whole visit came at the end when she asked whether he would be coming again: "Perhaps the thing that is so professionally frustrating about the kind of apathy reflected by this patient is the fact that it seems to contain no hope, while I see my role as 'bearer of hope.' How can I convey that hope?"

He went on to question the "standard reflective listening techniques" that he had been taught on the grounds that they seem "powerless to generate anything more than continued apathy unless there is opportunity to continue to be present to her on a regular basis, and thus support her by showing an interest in her. Perhaps, then, through such a caring relationship, one may engender some sense of personal value in the patient and, as a kind of incarnation of God's concern, imbue some sense of purpose and meaningfulness indirectly. But I wonder if even such consistency in relationship can penetrate the barrier of apathy?"

In a subsequent verbatim on Mary, he reported that he did attempt to provide such a caring, consistent presence over the next few months. He observed that Mary's "affect" remained flat except for a few bright spots. On one occasion, he was able to interest her in joining another patient in making some leather key-chain holders for Christmas gifts. They seemed to enjoy each other and the creative task they shared, but when the other patient was discharged, Mary returned to her previous mode of behavior, closing the door and withdrawing into television viewing.

After a few months had passed, she developed an abdominal infection and died within ten days. The student chaplain "deeply felt the loss. I did the memorial service at the hospital at the request of the staff and patients who knew her. In the message, I spoke about my own feelings of frustration over her apparent apathy and also spoke of my love and hope for her. At the conclusion, her family and a number of patients and staff approached me to thank me for putting into words such an accurate account of their own feelings about her. We felt her loss because we valued her but all wondered if she ever understood that value."

A major theme in this account is the pastor's sense of hopelessness that he perceived in the patient and the frustration that her apathy caused him personally, as it challenged his perception of himself as a "bearer of hope." Throughout the months that he ministered to her, he was unable to break through this wall of hopelessness, and, in the end, he concluded that, while there may have been an occasional bright spot for which he might take a little credit, she seemed to have died without hope. This, he perceived, was a direct affront to his view of himself as the bearer of hope, and he was aware that it frustrated and possibly even somewhat angered him.

Though he did not say so explicitly, one gathered that he also felt that her hopelessness contributed to her decline and eventual death; or that, at the very least, a more hopeful attitude would have enabled her to have experienced some inner joy and peace in the last months of her life. In the end, he found himself expressing more hope for her than she apparently held for herself, a clear indication that he saw himself as an upholder of hope, as if to suggest that if he could not instill hope in her, he could at least represent the interests of hope itself. Also, the woman's family and the hospital staff appreciated his hopefulness versus her hopelessness, and, far from being offended by his evident dissociation of himself from her own perspective on life, they conveyed to him at the memorial service that they agreed strongly with what he had to say.

It is possible, of course, that he exaggerated her sense of hope-lessness. From her perspective, she was responding to her situation with "patience" because there was nothing else for her to do. She could complain, but what good would that do? She could get angry with God, but, after all, "it isn't God's fault." Also, practically speaking, "it doesn't do any good to complain. I know that everyone is doing their best." Still, do we not share the chaplain's concern about her rather fatalistic attitude, especially since she represented this fatalism as the attitude that Christians are supposed to take toward situations like this? We notice the tone of resignation in her voice when she said, "It's just my body. It's just the way things are. If I'm meant to get better, I will, but there's nothing I can do about it now except be patient." And we, like the pastor, feel in our hearts that she could in fact have done something about it, namely, to have a hopeful attitude instead of a fatalistic one. It worries us, just as it did him, that she too readily accepted whatever might happen to her, and as it did him, it concerns us that she was using religion to validate this acceptance, an acceptance that was not based on hope, as it seemed to reflect so little desire or passion for life itself.

"I DON'T WANT TO STOP"

Our third case centers on a conversation that took place between a pastor and a young man at a young adults' fellowship meeting in a local church. The pastor, minister of another congregation in the city, had been invited to serve as facilitator for a workshop designed for young adults on the subject of interpersonal relationships. Ramon was eighteen years old and had been raised in the church where the meeting was being held. As a former member of the church himself, Pastor Acosta was well acquainted with Ramon and had had a number of conversations with him prior to this one. On this particular day, Pastor Acosta noticed that Ramon was unusually quiet and subdued through-out the first half of the seminar discussion. Normally a person who speaks his mind, Ramon was very pensive and seemed rather out of touch with the group discussion.

During the coffee break, Ramon came over to Pastor Acosta and began to talk about the workshop.

RAMON: Great workshop! I'm really glad I made it to this seminar. I really thought I wasn't going to make it. I had a hard time getting off from work, since I need to work on the weekends also. You know, it's really nice to hear other people going through some difficulties among their friendships. I thought I was the only one who has been going through so much. *(He hesitates.)* Do you have a few moments, or are you going out to talk with someone else?

PASTOR: No, let's get some soda and go upstairs.

RAMON: Why is it that every time you talk about a certain subject it hits home?

PASTOR: I don't know, maybe someone is trying to tell you something that you don't want to accept.

RAMON: Do you ever feel that when you're doing something wrong, you want to keep on doing it anyway?

PASTOR: I know that happens. I remember when I was in high school and in my third year I went dancing every Saturday. Although I was really lowering my school grades, I still kept going to all these clubs in the city. I know it was a growing experience because I once received my report card and saw the disappointed look on my parents' faces. I said, "No more!" And even *I* saw the waste of time, because I really didn't enjoy myself, but I saw myself trying to fit in with what everyone else was doing.

RAMON: You went out dancing?

PASTOR: Yes I did! And I was pretty good at it too.

RAMON: Well, let me just come out with it. I know that whatever I say you can understand. I've become really sexually active. I mean, it has come to the point that whenever I look at a woman my desires are such that I can't think straight. For instance, during this past week I went out and met this girl. We talked, and she was from out of state. She actually invited me to her hotel. I wanted her so much, not because of anything meaningful that might come out of it, but just for the good time. When I listened to the discussion and you described some of the basic points that we are all created in God's image and how we are to be relational beings and that we need to respect one another in relationships, I just don't feel that I am doing so. But I can't stop. I guess I don't want to stop. But it's like chewing a piece of gum and once the taste is over you put in another piece of gum. And that's the way I treat these women! Once it's done I don't speak to them the following day, and I don't see them the same way. I would only appreciate them if, well, you know.

PASTOR: So, whatever the excitement is at the time, it doesn't seem to last long.

RAMON: Right! I can't speak to them the following day, and even within myself I go to sleep feeling I'm on top of the world and then I wake up miserable—not knowing how I'm going to face this girl that I was with the previous night. You don't know how many excuses I've invented to avoid them. I don't want anything serious right now! I guess it's wrong! *(He bows his head and covers his face with both hands.)* I can't ask for an easy answer! But it's so hard. I go to school, after school I go to work, and when I get home it's so depressing. I need something else to relieve some of this tension. And who do I have to talk with? My mom won't understand, and if I talk to any of my friends that I'm doubting my actions, well. . . .

PASTOR: You're afraid you won't be seen the way you want them to see you?

RAMON: Yeah! That's it! But I still feel it's wrong.

Realizing that the coffee break was coming to an end, frustrated that there wasn't time to explore Ramon's problem in depth, Pastor Acosta tried to think of a possible solution.

PASTOR: You know, Ramon, I never have seen anyone as committed as you are to your music. The way you sing with the group is inspirational. If you need an outlet for expression with a purpose and to give some meaning to your relationships with others, why not pursue that avenue instead?

RAMON: But it's not the same thing. I don't know!

PASTOR: For a temporary pleasure it must be nice, but look at the way you're feeling at this point. How are you seen in the eyes of those who know what you're doing? How do you feel when you go home after it's done? Do you ever wonder about the health implications?

RAMON: You know, that's true, I go to sleep scared wondering how God is looking at me and, you know, I don't like what I see in myself. Or even what may happen. Imagine if I were to get AIDS?

PASTOR: I think you need to take a good look at yourself, your special talents, and see what you're going to do with them. If God has allowed you to go so far in your music ministry, just as God allowed me a second chance to restore my priorities in school and do the best I could in something worthwhile that would help me in the long run, I certainly believe that God can give you the strength and insight to make the proper decision. God has given you so much already. I don't doubt God's deep and patient love for you, but don't test your reluctance and hesitancy too long.

RAMON: You mean, I could get in so deep that it would be hard to turn back?

PASTOR: Yes, and it will continue being hard if you don't do anything about it.

RAMON: You're so right. *(Then, after a moment's pause:)* Are you upset with me?

PASTOR: Well, Ramon, at this point, I have to say that I'm very concerned! Let's go back to the seminar.

As the conversation ended, it was clear that no solution had been achieved. In fact, in his write-up of the case Pastor Acosta worried that Ramon might be looking for "ready-made answers" and was not taking seriously enough the fact that there were moral issues involved. Furthermore, Ramon was using sexual gratification as a way to avoid confronting the emptiness and purposeless of his life.

But while the conversation did not resolve Ramon's quandary about what to do, Pastor Acosta felt that he had at least given Ramon "some information to think about and make some decisions as a responsible individual." He also took some satisfaction from the fact that he communicated to Ramon his own theological view that "in order to develop meaningful and constructive relationships in life, there needs to be an awareness of the importance of our relationship with our creator. Our creator gives purpose and meaning in life. Although we have been created to relate with others in community, it is also our responsibility to be good stewards of this blessing by valuing and respecting each other's worth."

Pastor Acosta did not use the word "hope" in his pastoral encounter with Ramon, yet he sensed that he was trying to instill hope in his young friend. His ultimate objective was to help him find grounds for "long-lasting enthusiasm and encouragement and not disappointment and despair." Ramon's despair over his inability to cease behaving in a way that was distasteful and demoralizing to him was the underlying issue, and Pastor Acosta wanted to imbue him with the confidence that he could in fact do something about it. At the end of the conversation, he made clear that he did not view Ramon's situation as hopeless, but he warned him not to delay in making the proper decision, for there would come a point in time when it *would* be too late for him to act. Pastor Acosta wanted to shake Ramon out of his present attitude of despair so that he would act while there was still hope for him.

In contrast to the previous case involving the hospital patient, the pastor in this case felt that he had been an effective agent of hope. This was partly because the workshop theme was relevant to Ramon's situation and spoke effectively to it, as if God were speaking to Ramon through the pastor. He also felt that he had been appropriately firm with Ramon by warning him not to wait too long before he resolved his problem. Through such firmness he communicated his belief that the situation was not yet a hopeless one and expressed confidence in Ramon that, if he put his heart and mind to it, he would find a way to deal with his sexual urges and to avoid such situations in the future.

AGENTS OF HOPE

My purpose in presenting these three cases is not to open up discussion of how the three pastors performed or whether and in what ways they might have handled their situations more effectively. Rather, it is to make the point that pastors view hope as a critical issue in their ministry and that they often judge their ministry to be effective to the degree that it supports, instills, or inspires hope. Pastors do not necessarily believe that hope is always the primary issue in their pastoral interventions and activities, or feel obliged to make a self-conscious effort to instill hope in each and every situation they encounter in ministry. But the very diversity of these three cases suggests that hope is likely to have relevance for virtually everything that pastors do. The common link between the three pastors is that each viewed himself as an agent or bearer of hope, and this would have been just as true had all of these pastors been women, although a woman pastor would likely have viewed these pastoral situations differently and thus have carried out her role as agent of hope differently as well. These individual differences, however, make my point that pastors—men and women—see their primary task as nurturing and fostering hope, and they experience frustration and a sense of failure when their efforts to secure hope appear to be unsuccessful or in vain.

Of course, all three pastors in these case illustrations were aware that hope has its limitations. Looming against a hopeful attitude is the hard reality of life: an unplanned pregnancy, a chronic illness, a lonely existence. Against these tough and formidable realities, hope is not invincible. Yet the very fact of its vulnerability made these pastors the more concerned to instill and nurture hope in those faced with such hard realities. They were also aware that some human desires are conducive to hope, while other desires usually contribute to hopelessness and despair. Wanda's pastor wanted her to set aside her desire to marry the father of her child and to entertain desires relating to her future promise as a self-reliant young woman. Ramon's pastor friend wanted him to sublimate his sexual desires through his music, because his music was conducive to meaningful relationships with self and others, while acting on his sexual desires left him feeling even more alienated from self and others. Mary's chaplain wanted her to see that it was perfectly all right for her to entertain desires for herself. If she was reluctant to express the desire that she would get better, then he would show her the way by making this desire his own and lifting it to God in prayer on her behalf.

Pastors who see themselves as agents of hope do not celebrate all human desires in a promiscuous sort of way. They hold some desires to be clearly defensible, others not, and they are not reluctant to become involved in helping others distinguish the one from the other. Pastoral ministry involves the capacity for discernment,[1] and one way that these pastors sought to demonstrate and model such discernment was by helping another person develop a better, more discriminating understanding of what desires are likely to lead to a more hopeful life and which ones are likely to contribute to a life of despair.

Each of these pastors was also intuitively aware of the factors that undermine and support a hopeful attitude. In their case interpretations,

---

1. Edward Wimberly, *Prayer in Pastoral Counseling: Suffering, Healing and Discernment* (Louisville: Westminster/John Knox Press, 1990).

all three mentioned at least one of the major threats to a hopeful attitude that we will be discussing later, whether despair, apathy, or shame. Pastor Acosta alluded to Ramon's despair, Chaplain Reed to Mary's apathy, and Wanda's pastor cited her shame. While they did not directly mention the allies of hope that we will also be discussing—trust, patience, and modesty—these were introduced, if not in so many words, in the pastoral intervention itself. All three pastors operated on their belief that hope is ultimately grounded in trust. Patience figured prominently in the pastor's counseling of Wanda, and a questionable understanding of patience was much of the focus of Chaplain Reed's frustration with Wanda. Modesty (as the avoidance of a false grandiosity) was an important feature in the counseling of Ramon. Again, a false sense of modesty was present in Mary's view of herself.

But, in alluding to these allies and adversaries of hope, we are getting ahead of ourselves. These will be discussed in much greater depth in chapters to follow. Suffice it to say at this point that pastors understand themselves to be agents of hope. This is not my idea. It is *their* idea. But it is an idea I share with them.

This idea prompts us to wonder whether their ministry as agents of hope might profit from a more systematic understanding of the nature of hope. This is the premise that lies behind this book and the hope that has prompted me to write it.

two

THE ORIGINS OF THE
HOPEFUL SELF

As the cases in chapter one demonstrate, pastors are often involved with individuals who are in crisis, and the major thrust of their pastoral work in such crisis situations is to help these individuals find grounds for hope. Yet, an exclusive emphasis on crisis situations may cause us to overlook the fact that hope is not merely occasional—turned to when we need it—but is primarily attitudinal. It is an attitude or disposition that exists as an integral part of ourselves, whether or not we are entertaining specific hopes at any given time. Its attitudinal quality can be seen in the fact that the vast majority of us maintain a hopeful spirit toward life, as we live our lives from the implicit conviction or tacit belief that the future is an open one, and that it holds possibility for us. We do not necessarily believe that everything works out for the best, nor are we necessarily optimistic about what the future holds for us. But we are hopeful and act from hope, usually without giving conscious thought to the fact that our disposition is to be hopeful and not despairing.

In this chapter, I will use the writings of two psychologists, both in the psychoanalytic tradition, to argue that the attitude of hope can be traced to our earliest experiences of life as infants. The psychologists are Erik H. Erikson and Paul W. Pruyser. After exploring each one's work separately, I will use their insights to consider the role that personal autonomy plays in the genesis and maintenance of an attitude of hope. Our exploration into the origins of hope in infancy and early childhood will enable us to see that autonomy and hope go together. Also, because both Erikson and Pruyser trace the religious sentiment to infancy and early childhood, they help us to see the profound relationship between the religious view of life and the attitude of hope. In their origins, these are virtually indistinguishable from each other.

28

HOPE AS THE ORIGINAL
HUMAN STRENGTH

Erikson's major statement on hope appears in his article, "Human Strength and the Cycle of Generations."[1] Here he notes that psychoanalytic thought has tended to focus on our pathologies and has not given much attention to our personal strengths. This emphasis on pathology is understandable, as psychoanalysis is a therapeutic process. Yet, Erikson believes that through listening to life stories for more than half a century, psychoanalysts have developed an "unofficial" image of the strengths inherent in the individual life cycle and in the sequence of generations. This image enables an analyst to say that a given patient is "improved" and on the road to a "healthy life." There is more to this image than the loss of pathological symptoms. It is not the absence of symptoms but the presence of certain "strengths" that allows the analyst to say that the patient is getting well.

To make the case that he is not talking about personality traits that some people have and others do not, but about "basic human qualities" available to anyone, Erikson calls these strengths "virtues," a word that serves to make an important point. In Old English, virtue meant "inherent strength" or "active quality" and referred to the undiminished potency of well-preserved medicines and liquors. Thus, "virtue" and "spirit" once had interchangeable meanings. By calling these human strengths virtues, Erikson is able to ask: What virtue goes out of us when we lose a given vital strength, and what are the strengths that enable us to acquire that "animated or spirited quality without which our moralities become mere moralism and our ethics feeble goodness?" (p. 113).

Erikson is known for his life-cycle theory, developed together with his wife Joan Erikson, which includes the idea that the human career consists of eight developmental stages. As Erikson formulated this theory of development before he turned his attention to the basic human strengths or virtues, it was natural for him to propose that there are eight such virtues, each being closely linked to the psychodynamics of a given stage of the life cycle. I will not take time to discuss the life-cycle theory in detail, nor will I explore the question of whether eight basic human qualities exist or whether Erikson has merely identified the major ones. (These include hope, will, purpose, competence, fidelity, love, care, and wisdom, in this sequence.) What interests me

1. Erik H. Erikson, "Human Strength and the Cycle of Generations," *Insight and Responsibility* (New York: W. W. Norton, 1964), 111–57.

here is that hope is included among the eight and is given a significant priority, as it is identified with the first life-cycle stage.

To the extent that strengths build upon prior strengths, this means that hope is the basis for all other strengths. Erikson does not claim that hope is the most important in some normative sense, for, after all, he is well aware that St. Paul considered love to be greater than either hope or faith. Yet, developmentally speaking, hope is the most important because every other virtue depends on it: "Hope is both the earliest and the most indispensable virtue inherent in the state of being alive" (p. 115). If a hopeful orientation to life fails to develop, all subsequent strengths—including love—are thereby diminished.

Erikson characterizes hope as "the enduring belief in the attainability of fervent wishes, in spite of the dark urges and rages which mark the beginning of existence" (p. 118). His view that hope is an "enduring belief" suggests that it is not a strength that suddenly disappears as we move beyond the life stage in which this strength emerged, but, rather, it continues to influence our development throughout life. Furthermore, his suggestion that hope endures "in spite of the dark urges and rages which mark the beginning of existence" indicates that hope is threatened by other perceptions and emotions with which it coexists and which may themselves develop into enduring life attitudes as well. Since these "dark urges and rages" are coterminous with hope, we cannot say that there is ever a time in life when hope is not endangered. Yet Erikson believes that it is better that way: "An exclusive condition of hopefulness, translated into various imaginable worlds, would be a paradise in nature, a Utopia in social reality, and a heaven in the beyond. In the individual, here and now, it would mean a maladaptive optimism" (p. 118).

What inspired Erikson to locate hope in the earliest stage of life? He notes that other psychologists, notably Therese Benedek, had called the earliest positive attitude "confidence," and that he himself has called it "trust." But he asks, "What is it that sustains life even where confidence is wounded and trust impaired?" The answer, he says, is hope. Hope is a basic strength precisely because it persists even when we have no objective grounds for trust. Thus, the very fact that our trust is constantly countered by experiences that evoke mistrust is basis for viewing hope as the basic strength that sustains human life. Throughout life, hope, as a basic human quality, exists independently of the realization of specific hopes: "Hope, once established as a basic quality of experience, remains independent of the verifiability of 'hopes' for it is in the nature of our maturation that concrete hopes will, at a time when a hoped-for event or state comes to pass, prove to have been quietly superceded by a more advanced set of hopes" (p. 117). Thus, hope becomes an attitude toward life and, as an attitude, it does not depend solely or even primarily on the attainment of specific hopes.

Another basis for viewing hope as the quality that emerges in the earliest stage of life is the fact that "there is something in the anatomy even of mature hope which suggests that it is the most childlike of all ego-qualities" (p. 116). One can observe such childlikeness in the petitionary prayers of adults as they assume "a measure of childlikeness toward unseen, omnipotent powers." Hope is also essential to the interactions that occur between the infant and the caring adult with whom the infant interacts: "The infant's smile inspires hope in the adult and, in making her smile, makes her wish to give hope" (p. 116). This experience is very important, for even though hope "is verified by a combination of experiences in the individual's 'prehistoric' era, the time before speech and verbal meaning," the critical factor in infancy is "the secure apperception of an 'object.' The [genetic] psychologists mean by this the ability to perceive the *enduring quality* of the *thing world* while psychoanalysts speak loosely of a first love-object, i.e., the experience of the care-taking person as a *coherent being,* who reciprocates our physical and emotional needs in expectable ways" (pp. 116-17). These objects, the "thing world" and the "coherent being," are for the infant "the first knowledge, the first verification, and thus the basis of hope" (p. 117).

Of the two—the "thing world" and the "coherent being"—Erikson places particular emphasis on the "coherent being" as verifier of hope. This is because the "caring person" is the original verifier not only of the world of persons but also of the world of things: "To the human infant, mother *is* nature." She is not only "coherent being" but also "thing world" for the infant, and through her the infant discerns the enduring quality of things as well as of beings. Thus, Erikson stresses the unique role of the caretaking person as the basis of hope: "She must *be* that original verification, which, later, will come from other and wider segments of reality" (p. 117).

For Erikson, there is nothing magical or mysterious about how the caretaking person verifies the enduring quality of the world of persons and things. This results from doing what caretakers customarily do for infants: responding to the infant's need for intake and contact with a warm and calming envelopment, providing food both pleasurable to ingest and easy to digest, and preventing experiences of the kind that may regularly bring too little and too late. Through such responses, she provides "a convincing pattern of providence" in which hopes are met and hopefulness is inherently rewarding (p. 116).

A sense of our own enduring nature emerges in these early encounters with the maternal person. Since verification of the infant's "beingness" is provided through continued interaction with this "coherent being," all "self-verifications" begin in the "inner light of the mother-child world, which Madonna images have conveyed as so exclusive and so secure" (p. 117). This means that our perception of ourselves as having identity, a sense of I-ness,[2] is rooted in the same experiences that engender and verify hope. In these experiences in which the infant and the maternal person express and give each other hope, the infant acquires a sense not only of the enduring quality of things and other beings, but also of his or her own enduring nature.

If hope has its origins in these interactions between the infant and the maternal person, it begins to transcend this relationship as the infant becomes a child: "The gradual widening of the infant's horizon of active experience provides, at each step, verifications so rewarding that they inspire new hopefulness."[3] Learning to crawl and then to walk, for example, are acts of will, but they are inspired by hope. While the earliest experiences of hope in infancy involve initiative (e.g., the infant's smile or outstretched hand), this initiative increases as the infant becomes a child and hoped-for events are not just longed for but are sought after as we become active agents of hope.

With increased agency also comes a greater capacity to renounce one's hope, to "transfer disappointed hopes to better prospects," and to train our expectations "on what promises to prove possible."[4] Hope stays aligned with the maintenance of a stable, reliable, and verifiable world, but it becomes increasingly identified with change, new prospects, and widening horizons. In this new milieu there will be more experiences of unrealized, inappropriate, and impossible hopes. In this more unpredictable setting, hope becomes more flexible and adaptable. We may not insist on having the precise object of our desire, but may accept substitutes of comparable worth. We become more discriminating in what we hope for as we discern a closer fit between what we desire and what is possible. And most important of all, we remain hopeful even when we do not attain what we hope for. This continued hopefulness arises partly from our increased capacity for

    2. Erik H. Erikson, *Identity: Youth and Crisis* (New York: W. W. Norton, 1968), 216–21; idem, *The Life Cycle Completed* (New York: W. W. Norton, 1982), 85–88.
    3. Erikson, "Human Strength and the Cycle of Generations," 117.
    4. Ibid.

renunciation of our desires but primarily from the projective character of hope. Even as certain hoped-for events are coming to pass, they have already been "quietly superceded by a more advanced set of hopes."[5] Thus, our hopefulness does not depend on the realization of any particular hope.

In infancy, hope is based on specific hopes and has not yet developed into an attitude or spirit of hopefulness independent of these specific hopes. It is when this spirit of hopefulness achieves its own independent existence, in the second stage of life, that we can begin to talk about hope as a formidable human strength. As long as hope is tied to the fulfillment of each and every hope we entertain, it is more liability than strength. As hope matures, an attitude of hopefulness forms that does not depend on the realization of a specific hope because hopefulness is inherently rewarding. Hence, even when some or many of our hopes go unmet, when it would make sense for us to abandon hope, few of us actually do. This is because we have become hopeful selves, and hopefulness has become intrinsic to who we are.

Later in this chapter, I will comment further on Erikson's view that hope assumes new dimensions in the second and third stages of the human life cycle. We now turn, however, to Paul W. Pruyser and his views on the origins of hope.

HOPING AND WISHING

Pruyser published an article on hope in 1964, the same year that Erikson's essay on the basic human strengths appeared.[6] He returned to the subject of hope again and again, most recently in an article published in 1986 entitled "Maintaining Hope in Adversity."[7] In the intervening years he addressed the issue of hope in two major books.[8]

Each time that he has written about hope, Pruyser has cited a brief paper by W. C. M. Scott on depression.[9] In this paper, Scott suggests that hope is part of a dynamic sequence. When we fail to realize the

5. Ibid.
6. Paul W. Pruyser, "Phenomenology and Dynamics of Hoping," *Journal for the Scientific Study of Religion* 3 (1964): 86–96.
7. Paul W. Pruyser, "Maintaining Hope in Adversity," *Pastoral Psychology* 35 (1986): 120–31.
8. Paul W. Pruyser, *Between Belief and Unbelief* (New York: Harper & Row, 1974); idem, *The Play of the Imagination: Toward a Psychoanalysis of Culture* (New York: International Universities Press, 1983).
9. W. C. M. Scott, "Depression, Confusion and Multivalence," *International Journal of Psychoanalysis* 41 (1960): 497–503.

satisfaction of our basic wishes, the following sequence may occur: (1) waiting; (2) anticipation; (3) pining; and (4) hoping. Scott assigns the generic name "wishing" to all of these stages, but Pruyser believes that wishing applies only to the earlier phases of the sequence, and distinguishes between wishing, which is not oriented to reality, and hoping, which is.

For Scott, each stage has an effect or mood that differentiates it from the others. Waiting involves diffuse aggression visible in physiological restlessness over the frustration caused by the absent and urgently needed object. Anticipation involves a lighter affect, a foretaste of libidinal fulfillment. Pining involves "concern" and is a kind of languishing or yearning for the one who has bestowed goodness in the past and may do so again. Pining also presupposes a fairly entrenched "memory image" of the person who has provided satisfaction in the past. In hoping, the fourth stage, there is a "positive balance of love, which can encompass, restitute, and repair effects of hate."

As these four stages interact in very subtle ways, Scott suggests viewing their relationships as "multivalent" because the more standard term, "ambivalent," alludes to an all too stark contrast between two phases.

Waiting. In this phase, in the absence of the gratifying object, wishes give rise to hallucinations, and the subject waits for the hallucinatory images to be transformed into sensations. Hallucination as used here does not necessarily have a pathological connotation. It simply implies the "apparent perception of something external to us that is not actually present." Thus, as Pruyser points out, a very hungry infant may hallucinate an image of food. But, as this hallucination does not satisfy the desire for food, it produces a waiting posture, that is, a waiting for the image to be transformed into more powerful sensations (of smell and taste).

Anticipation. In this stage, we are able to experience the absent object of our desire in a more visceral way as our senses become involved. We feel a tingle of excitement as we anticipate meeting a loved one from whom we have been separated for what seems an unendurable length of time. On such occasions we have more than a visual image of the person for whom we wait. Instead, we "feel" the presence of the other and may even "feel" the other's embrace. Thus, anticipation is much stronger and proactive than waiting. In anticipation, our senses are involved and our emotions are running high.

We may even experience pain because our longing is so intense, and the delay of the object of our desire becomes excruciating. If such anticipation is a projection, it involves much more than a mental image of the desired object, as there is a physical sensation of the desired object's presence.

Pining. The next phase is pining, in which the focus is less on the anticipated meeting and more on the recollection of what we are missing as a result of the other's absence. The infant pines for the satisfactions that the maternal person is able to provide. Often, anticipation and pining alternate with one another. The mixture of laughing and crying that sometimes occurs in intense desiring testifies to this alternation. In pining, we have an overwhelming sense of the absence of the missing object; so strong is this perception that even when the missing one appears to us, we often find it difficult to feel her presence because it takes a while to terminate our pining. The other may sense our difficulty and ask, "Aren't you glad to see me?" or "You can stop crying now, I'm here, and everything is all right."

Hoping. The fourth stage is hoping, which "completes the developmental sequence by adding motivational, affective, and temporal complexity."[10] Hoping involves the "belief that an object is forthcoming which has itself the desire to satisfy the longing infant."[11] As the "object" is believed to have its own desire, Pruyser associates hoping with the infant-mother relationship and with the infant's "belief that the mother herself has a need to give to her child what she can" and is therefore "benevolently disposed" toward the child.[12]

Thus, hope involves the belief that our desire is reciprocated by the one whose presence is desired. Even as we know that we want the other to come, we believe that the other wants to come and therefore will come. Our desire and that of the other are reciprocal. It is not that infant and mother necessarily desire the same thing, but that their desires are interrelated. What the infant desires, the mother desires to provide. Also, each discerns that the meeting of the desires of the one will fulfill the desires of the other. It is this discernment that enables one to hope, to replace hallucinatory images and sensations with a kind of intuitive knowing or subjective certainty.

Because the belief that one's desire is reciprocated is an accurate belief, Pruyser suggests that hoping is reality-oriented: "It seems to me

10. Pruyser, *The Play of the Imagination,* 19.
11. Pruyser, *Between Belief and Unbelief,* 185.
12. Pruyser, "Maintaining Hope in Adversity," 123.

that Scott's continuum moves from primitive wishful thinking at one pole to reality-oriented thought at the other."[13] Hoping is the stage in the process that takes the reality of the situation into account. Waiting and anticipating are not under the constraints of reality, as these stages focus on images and sensations in lieu of the other's presence. Pining is more reality-oriented, as one is profoundly aware of being bereft of the other's presence. Because it differs in this respect from waiting and anticipating, Pruyser suggests that pining, together with hoping, are the "hoping" stages in the process, whereas waiting and anticipating are based on "wishing." Still, pining does not include the belief that the other is forthcoming, nor does it provide grounds for the belief that self and other have reciprocal desires. Hope alone is based on confidence that the desired one will appear, precisely because she is believed to desire this herself and is also believed to be able to act on this desire of hers.

While Pruyser uses Scott to inform his own analysis of hope and hoping, he goes beyond Scott in applying the schema to religion. In *Between Belief and Unbelief,* he notes that the infant has "vested his hope not in food or taste or smell or the sound of his mother's steps as she walks to him, and certainly not in hallucinations of all these, but in the mother herself as the good object who desires the infant as much as he desires her." He infers from this that "hoping requires trust in benevolence as an actual trait of another human being or as a quality of the universe."[14] In "Maintaining Hope in Adversity," he strikes a similar chord as he generalizes from the infant-mother relationship and says that Scott's model "implies that hoping is based on a belief that there is some benevolent disposition toward oneself somewhere in the universe, conveyed by a caring person" (pp. 123–24).

This belief, he notes, has been central to the thought and experience of mystics, and he cites two Christian mystics who say that our desire for God is reciprocated in God's desire for us. Thus, Angelus Silesius: "I know that without me God could not live one moment," and the poet Rilke: "What will you do, God, when I die?" There are traces of "infantile grandiosity" in such statements, but we should not be so concerned about the grandiosity that we overlook these writers' "stunning discovery that the creator and the created, or the universe and the solitary person, are interdependent and engaged in patterns of mutuality" (p. 124).

13. Pruyser, "Phenomenology and Dynamics of Hoping," 89.
14. Pruyser, *Between Belief and Unbelief,* 185.

Erikson has made much the same point in various writings, as he views the infant-mother relationship as paradigmatic of the self's relationship to the universe. In his article on the sayings of Jesus, he notes that the interaction in infancy of the "budding I" with the "primal Other" continues "into adulthood as a mutuality between growing perceptiveness and a discernible order in the universe."[15] He too cites the views of mystics concerning the mutuality of the individual self and a responsive universe, noting Meister Eckhart's exclamation that "the eye with which we see God is the same as the eye with which God sees us."[16]

Pruyser also discusses the subject of hope in a chapter on providence in *Between Belief and Unbelief,* noting that we can view the benevolent disposition of the universe from the perspective of wishing and can therefore anticipate that Providence will deliver specific goods "as promised," and, if they are not, react as though "we have a case against God." Or we may view Providence from the perspective of hoping and see it "predominantly as Benevolence, whose benevolent intention will come through even in incalculable events and unforeseeable forms."[17] Citing psychoanalyst Ernest Jones's observation that "what one really wants to know about the Divine Purpose is its intention toward oneself," Pruyser concludes that "the foremost discovery to be made [regarding Providence] is that one must come to terms with benevolence," and this means that divine benevolence, like human benevolence, is a promise to be with us in trouble, to be present in our hours of agony, but not to perform magical cures and miraculous healings, to send forth angels of mercy, to bestow horns of plenty, or to postpone the hour of our death.[18]

IMAGES OF HOPE

By emphasizing the difference between a view of divine providence based on hoping and one based on wishing, Pruyser makes a stronger distinction between wishing and hoping than Scott does. Where Scott views all four stages as a process of wishing, Pruyser sees in this sequence a progression away from wishing and toward hoping. By distinguishing hoping from wishing, he clarifies the role that imagination plays in hoping and shows that images of hope are very different

15. Erik H. Erikson, "The Galilean Sayings and the Sense of 'I'," *The Yale Review* 70 (1981): 321–62. Quotation is from pp. 349–50.
16. Ibid., 361.
17. Pruyser, *Between Belief and Unbelief,* 187.
18. Ibid., 187.

from the images that occur in wishing. In the waiting stage, hallucinatory images occur as we experience the frustration caused by the absent and urgently desired object. In the anticipation stage, such images give rise to sensations of the presence of the missing object. In pining, which marks the shift from wishing to hoping, there is a well-established "memory image" of the missing object. In the hoping stage, hallucinatory images no longer play a significant role, for hope is reality-oriented.

This does not mean, however, that images have no place in the hoping stage. What it does mean is that our disposition to create images is chastened. This can be seen, for example, in Pruyser's contrast between the apocalyptic and eschatological attitudes. Apocalyptic literature "teems with imagery of terrestrial experience and with speculative imagery about heaven and hell which turns out to be derived from terrestrial perceptions, vastly expanded, such as pearly gates, crystal seas, blazing fires, and sulphur rains."[19] Such apocalyptic imagery is the product of wishful fantasizing. It is like Scott's waiting stage, in which wishing predominates, and it shares the waiting stage's diffuse aggression, as it has a "revengeful intention." In contrast, the "eschatological attitude" reflects a more cautious use of images, as it "rests hope quite soberly in the apostle Paul's affirmation, 'Now we see in a glass darkly, but then we will see face to face.' Paul abstains from speculating about what he will see; his only certainty is that the Creator who presided over his birth and his life will also be present at his death."[20] This sober conviction "controls wishing, abstains from selfish claims, and keeps imagery to a minimum." Pruyser calls this "the eschatological attitude and the essence of hoping."[21]

Thus, a critical difference between hoping and wishing is the controlled use of imagery in hoping in contrast to its flamboyant use in wishing. Imagery appropriate to hoping bears directly on the conviction that sustains the hope, that is, the conviction that the object of desire will appear and that this object has the desire to satisfy the one who hopes. The images are those that sustain the belief itself and do not cater to other emotions, such as revenge and vindictiveness. Also, they do not attempt to describe in minute detail how the hoping person's desires will be satisfied, but instead leave this to the initiative and imagination of the other.

Again, Scott's model enables us to see why these three limitations are vital for images of hope. In the waiting stage, the maternal person's

19. Pruyser, "Maintaining Hope in Adversity," 129–30.
20. Ibid., 130.
21. Ibid.

absence, especially if prolonged, may cause diffuse aggression visible in physical restlessness. Images produced under this condition will reflect such aggression. Not only the maternal person herself but also the objects in the child's environment are considered agents of frustration. Such objects are kicked, thrown, and bitten as the infant's world becomes a combat zone. Given the emotional climate in which hallucinatory images originate, it is not surprising that adult hallucinations often express paranoid feelings.

With the shift from waiting to anticipation, the infant's imagination takes on a very different form. Now she expects the mother's return, whereas before she felt only the frustration of her absence. Images reflect this shift. As anticipation provides a foretaste of libidinal fulfillment, the images focus on what will happen when the infant's mother returns and are accompanied by bodily sensations. They are highly specific. If the infant craves food, the anticipation is not of just any "good tasting" food, but of a particular food with a particular taste. If she wants an embrace, the anticipation is not just of any warm embrace, but of a particular kind of embrace done in a particular way. Thus, imagination is involved, but in a ritualistic, almost obsessive manner. The images are not a more relaxed and self-confident expression of desire, but are overly precise and detailed as they reflect urgent cravings. Nor do they envision novelty or originality in the anticipated encounter. Thus, anticipation marks a gain in the infant's coping with the situation of the absent mother, as anger and hostility are replaced with expectations of needs being met. Yet, there is a cost involved. The imaginal thinking of the anticipatory stage opposes spontaneity and novelty. Paranoia is dispersed, but obsessiveness—overspecific cravings—takes its place.

The images produced in the pining stage are as different from the anticipation stage as anticipatory images were from those of the waiting stage. Pining involves languishing and yearning. The infant tends to focus on an entrenched "memory image" of the person who has provided satisfactions in the past. Here, the "image" reflects and evokes feelings of the vast gulf that separates oneself from the other, of the radical discontinuity between present experience without the other and past experiences when the other was present. With thoughts so focused on the memory image of the absent one, the infant is unable to visualize the other as a "future image" or an "image of hope." The other is associated with past experiences only, and even then with a very romanticized perception of the past. The image of the other is much like the image we have of an old friend, perhaps one with whom we were romantically involved, whom we have not seen for twenty or thirty years. Our image of him is fixed at the time we knew him, and the fact that he has aged, as we have, is conveniently overlooked. Also, any unpleasant features of our experience with the "object" are conveniently forgotten. Thus, the "fixed" image is also an "ideal" image.

If waiting is associated with feelings of paranoia, and anticipation has elements of obsessiveness, the pining stage is one in which masochism prevails. Of the three stages, it is the most painful, and yet it is also strangely pleasurable, as it makes us feel heroic and vindicated. As Theodor Reik points out, the essence and aim of masochism can be summed up in three words: Victory through defeat. It "is characterized by unconscious defiance in defeat and by the secret foretaste and foreknowledge of coming conquest." The masochist "faithfully believes that misery, humiliation, disgrace will be made up for by what is to come after. Foreseeing future appreciation and sure of the praise of posterity, he enjoys divine raptures."[22] In pining, then, one feels that one is the object of neglect or rejection, the victim of the other's inexplicable and undeserved absence. But, alongside these feelings of abandonment is a sense of defiance, the feeling that "I can get along perfectly well without you." Pining is therefore quite literally the stage in which one hopes *against* hope. One longs for the return of the other, but one also opposes this very hope, defiantly asserting one's ability to go it alone. If images of the other are idealized, so are the corresponding images of the self rather grandiose, as one perceives that through one's sufferings one will be the ultimate victor, the heroic survivor, the vindicated one.

In contrast to images of wishing, images of hoping are more reality-testing and thus inherently healthy. As they reflect an eschatological rather than apocalyptic attitude, they are chastened or purified of the pathological emotions that arise in the stages of waiting, anticipating, and pining. However, because hoping is so closely associated with wishing, some images of hoping will inevitably reflect the pathological emotions of the preceding stages. There is probably no such thing as pure hope, so our images of hope will inevitably be contaminated by elements of wishing. Still, the characteristics of the images that hoping generates can be identified. While Pruyser does not offer a systematic treatment of this issue, we can construct his conception of images of hope from his various writings.

22. Theodor Reik, *Of Love and Lust: On the Psychoanalysis of Romantic and Sexual Emotions* (New York: Farrar, Straus and Cudahy, 1949), 363.

First, images of hope reflect our perception of the future as novelty. In both the apocalyptic and eschatological attitudes toward the future, reality is considered unfinished because it is a process and therefore "there is novelty in the making." Yet, in the eschatological attitude, there is a much greater sense that "we may not know the shape of things to come." For the eschatological attitude, the future may be knowable in its broad outlines, but the actual shape of the future cannot be anticipated with any precision. Whereas the apocalyptic attitude is concerned to eliminate novelty—the unexpected—the eschatological attitude is comfortable with it, for who knows but what the future may exceed our greatest expectations? This means that images of hope differ from images of wishing because they recognize that the anticipated encounter cannot be staged in advance. Images of hope anticipate novelty in each new encounter. They are in this sense nonritualistic. The object of desire is known, but the circumstances of the encounter are unknown as these depend on the initiative and imagination of the object and on what each party to the encounter evokes in the other at the time of meeting.

Second, images of hope concern the transitional experiences of life. One of Pruyser's major contributions is his application of D. W. Winnicott's famous notion of the "transitional sphere" to religion. Winnicott noticed that infants tend to become strongly attached to a piece of their blanket, a soft toy, a rag doll, or some other special object that they keep close to their bodies, often near their mouths. Sometimes they suck a finger while the rest of the hand holds the special object. Such action often occurs before the child falls asleep (in the transitional stage between waking and sleeping) or when frustrated, fidgety, anxious, or depressed. Winnicott called these "transitional objects" because they combine "many fragmentary elements of the total mothering situation," yet, at the same time, help the infant to come to terms with the fact that this exclusive relationship between her mother and herself is being replaced by new experiences in which her mother is no longer the primary mediator of encounters with the objective world. The transitional object helps the infant make the transition from the exclusivity of the mother-infant relationship to a direct engagement with the world around her.[23]

Pruyser's contribution has been to develop Winnicott's own suggestion that the transitional object is closely associated with the origins

23. Pruyser, *The Play of the Imagination*, 110–11.

of religion. As Pruyser suggests, the transitional object is related to the holy and the mysterious because it is invested with a sacred aura. It is also the focus of family rituals as other members of the family accept the infant's view that the object is special and has unique powers. They treat the object with uncommon respect and caution, mindful of the righteous indignation they will provoke in the infant if they fail to reverence the object.[24]

Pruyser does not claim that transitional objects are symbols of hope, but he implies some relationship between the two when he notes that the transitional sphere may remain undeveloped either because of the "overactivity of the inner world of dreams and hallucinatory wish fulfillment" or because one has "been goaded to notice only the outer perceptual world with its facilities and its inherent laws."[25] Thus, those in whom the transitional sphere is well developed are neither captive to wishful fantasy nor controlled by the world of immutable facts. As hope falls between these two extremes—that is, is more reality-testing than wishing but at the same time views reality as a sphere not of immutable but of ever-changeable facts—it is reflective of a well-developed transitional sphere.

Pruyser notes that the transitional object enables the infant to make the transition from one state of affairs to another, as from wakefulness to sleeping. It is especially valuable in helping the infant deal with the negative emotions that the transition produces in her, especially the anxieties and fears that occur when she leaves a situation in which she is secure for one of uncertainty and doubt. The transitional object assuages her anxieties and fears. Yet, as we know from observation, the infant will eventually relinquish the transitional object, no longer feeling the need of it. This is partly because, as pointed out by W. W. Meissner, the transitional object is replaced by playing, but also because the capacity to form good transitional objects evolves in the direction of "a healthy capacity for symbolization."[26] It would seem, therefore, that we relinquish transitional objects as we develop the capacity to form images of hope, and that such images do for us what the transitional object did for the infant, that is, enabling us to feel that we are not alone as we move from one state of affairs to another.

Much has been written about "rites of passage" and of our need for rituals to help us negotiate the various passages that occur in life, not

24. Pruyser, *Between Belief and Unbelief,* 198–213.
25. Ibid., 114.
26. W. W. Meissner, *Psychoanalysis and Religious Experience* (New Haven: Yale University Press, 1984), 169.

only the passages from the single to the married state and from life to death, for which we have well-established rites, but also passages involving children leaving home, marriages breaking up, dramatic changes in lifestyle and self-definition, and so on. Pruyser's observation that the transitional object requires family support and thus becomes the focus of a family ritual supports such appeals. So does Meissner's observation that the transitional object evolves into play, the child's form of healthy ritual. But, however important these ritualizations may be, the capacity for symbolization is also a tremendously important resource for the individual who is going through a certain "passage" in life, and images of hope may play a central role in such symbolization.

One thinks here of the enormously popular image of hope in Psalm 23: "Even though I walk through the valley of the shadow of death, I fear no evil, for thou art with me; thy rod and thy staff, they comfort me." Many of the images employed in the book of Psalms concern the experience of transition. One walks through the valley of the shadow of death (Psalm 23), one is drawn up from the miry bog (Psalm 40), one is like a leaning wall or a tottering fence, about to be brought down (Psalm 62), and one is like grass that flourishes in the morning and fades and withers by evening (Psalm 90). In the psalms, we live between the times and experience God in the process of moving from one secure point to another. As Psalm 121 (vs. 7-8) has it: "The Lord will keep you from all evil; the Lord will keep your life. The Lord will keep your going out and your coming in from this time forth and for evermore."

It is no accident, then, that the God who is addressed in the psalms is preeminently identified with hope. Nor it is surprising that, in many of the psalms, emotions reflective of the three stages of wishing are often intermingled with feelings reflecting hope: the paranoia of the waiting stage, the obsessiveness of the anticipation stage, and the masochism of the pining stage. Yet, these only make the psalms' convictions of hope all the more impressive, as hope is the predominant theme of each psalm and of the psalms as a whole.[27]

Because images of hope arise from our experience of life as transitional, they are, as Walter Capps has pointed out, kinetic.[28] They involve movement, not stasis; action, not immobility; emotion, not

27. See my *Biblical Approaches to Pastoral Counseling* (Philadelphia: Westminster Press, 1981), 206–8.

28. W. H. Capps, *Time Invades the Cathedral: Tensions in the School of Hope* (Philadelphia: Fortress Press, 1970), 142.

passivity. If they are visual, they are more akin to film than to portraiture. As kinetic, they are also identified with sounds and are often associated with music. In *The Play of the Imagination,* Pruyser considers the various forms that imagining or image-making may take, and concludes that the "highest" form of imagining is music, which involves the creation of sound images. In a section of his chapter on imagery in music, he points out that "toddlers often sing or hum just before falling asleep, and it is also true that wise parents teach their children to hum a tune to ease them into assuming the solitariness of sleeping."[29] He also notes that music is often performed at major transitional events in life, including graduations, weddings, and funerals. Also, "The use that children and adults make of so-called background music, especially when they feel saddled with irksome or ominous tasks that must be discharged, strongly suggests that in such situations music functions as a transitional object or parental substitute. . . . The student who can do his homework only in the presence of music appears thereby to strengthen what Winnicott calls his 'capacity to be alone'—that is, not radically alone but with a symbolic token inside him or nearby, of the reliable mother."[30]

Our internalized image of the mothering one is as much sustained by the sound of her voice as by the sight of her face; normally, her voice image is more lasting and less subject to distortion than her facial image and is less subject to change as she grows older. So, too, the feelings associated with her voice are more poignant, more expressive of our deepest yearnings and longings, and more the source of our nostalgias. The voice instills desire as no other. As Erikson says of Luther: "I will state, as a clinician's judgment, that nobody could speak and sing as Luther later did if his mother's voice had not sung to him of some heaven."[31] The night that William Styron was intending to take his life, he was watching the tape of a movie set in late-nineteenth-century Boston. At one point in the film the main characters moved down the hallway of a music conservatory and, in the background, a contralto voice could be heard singing a soaring passage from Brahms's *Alto Rhapsody,* a passage that he had heard his mother sing when he was a child. Hearing it again, he could not bring himself to commit suicide, but instead awakened his wife and asked her to take him to the hospital.[32]

29. Pruyser, *The Play of the Imagination,* 190.
30. Ibid., 192.
31. Erik H. Erikson, *Young Man Luther* (New York: W. W. Norton, 1958), p. 72.
32. William Styron, *Darkness Visible: A Memoir of Madness* (New York: Random House, 1990), 66–67, 81.

Again, it is no accident that images of hope are found preeminently in the psalms, which are, after all, songs or hymns. Nor is it surprising that the transition from our present life to the life that awaits us after death is most effectively portrayed through music. As the book of Revelation has it: "And I heard a voice from heaven like the sound of many waters and like the sound of loud thunder; the voice I heard was like the sound of harpers playing on their harps, and they sing a new song . . ." (14:2-3). Thus, music has a unique association with hoping. We know this, of course, from the fact that groups and movements that hope for a better tomorrow are often sustained in their hope by shared songs and the ritual of communal singing ("We Shall Overcome"). Conversely, hopelessness is often experienced as soundlessness, or, at best, the almost inaudible sounds of low moaning with which we associate the pining of unrequited love and inexpressible grief.

In short, images of hope involve *transitional* experiences of life and are at least as valuable as rituals in assisting us in negotiating these transitions, for they enable us to feel that we are not alone when we undergo life's inevitable transitions, even in situations where there are no other human persons nearby. Moreover, the "rites of passage" in which we engage in order to make the transition from one state to another less terrifying are effective precisely because they contain images of hope. A rite of passage "works" for us because it enables us to view the new state of affairs with at least some degree of hopefulness.

A third characteristic of images of hope, briefly alluded to above, is that they reflect the capacity to be alone. Pruyser develops the relevance of this idea of Winnicott's to hope when he focuses on Winnicott's question, "How is it that children develop the capacity and the wish to be alone, seemingly unprotected?" While much has been written about children's fears and their desire for protection by clinging to their loved ones, Winnicott was interested in the opposite phenomenon, whereby children are content to be alone and do not experience solitariness as threatening or anxiety-producing. What makes this possible? Following Winnicott, Pruyser says that it depends "on having a good internal object—a rich, pleasurable, and peace-producing image of the mother present in the psychic reality of the child. The child feels related to the mother even when she is absent."[33]

33. Pruyser, *Between Belief and Unbelief,* 180.

Thus, a critical difference between hoping and wishing is that, in hope, the absent other has been internalized and one "feels related" to the other even when she is absent. This feeling of relatedness is lacking in the wishing stages, as the other is not internalized, causing the infant to become frustrated, fidgety, hostile, and defiant. In contrast, where the mother is experienced as successfully internalized, the child can be at peace in spite of her absence.

It would seem, therefore, that images of hope originate in the capacity to be alone. They are stimulated by the felt sense that one is not in fact alone, that while the other is objectively absent she is subjectively present. As a result, images of hope reflect a greater sense of equanimity and reassurance than images of wishing. The conviction that the absent one wants to come to us is experientially based on the sense or realization that she is already present to us.

It is not difficult to draw the religious implications of this phenomenon of the capacity to be alone and its relationship to hope. If the relationship of maternal person to infant is paradigmatic of the relationship to God to self, then images of hope in God are based on our internalization of God, our felt sense that God is "within" us and is therefore always present to us. The one for whom I wait is, in another sense, already here, inside of me, having taken residence in my heart or soul. Like pining, images of hope are fueled by longing for the awaited encounter, but, unlike pining, they reflect the sense of the other's "here-and-nowness." Religious images of hope are therefore noteworthy for their affirmation that God is always with us, wherever we are, and is closer to us than our very own breath.

The danger, of course, is that religious images of God, precisely because they are rooted in hoping, will routinize the presence of God and speak too easily and too glibly about the accessibility of God. Yet, life itself has a way of challenging this danger, as life's circumstances often cause us to regress to the earlier stages of pining, anticipating, and waiting, and we find ourselves again confronting the fact that we are never far from our masochisms, our obsessions, and our paranoias. The pathologies of our lives are always just below the surface, and they keep us honest in our imaginings of hope.

HOPE AND AUTONOMY

We have seen that both Erikson and Pruyser consider the origins of hope to be rooted in the relationship between the infant and the maternal person. Yet, both also emphasize that hope takes the form it does because this relationship is also transcended. For Pruyser, its transcendence occurs in the child's adoption of a transitional object. For Erikson, the maternal person is the child's first verification of hope, but as the child grows, its sphere of activity expands and hopes are no longer limited to expectations of the maternal person. The child's whole environment becomes a venue for hope.

Erikson is especially interested in how hope continues to develop in the second or "autonomy vs. shame and doubt" stage of life and in how the child participates actively in the realization of hoped-for outcomes. Hope has its origins in trust that the maternal person will appear because she shares the infant's desire to be together. But Erikson also affirms the importance of self-trust, which originates in the infant's struggle to control her hostile urges toward the maternal person so as not to cause her to withdraw. This self-trust, which takes a very rudimentary form in infancy, becomes the basis for the development of autonomy in early childhood: "For the growth of autonomy a firmly developed early trust is necessary. The infant must have come to be sure that his faith in himself and in the world will not be jeopardized by the violent wish to have his choice."[34] Autonomy emerges in the second stage of life as the child learns to exercise self-control over his willfulness.

Thus, in the second or early childhood stage, hope itself assumes a new dimension. Hope is less associated with awaiting the maternal person and more related to the child's emerging capacity to take independent actions, some of which may be contrary to the desires of the maternal person. At the same time, a sense of autonomy emerges as the child learns that a chastened will is more effective than a will that is out of control. Temper tantrums usually fail to secure what the child desires, while learning to compromise and to forego certain desires in a spirit of give-and-take often results in the realization of other, more valued desires. So, as the infant becomes a child, hope is closely associated with the formation of personal autonomy, with the child's desire and capacity to have and make choices. Now there is much personal agency in hoping. The child is actively engaged in the world and her hoping reflects this engagement. Hopes are based less on waiting for one's benefactress to appear and more on causing the world itself to change. Or, to put it another way, the desire behind the child's hope is not for the expected appearance of the other, but for the freedom to exercise personal choice. The chastening of desire

34. Erikson, *Identity: Youth and Crisis,* 110.

is less related to feelings of potential abandonment and more to the necessity of exercising self-restraint in the choices one makes.

In emphasizing the association of hope and personal autonomy, I am aware that Erikson's views on autonomy have been sharply criticized by Carol Gilligan and other feminist developmental psychologists on the grounds that autonomy is more reflective of male than of female development. As Gilligan puts it: "Although the initial crisis in infancy of 'trust versus mistrust' anchors development in the experience of relationship, the task then clearly becomes one of individuation. Erikson's second stage centers on the crisis of 'autonomy versus shame and doubt,' which marks the walking child's emerging sense of separateness and agency. From there, development goes on through the crisis of 'initiative versus guilt,' successful resolution of which represents a further move in the direction of autonomy."[35] She goes on to note that with each succeeding stage, there is increasing sense of personal autonomy and diminishing emphasis on relationship and attachment. Thus, with adolescence comes "the celebration of the autonomous, initiating, industrious self."[36]

Gilligan contends that Erikson's developmental schema has a systematic bias toward separation and against relationship and is therefore far more descriptive of male than of female development. She points to Erikson's own admission that among adolescents girls tend to experience the tasks of separation and attachment as fused, whereas for adolescent boys the task of attachment is indefinitely delayed as they continue to focus on the task of separation. For her own part, Gilligan acknowledges that in the essay that formed the basis of our discussion of his views on hope ("Human Strength and the Cycle of Generations"), Erikson attempts to grapple with the problem of attachment, or the integration of self and other. Yet, "when he charts a developmental path where the sole precursor to the intimacy of adult love and the generativity of adult work and relationships is the trust established in infancy, and where all intervening experience is marked as steps toward autonomy and independence, then separation becomes the model and the measure of growth."[37]

This is not the place to engage in a detailed discussion of Gilligan's critique of Erikson, as many of the issues she raises are somewhat tangential to our primary concern here with hope. But, as her critique

35. Carol Gilligan, *In a Different Voice* (Cambridge, Mass.: Harvard University Press, 1982), 12.
36. Ibid., 12.
37. Ibid., 98.

of Erikson centers on his emphasis on personal autonomy, and my own favorable view of his understanding of hope is based in part on the fact that he sees autonomy playing a very significant role in the maintenance of a hopeful attitude toward life, I need to comment, however briefly, on Gilligan's own view of autonomy.

As we have seen, Erikson understands autonomy primarily in terms of the exercise of choice. Thus, of the two words that Gilligan uses to characterize autonomy—separateness and agency—he comes down strongly and positively on the side of agency (the exercise of one's own will). As far as separateness is concerned, this is a different matter. He certainly characterizes the young toddler as less dependent on her mother for nurturance, but this does not necessarily imply separation. Separateness was already a major feature of the infancy stage, for hope emerges in infancy precisely because the maternal person is experienced as absent. In fact, it could be argued that there is *less* separation in early childhood than in infancy precisely because the child is able to take initiatives to secure the mother's presence. If there is greater separation in the second stage of life, this is, for Erikson, experienced more as an intrapsychic problem than an interpersonal matter, as it is in the second stage of life that the child begins to experience herself as internally split, as self-contradictory.[38] This is William James' divided self, Augustine's sense of two wills competing within him, and St. Paul's sense of a warring in his members. Against this "inner split," judicious parenting is essential, for only it "can convey a healing sense of justice."[39]

On the other hand, this intrapsychic split does have its interpersonal costs, with separation being one of them, as the child may have serious doubts that the mother wants to be with her, because there is a part of herself that she herself would avoid if only she could. The infant's confidence that she and her mother have reciprocal desires may thus be shattered in early childhood. While separation between the child and maternal person may be somewhat greater among male children, as the need to differentiate from the mother is greater for them than for female children, the deeper issue is the child's sense of self-alienation and awareness that she has desires that place her in conflict with the maternal person.

Thus, while recognizing the validity of Gilligan's argument, we need also to stress that Erikson's own view of autonomy is far more concerned with agency, specifically the opportunity and capacity to make choices,

38. Erikson, "Human Strength and the Cycle of Generations," 120.
39. Ibid.

than with separation of self from the maternal person. In this regard, Erikson's understanding of autonomy is quite similar to the view articulated by the philosopher Gerald Dworkin in *The Theory and Practice of Autonomy.* For Dworkin, autonomy "is conceived of as a second-order capacity of persons to reflect critically upon their first-order preferences, desires, wishes, and so forth, and the capacity to accept or attempt to change these in light of higher-order preferences and values. By exercising such a capacity, persons define their nature, give meaning and coherence to their lives, and take responsibility for the kind of person they are."[40] In Dworkin's view, the adversary of autonomy is paternalism, which occurs when another person or agency makes our choices for us on the grounds that they know better what is in our own best interests.

Dworkin also points out that what matters is not the sheer quantity of our choices but the opportunity that a range of choices affords us to live a life shaped by our choices: "If one wants to be the kind of person who makes decisions and accepts responsibility for them, or who chooses and develops a life-plan, then choices are valued not for what they produce nor for what they are in themselves, but as constitutive of a certain ideal of a good life."[41] Hope, then, does not depend on our having unlimited choices, but on having a range of opportunities sufficient for us to experience ourselves as choosing beings. In this sense, autonomy, the ability and capacity to make choices for ourselves, is vital to the development of a spirit of hopefulness.

Dworkin stresses that autonomy is not the only important human value, that there are others, such as loyalty, commitment, benevolence, and love, with which autonomy is related in complex ways. Sometimes, these other values place appropriate constraints on our exercise of autonomy. At other times, our exercise of autonomy fosters these other values. In fact, the exercise of autonomy may well be the means by which separation from another is overcome. Sometimes, children are content to wait quietly for their mothers to come, as their capacity to be alone sustains them. Other times, they exercise the autonomy that their locomotor skills affords them, and they go looking for their mothers. In both instances, they are confident that their mothers *want* to come. The difference is not in the depth of conviction that child and mother have reciprocal desires, but in the degree of autonomy that is needed to make it happen. As for mothers, so with God. As Jesus said,

---

40. Gerald Dworkin, *The Theory and Practice of Autonomy* (New York: Cambridge University Press, 1988), 20.
41. Ibid., 80–81.

"Ask, and it will be given you; search, and you will find; knock, and the door will be opened for you. For everyone who asks receives, and everyone who searches finds, and for everyone who knocks, the door will be opened" (Luke 11:9-10). Without autonomy, the capacity to act on our desires, hoping is often reduced to wishing. Autonomy often makes the crucial difference between hoping and pining and is therefore our means to avoid succumbing to masochism, where the capacity to be alone degenerates into a defiant declaration of one's capacity to go it alone.

Images of hope are characterized by our perception of the future as novelty, they are prominent in the transitional events of life, and they reflect our realization of the capacity to be alone. The conditions for hopelessness exist when the future evokes no perception of novelty but just more of the same, when the transitions in life are ignored, and when there is no capacity to be alone because the object of our desire exists only outside of us. We are perhaps more consciously aware of the first condition for hopelessness, since we have an intuitive sense that hope cannot exist where the future is closed or is condemned merely to repeat the past and present. We may also be conscious of the fact that images of hope help us to negotiate the transitions in life. What we are least likely to be conscious of is the role played by the capacity to be alone—solitary—in the maintenance of hope. What does solitariness have to do with hoping? According to our analysis here, it is vital to hoping, because it means that we have internalized the object of our desire, that it is "out there" and "in here" at one and the same time. Without such internalization, we would be consumed by anxiety as we await the one who is to come. With it, we have a stable attitude of hope, for the one for whom we wait is, paradoxically, already here.

As a necessary condition for hopefulness, the capacity to be alone is not, then, the same thing as separation. It is the experience of a powerful paradox, the paradox that something can be both "here" and "not here" at one and the same time. For the autonomous self, this paradox is not only a fact of life. It is the crucible in which a hopeful attitude begins to assume a life of its own.

three

THE EXPERIENCE
OF HOPING

I n discussing the origins of hope, we have already embarked on a
discussion of what hope is. We have talked about it as being an
expression of desires, of being reality-testing, of having an object,
and so forth. In this chapter, I want to pull these various strands together
and add a few new ones, in order to develop a more systematic picture
of the nature of hope.

Like those who write about love, those who have written about hope
have frequently commented on the difficulty of defining or describing
it. It is one of those features of human life that we think we know and
understand until we try to say something about it. The more we try to
say what we think it is, the more it seems to defy our best efforts to
do so. I do not claim that my own effort to capture it in words will
necessarily be more successful than previous efforts. Yet, I believe it
will offer a reasonably accurate picture of how most of us experience
hope in our lives and will provide insights into why a hopeful attitude
toward life is so important for us. As our concerns here are more
practical than philosophical, the real test of its adequacy will come in
subsequent chapters, when we apply it to another pastoral care case
and relate it to the factors that challenge and support the attitude
of hope.

My own efforts to get at the phenomenon of hope suggest the wisdom
of making a distinction between "hoping" and "hopes." Some of the
confusion in talk about hope is due to the failure to make this distinction. "Hoping" indicates that we are concerned with a process or
form of experience, one that may be compared with other experiences,
like "loving," "hating," "creating," and the like. "Hope" or "hopes," on
the other hand, concern a phenomenon or thing, one that may be
compared with other things, like "beliefs," "judgments," or "skills."

While it might be easier to focus on one or the other and not both, this would give a distorted picture and would inhibit the very understanding we are trying to achieve. Thus, I will begin with "hoping" and will suggest the following working definition: Hoping is the perception that what one wants to happen will happen, a perception that is fueled by desire and in response to felt deprivation. Our working definition of a "hope" or "hopes," to be discussed later, is this: Hopes are projections that envision the realizable and thus involve risk.

THE PROCESS OF HOPING

The Perception That What Is Wanted Will Happen

Alexander Solzhenitsyn, the Russian author, was arrested by the KGB in 1974 and forced into exile in the United States. Shortly after he came to the United States he told an interviewer, "I have no proof of it, but I have a premonition, a feeling. . . . I think—I am sure—that I will return to Russia and still have a chance to live there."[1] His intuition that he would someday return to Russia was an indication of hoping. He had no "proof" for it and no specific plan for realizing it, and yet he felt "sure" that it would someday come to pass. As it turns out, his hoping proved to be accurate.

I suggest that hoping is a particular kind or type of *perception.* It is the perception or felt sense that what is wanted will happen, and therefore it involves investment of self: "I think—I am sure." Without the sense that what we want to happen will in fact happen, there is no hope. Without this sense of things, we are hopeless, bereft of hope. Of course, our confidence that what is wanted will happen varies with the nature of what is hoped for and our own unique situation. Some things that humans hope for are quite rare and happen only to a few. The Presidency of the United States is one of these. Only a few persons ever attain this. Because this office has only been held by white men, the hope of being the President of the United States is extremely rare among women and any men who are not Caucasian. Also, our confidence that what is wanted will happen can fluctuate over time. There are times when we firmly believe that a given hope will come true, and times when our confidence sags. Students who anticipate a major exam often go through this up-and-down cycle. One day, they are quite

1. "Solzhenitsyn Asked to Come Home," *The Trenton Times,* August 19, 1990.

confident. The next day, they are close to despair. The very fact that hopes produce such fluctuating emotions tells us that emotions play a role in hoping, but hoping is not primarily a matter of emotions. The sense or intuition that what is wanted will happen can persist even when we do not "feel" this to be the case. This disparity between our current feelings and our longer-range intuitions suggests that hoping is primarily a perceptual phenomenon. Emotions are involved, but hoping is primarily a way of seeing or perceiving.

By the same token, hoping always has a cognitive element—as it could not occur without thinking—but hoping is more than the entertaining of an idea. As we will see later when we discuss the nature of hopes, hoping involves an imaginative projection and is therefore more than a cognitive act, as cognition has primarily to do with reality as we know it. Because hoping envisions the not-yet or the yet-to-be, it is more appropriate for us to describe it as an intuitive or perceptual process than as a cognitive one. Hoping is therefore sustained more by our intuitive skills than by our cognitive capacities or by our emotions. These others are involved, but emphasis is given to our senses. This is confirmed by the fact that the language we use when we talk about our hopes is one in which neither thinking nor feeling predominates. What predominates is the language of the senses, as hoping often prompts us to use the language of seeing or foreseeing. Also, some hopes are so real to us that we are virtually forced to speak of them in tactile terms, as though they are objects of human touch.

Hoping as unexplainable.   When we engage in hoping, we readily acknowledge that there is no proof that what is wanted will happen, and perhaps not much evidence in support of it either. When we say, "I know that they will offer the job to me," or "I'm sure I will lick this infection before it licks me," we frequently add something like, "I can't explain it," or "Don't ask me to explain it." We cannot explain the sense we have that things will turn out as we want them to. We might go on to elaborate, "It isn't anything they said to me in the interview that makes me feel this. In fact, all they said was that they had ten more interviews to conduct, so I wouldn't be hearing from them for several days. But I know that I am right for the job, and I think that they know this too." Or, "I don't have any real basis for believing that I'll get better. The doctors say they are 'cautiously optimistic,' which to me really means that they are pretty doubtful about my chances. But I just know deep inside of me that I'll get better. Don't ask me to explain it, because I can't, but I just have a sense that it's not my time to die."

Because our intuitive sense that what we want will happen is unexplainable, not based on objectively verifiable evidence, we often have difficulty making the other person to whom we are talking experience what we experience and thus share our hope. The other person wants some concrete evidence: "What were your scores on the computer competency test? Were they impressed when you told them about your work background and experience? Did they give you any indication at all as to how they perceived you?" Or, "What do the lab tests show? Were they improved over last week? I know they also took X-rays. Are those results in yet?" We answer these questions as best we can and then say something like, "But I just know they will offer me the job," or "I know I'm going to come out of this ordeal alive. I just know my time hasn't come." In effect, we have a premonition that is not based on anything actually said by the interviewers or the medical staff, or that is supported by objective facts that we might marshal. It may not even have to do with the interviewers' nonverbal communications, such as a certain look that passes between them, or the way they suddenly become engaged in the conversation, or the rapport that develops between the candidate and the interviewers. The medical staff may communicate through their personal solicitude that they believe a positive outcome is possible. But, as their kindness could mean just the opposite, that they fear the worst, their behavior cannot be the sole or even primary basis on which one's hopes for survival are entertained.

So, the first thing that we can say about hoping as the intuition that what is wanted will happen is that this intuition is *unexplainable* in purely objective terms. It may have something to do with the objective world of facts and evidence, but there is always more to it than that. There is a subjective element in hoping which we may call an intuition or distinct impression, and it is this element of the sense that what is wanted will happen which is beyond explanation. We can affirm our hope, but we cannot adequately defend it on objective grounds if challenged to do so. As Pruyser points out, "It makes no sense to say to a person who hopes: 'You better give up hope, because things have never turned out that way.' " The person who hopes can point out, says Pruyser, that "such a statement is only a conjecture derived from the past; it closes off the possibility of novelty, and takes present knowledge to be final."[2] The hopeful person says to the skeptic, "How do you know that it *cannot* be as I envision it to be?" Even the fact that the

2. Paul W. Pruyser, "Maintaining Hope in Adversity," *Pastoral Psychology* 35 (1986): 126.

hopeful person has often been wrong in the past, that her track record is not very good at all, is insufficient grounds for skepticism, because each situation is new: "This time, I know that Jack's decision to quit drinking will last." "Oh, Milly, you know how many times you have thought this, and how many times you've been deceived." "I know, but that doesn't matter. This time, it's different. I can sense it."

On the other hand, we must acknowledge that there are times when it is futile to be hoping because our hoping is based on inadequate knowledge of what has already been decided by others. Supposing that the job interviewers have already made their decision and are simply going through the interviewing process to satisfy certain legalities about equal opportunity employment. What seems to be a situation in which the future is still open is not the case. The interviewers are going through the motions, and their interest in the interviewee is merely feigned as they have already made their choice. Still, if the person who is hoping in this instance were informed that the interview process is a charade designed to satisfy legalities, would she abandon hope that she will be chosen for the job? Not necessarily. Until the decision is actually finalized and the appointment has been officially announced, there is the possibility, however remote it may seem, that she will be chosen for the job after all. Those responsible for hiring may begin to have second thoughts about the moral issues involved in carrying out this charade. They may also be so impressed with her qualifications and her performance in the interview that they begin to question the wisdom of their original decision. They may arrive at this revised perspective solely on the grounds of self-interest: "This woman can work circles around the boss's nephew. She can make our own work that much easier. I think we should stand up to the boss on this one." So, even if she had known the interview was for appearances only, she may have believed that she would be hired. In that case, her hoping is even more unexplainable, because it is directly challenged by strong objective evidence to the contrary.

Hoping as a solitary act. Because hoping is unexplainable, we often express it in apologetic and defensive terms: "I know it's silly of me to believe this," or "I can hardly expect you to agree with me on this, but. . . ." Patients with terminal illnesses are often apologetic in this way, aware that the persons with whom they are communicating are unlikely to believe it but have instead resigned themselves to the "inevitability" of death. Persons who are hopeful regarding the survival of the human spirit after death also find themselves expressing this intuition in rather apologetic language, and often defensively. They sense that what they are persuaded will happen is not shared by the other, and they feel alone in this, as though their hoping has driven a wedge between them and the other. Hoping is often experienced as a solitary act.

A chaplain visited the hospital room of a woman who was dying of cancer. In the course of their conversation, she said that she had no belief in any kind of life beyond death, and that she was just waiting for the end. The chaplain commented, "I have the same hope for you that I hold for myself." She exclaimed, "Hope? What hope have I? I just lie here and suffer, waiting for the end." He responded, "The hope of the spiritual, beyond the physical. The physical drops away. This happens to all of us one way or another but the spiritual gains strength. I don't know why such suffering comes, I suppose we shall never know." She responded, "Why! There is no why. There can be no why." He continued, "But I am convinced that That which creates and sustains the world as we know it, complex and minute, is able to know and claim every one of us, regardless of who we are." To this affirmation of hope, the woman simply replied, "It is too terrible, terrible, terrible," and, after a brief pause, she changed the subject: "How is Miss Duncan?"[3]

Here, the chaplain engages in hoping, a hoping that the dying woman does not share. At first, he simply expresses it: "I hold the same hope for you that I hold for myself." When she questions this statement, wondering how he could see any similarity between her situation and his own, he tries to clarify what he means, namely, not hope in the here and now, but hope for life after death, for as the physical "drops away" the spiritual "gains strength." Then, to explain further, he offers his conviction that the one who creates and sustains the world is also able to know and to claim everyone, so that in effect when we die we are not lost. The woman's response, "It is too terrible," and her abrupt attempt to change the subject suggest that his hope, even after his effort to explain it, is incomprehensible to her. But to him, the "terrible" thing was her feeling of hopelessness. What must it be like to lack the sense that what is so dearly and passionately wanted will not come to pass?

Thus, wherever hoping occurs, we are likely to see deep disagreements among individuals, as those who do not share the other's hope

3. Richard C. Cabot and Russell L. Dicks, *The Art of Ministering to the Sick* (New York: Macmillan Company, 1936), 344–45. I am indebted to Gene Fowler for bringing this case to my attention.

are likely to say that "wishing won't make it so." Knowing that others are likely to make this observation, our intuition that things will turn out as we want them to leaves us feeling alone and isolated. As the chaplain in this case knows only too well, hoping can be a very lonely act. More often than not, our hopes are not shared by others, and this is what makes hoping a most remarkable thing. Most of the time, our hopes are entertained in the face of the skepticism of others. And we ourselves are often among the skeptics where others' hopes are concerned.

Fueled by Desire

Julia Kristeva, who was trained in the French psychoanalytic tradition of Jacques Lacan, has written eloquently about desire in several of her writings, and in doing so she has introduced desire—a central theme of the Christian mystical tradition—into contemporary theological discussion of the self-God relationship. In *In the Beginning Was Love,* Kristeva explores religion from the perspective of desire, and notes that "religion for Freud is a rather unrealistic construct which nevertheless gives an accurate representation of the reality of its subjects' desires."[4] Kristeva emphasizes the fact that desire is "a feature of Christian discourse," that it is identifiable in and behind Christian affirmations of belief (i.e., in the Credo).[5] Desire is also key to the relationship between self and God. In an especially compelling discussion of the writings of Bernard of Clairvaux, she notes that Bernard "considers psychological desire as being germane to any man who longs for what he does not have," and that, while desire for God is on a different plane from all other human desires, it is nonetheless rooted in these psychological desires. Moreover, for Bernard, the believer's desire for God is fulfilling only if he or she "recognizes that God desired us first to the extent of creating us in his image. That is why God is defined as also desiring, and desiring first. . . . Consider this mirrorlike motion: My desire will be fulfilled through Him, for He has fulfilled his own by creating me in his image."[6] We are, then, desiring beings, and it is in our desiring that we share a likeness to God, for it was God's nature to desire us even before we desired God.

    4. Julia Kristeva, *In the Beginning Was Love: Psychoanalysis and Faith,* trans. Arthur Goldhammer (New York: Columbia University Press, 1987), 11.
    5. Ibid., 44 and 37ff.
    6. Julia Kristeva, *Tales of Love,* trans. Leon S. Roudiez (New York: Columbia University Press, 1987), 159–60.

Hoping as named desire. In her discussion of Bernard and other mystics Kristeva is concerned with the relation of desire to love: love for the other, love for self, love for God. Instead, we are concerned with the role of desire in hoping. Even so, Kristeva's understanding of desire is important for us here as it emphasizes that desire expresses the self in its deepest and truest sense (i.e., in its sharing of the very image of God). Thus, to the extent that hoping is also an expression of desire, there is a deep investment of our God-given self in the human disposition to hope. When we hope, it is our true self that comes to expression, that manifests itself.

Yet, if desiring contains investment of our true self, it is often the case that our desires are difficult even for ourselves to understand. As Joel Kovel, another psychoanalytic thinker, has pointed out, "Desire consists of striving toward an object that cannot yet be named."[7] The infant longs for something but does not know "what" it is that she longs for. All that she "knows" is that she lacks something, misses something, something for which she longs and yearns. In contrast, her mother may know exactly what she desires, and, knowing what it is, she gives her something to drink.

I suggest, therefore, that hoping occurs as the identity of that which is desired becomes known to us. In this sense, hope does not exist until desire has been able to "name" its object, to say, *this* is what I long and yearn for. Thus, hoping reflects the clarification of our desires, enabling us to "know" where our desires lead and are leading us. Hoping entails the capacity to identify the object of our desire.

Hoping as persisting desire. Desire also draws our attention to the intensity of the intuitions involved in hoping. Desire may be compared with wishing, which is not as strong a term as desire in that wishing is less intense. On the other hand, desire is less intense than "craving," which reflects a more urgent need. As hoping is associated with desire and not with wishing or craving, it involves moderately intense feelings—longings and yearnings, not strong and uncontrollable cravings. What is most significant about desire, and what distinguishes it from both wishing and craving, is that its intensity is expressed in its persistence, as it continues to strive until its object is realized or proven to be unrealizable. Jacob's desire for Rachel was notable for its persistence. No substitute could satisfy his desire for her. In fact, the offering of a substitute, her sister Leah, only strengthened his desire

7. Joel Kovel, *The Age of Desire: Reflections of a Radical Psychoanalyst* (New York: Pantheon Books, 1981), 70.

for Rachel, and he was willing to continue working for seven more years for the object of his desire. Cravings are more urgent, but they are not as lasting. If we crave a certain food and know that we should not have it, we can sometimes talk ourselves into the fact that if we wait a half hour or so, the craving will pass. We are not as willing to dispense with our desires.

Because desire persists, it gives hoping a stability that other human propensities may lack. Because it is fueled by desire, hoping has staying power. Where wishes come and go, hopes persist because they are fueled by desire that, having identified its object, anticipates its realization. When we wish, we anticipate that it will not come to pass, and we normally wish about those matters whose outcome we are in no position to influence, even by the simple act of entertaining the wish itself: "If wishes were horses, then beggars would ride." The wish that it will rain tomorrow so that I don't have to wash my car is not something that I can influence. As God said to Job: "Can you lift up your voice to the clouds, so that a flood of waters may cover you?" (Job 38:34). But when we hope, we not only anticipate that the object of our desire will come about, but we also marshal our own energies and resources to make it so. Wishes have little staying power, little persistence, because they are not so invested with desire. When a wish becomes invested with desire, it is then on its way toward becoming a hope.

Response to Felt Deprivation

The third feature of hoping is that it is a response to felt deprivation. We hope because we sense or perceive that something is lacking in our lives, usually something that we believe we cannot live without. As Pruyser points out, "In order to hope one must first have some sense of captivity."[8] But I prefer the word "deprivation" to "captivity," as deprivation is more inclusive. Hoping is not frivolous. It is not an idle fantasy. It occurs because we want a change in the situation we are in. Something is missing or lacking in our lives. Oftentimes, what we lack is something that we have never experienced but that we have a strong sense of wanting and needing. We want the love we have never had, the recognition that we have never been afforded, the joyful life that has never been ours. Other times, what we lack is something we once had but have since been deprived of. We long for the presence

8. Paul W. Pruyser, "Phenomenology and Dynamics of Hoping," *Journal for the Scientific Study of Religion* 3 (1964), 87.

of our life's companion, now deceased. We are filled with nostalgia for our childhood home or childhood friends. Our sense of deprivation may involve something we took for granted until we lost it: our health, our work, our freedom to move about. Then we realize how important these things have been to us, how much we want them back, and what we would be willing to do to have them again.

An inner sense of deprivation. People often talk about hope as if it were primarily concerned with desiring what other people have. In this view, hope is typically spurred by envy or the desire to compete favorably with others. Certainly, many hopes are born out of the sense that we lack what others have: "Look at that big mansion with the swimming pool in the yard. I hope some day I'll have something like that." But our deepest hopes are generated by our own personal experience of deprivation. What other people have and we lack may stimulate us to hope for what they possess, but it is our own deep sense of lack, coming from inside us, that causes the yearnings that lead to our most heartfelt hope. One reason our hopes are sometimes so difficult to identify or define is because the lack we feel is deeply personal, and these deep personal deprivations are hard to put into words. We sense that our lives are unfulfilled, or that our existence seems purposeless and devoid of meaning. Or we have a deep sense of personal inadequacy, of not having the capabilities we want or need. Why we have these felt deprivations is difficult to say and difficult to talk about in a coherent and meaningful way. How to talk about something that we know only by its absence? This is our dilemma, yet it is precisely this dilemma, and our effort to think and speak meaningfully about it, that enables us to begin, first haltingly and then more self-confidently, to express our hopes. Our hopes get identified and formulated as we struggle with our perceived sense of deprivation, with what we sense is missing in our lives.

The experience of loss. Deprivations are not synonymous with loss, as we may experience a sense of deprivation over something that we have never had. Yet, losses are a major cause of a felt sense of deprivation and are therefore of great importance to the subject of hope. One reason the death of a loved one has been the single most prominent topic of pastoral care is that this is an experience of personal deprivation that is so profound, we do not know whether there could be anything we could ever hope for again after suffering such a loss. The hoping against hope that occurs in the wake of the loss reveals how deeply related hoping is to deprivation. Death takes from us the one with whom so many hopes, large and small, were shared. It also makes us desperately aware of our deprivation. Having taken our loved one from us, it deals the second blow of making painfully, irrevocably clear that there is a limit to what we can hope for. If we hope for our loved one to be restored to us, we hope in vain, and we face the stark and bitter truth that our deprivation cannot be erased, however long we live. We learn instead that we must make do with secondary hopes, with the compensatory hopes to which we manage in time to orient our lives.

Thus, the loss of a loved one and the way this loss threatens our very capacity to hope reveals that hopes are typically inspired by our sense of personal deprivation. What we hope for is determined by what we perceive ourselves to lack, either because it was never ours or because we no longer have it. Because many of our deepest hopes arise from the experience of having lost what we once had, our hopes are as likely to be addressed to the familiar as to the new and novel. At times, our hopes involve the envisioning of something genuinely and uniquely new for us, something we can only know in our imaginations, but, at other times, we envision the recovery of the familiar and the customary. The prisoner who anticipates parole wants to be able to walk the same streets he walked before and to sleep in the bed he slept in before his arrest and conviction. The released hostage informs the press that throughout his ordeal he thought mainly of being able to hug his wife and children once again and to sit down at the kitchen table to a large steak and a beer. These are not exotic dreams at all. These are hopes that are not directed toward some new experience, but toward the restoration of what one used to have.

In noting that hope is often about recovery and retrieval, we are able to see why hope has special poignancy for middle and older adults, for they are faced with the fact that some things are gone forever, while others can be recovered through effort and persistence. Herein lies the ambiguity of hope and of our need to develop discrimination and judgment. The wisdom that we often ascribe to the old is often nothing more and nothing less than the capacity to differentiate between reversible and irreversible deprivations.

The need for something new.   That hopes often center around losses should not, however, be exaggerated, as many of our hopes have to do with the realization of something never previously possessed or experienced, something that is genuinely new. Client-centered therapists in the 1960s pointed out that many of their counselees came to therapy from a deep sense of wanting and needing new experiences. Their lives had settled into a predictable routine, and this concerned them: Is this my life from here on out? Is my future just more of the same? If our felt sense of deprivation is deeply personal, this means that hopes are not for mass production, and what makes for hope in one case is cause for despair in another. If the deprivation is due to loss, our hope is not for something different, but for that which has been lost or, failing that, its nearest approximation. But, if the deprivation concerns the sense that there is more to life than one has experienced thus far, then we hope for something new and novel, and hopelessness is identified with the status quo. Where hopes are linked to deprivations due to loss, they hold promise insofar as these deprivations are perceived to be reversible. Where hopes are linked to deprivations associated with the sense that surely there is more to life, they hold promise insofar as we believe that our future can be different from our present and our past. As Frederick Townes Melges puts it, "With hope, the personal future is not certain and fixed but is viewed as being open, unfrozen, and full of opportunities."[9] Indeed, all hopes share the anticipation that the future is open and not closed, for whether we anticipate a future where things are like they used to be, or whether we envision a future where things are very different from what they are, these anticipations gain strength and credibility for us from the conviction that the future is not closed but open, that it is not frozen but brimming with possibility.

Hoping, then, is the perception that what is wanted will happen, a perception fueled by desire and in response to felt deprivation. Hoping involves all of these elements, and if any one of them is missing, we are probably witnessing something that approximates hoping but is something else. On the other hand, this understanding of hope reveals that it is not a rare thing at all. We are all creatures of desire, and all of us feel deprived in one way or another, so the necessary conditions for hoping are always present.

Yet, if this is so, why is it that we are so often despairing, so often lacking in the perception that what is wanted will happen? One obvious answer is that we cannot always have what we desire. Our desire is met by hard reality, and something has to give, and what gives, more often than not, is hope. There is another reason, however, that is more subtle and less frequently noted, and this is that we do not know what it is that we desire. If it is difficult to put our finger on why we feel

9. Frederick Townes Melges, *Time and the Inner Future* (New York: John Wiley and Sons, 1982), 178.

deprived and what we feel deprived of, it is also difficult to know what it is that we really want. This brings us to the matter of our hopes: If hoping involves the perception that what is wanted will happen, what is the "what" that is wanted? What is the "object" of our desire?

THE NATURE OF HOPES

Earlier, I suggested that hopes are projections that envision the realizable and thus involve risk. This understanding of hopes grows out of our previous consideration of the experience of hoping, as it implies that hopes are not vague imaginings but are specific as to what is wanted or desired. They are purposeful, giving focus and intentionality to desires, by envisioning anticipated outcomes.

Hopes as Projections

The idea that hopes are projections was anticipated in our earlier comments on desire, when we noted that desire becomes hoping when it is able to identify its object. Because hoping is primarily a matter of sensing or perceiving, we should expect that hopes would express themselves in imagistic form and not as concepts or ideas. If so, this invites us to consider hopes to be projections.

In psychology, a projection is the unconscious act or process of ascribing to others one's own ideas or intentions, especially when such ideas or intentions are considered undesirable. We may, for example, ascribe to another person sexual fantasies or aggressive intentions that are really our own. In photography, however, projection is the process of causing an image to appear on a screen. In a sense, both types of projection are based on an illusion and are therefore inherently false. Yet, we generally view the photographic representation on the screen as artistic, whereas the ascription of ideas or intentions to another person is viewed as inappropriate, unacceptable, and often pathological. Paranoia, for example, involves the false belief that someone wants to harm me.

One reason, and perhaps the major one, that we take a more positive view of photographic over psychological projection is that we understand the photographic projection to be the work of a creative mind, whereas psychological projection is the work of a mind that is disoriented or disturbed. The psychological projection is based on an error, the erroneous ascription of ideas and intentions to another, and once we become aware of the error, no useful purpose is served by retaining the projection. So, we set about the task of learning how to withdraw it, usually by putting something else—an accurate ascription of the other's intentions toward us—in its place. In photographic projection, the image has an artistic function, not in spite of but because of its illusory character. Such projections continue to be valuable precisely because they are illusory and thus allow us to imagine a reality other than our own everyday experience.

Hopes as creative illusions. Hopes are projections in the photographic sense, not the psychological sense as described here. They are illusions because they envision something that does not in fact exist, but they are the work of a creative mind, allowing us to imagine a reality other than our ordinary, everyday experience.

In his poem "Bright Star, Would I Were Steadfast as Thou Art,"[10] John Keats describes the stars as eternal watchers over the events of earth. He notes how they observe the motions of the sea, and how they watch the snow falling from their privileged vantage point far above the earth. He also pictures them watching his beloved at sleep. Stars, of course, do not literally "watch" what is taking place on earth. In fact, it is we who watch the stars, and not the stars that look down on us. Yet, by projecting onto the stars the ability to watch, and to watch forever, Keats expresses his own desire to be as the stars, to be able, like them, to gain a privileged vantage point from which to watch the scenes of earth. If only he could become an eternal watcher over the natural, recurring events of the sea's ebb and flow and the snow's descent. If only he could watch his beloved, night after night, as she sleeps peacefully in quiet repose.

Keats wrote this poem a few months before his death at the age of twenty-six and in full awareness of the fact that he was suffering from an incurable disease. But the projection itself was anything but diseased. It was not an expression of his disturbed mind, although, given his physical condition, some such disturbance was probably inevitable. Rather, it derived from his creative mind, as his image of the stars as eternal watchers expressed his agony over having to leave the earth and its wonderful scenes, and his yearning to be able to remain in touch with it somehow, if only from a distance. We would not want Keats to have concluded that he had falsely projected his own ideas and intentions onto the stars, and thus to withdraw the projection, possibly by destroying the poem. The image of stars as eternal watchers

10. Aileen Ward discusses the personal meaning of this poem for Keats in *John Keats: The Making of a Poet* (New York: The Viking Press, 1963), 297–300.

has an artistic function in spite of or even because of its illusory character, as it allows Keats—and those of us who have yearnings similar to his—to envision a reality other than our own everyday experience, which, in Keat's own case, was the experience of impending death.

Yet, more than an artistic image, Keats' eternal watchers are an image of hope: the hope that, as his earthly life draws to a close, he will be "lifted up" to take his place among the eternal watchers and will then be able to see with clarity what he now sees only in partial and distorted ways. To withdraw the projection would be in this case to withdraw hope itself. Hope is created and sustained through the image, and the image is a stay against the personal despair that he found himself fighting, day after day, as death drew nigh.

Hopes, then, are projections because they envision a future that is technically false and unreal, as it does not exist, and yet is profoundly true and real, as it expresses yearnings and longings that not only exist but are often more real than the objective world. When we hope, we envision eventualities that are not yet realities but yet appear to us as potential realities. Also, because hope is a projection, and thus involves images that play against the screen of the future, hope is a certain way of seeing, of visualizing, of foreseeing. We see or image forth realities that are not yet present to us and yet are made closer—almost within reach—by the images we project. In this sense, hopes are always a future projection, but through imaging, they make the future more palpably real and present to us.

Freud's criticisms of religion are relevant here, as they focused on religion's tendency to place severe limits on allowable projections. Noting that religion assures us of "a careful Providence" who watches over our lives and compensates us in a future existence for any frustrations suffered here, he contends that most people "cannot imagine this Providence otherwise than in the figure of an enormously exalted father."[11] As he expressed little sympathy for the idea of there being such "a careful Providence," Freud has usually been understood to be an atheist. Yet, his point that most of us cannot imagine this Providence except as "an enormously exalted Father" is important for two reasons. It suggests that religion, at least the religion of which Freud himself had experience, severely restricts our capacity to imagine Providence, or the ultimate source of hope, as it limits us to a single image of God. It also suggests that to image God as an enormously exalted father is

11. Sigmund Freud, *Civilization and Its Discontents,* trans. James Strachey (New York: W. W. Norton, 1962), 21.

to take the infant's rather than the adult's perspective on God, so that religion, in effect, never grows up. As Freud puts it, "The whole thing is so patently infantile."[12]

Freud believed that unlike religionists, artists are allowed much greater freedom to make and devise images (this, after all, is what art is all about); and that, in art, there is much more affirmation of the grandeur of the human self. Artistic images are not as likely to represent humans in abject and impotent forms (i.e., as helpless infants). If a poet ascribes to stars the capacity for seeing, he does not thereby diminish himself, for the metaphor of the seeing stars is, as it were, his own act of seeing and thus affirms a personal grandeur not unlike that of the stars.

The imaging of God. When we say that hope is a projection, it functions more the way it functions in art and less the way it functions, according to Freud, in religion. It is noteworthy, in this connection, that the "theology of hope" does not portray God in terms of immutable qualities or singular characteristics. Instead, theologians like Jürgen Moltmann view God in dynamic and future terms, such as "I will be what I will be" (Exod. 3:6) or "the coming of God."[13] In this sense, the theology of hope seems much closer to artistic forms of projection than to religious ones. At the same time, unlike the philosophers whom Freud criticizes for avoiding the problem of projection altogether by using abstract concepts and principles in their writings about God, these theologians have not been reluctant to use concrete images for God, as in Moltmann's use of various biblical images for the coming God.

As these biblical images were themselves the work of poets, we should not be surprised that poets are able to give us a richer collection of God images than theologians, who are often more involved in debates as to which images are legitimate and on what basis. Note the plethora of images of God in this poem by Rainer Maria Rilke:[14]

> You are the future, vast red dawn
> over the plains of eternity.
> You are the cock-crow ending the night of time,

12. Ibid., 21.

13. See W. H. Capps, ed., *The Future of Hope* (Philadelphia: Fortress Press, 1970), 28; also Jürgen Moltmann, trans. Margaret Kohl (San Francisco: Harper & Row, 1983), 19–27.

14. Rainer Maria Rilke, *Twenty Poems from The Books of Hours,* trans. Joan M. Erikson (Taucross Farm Press, 1988), 12.

the dew, the early matins and the maiden,
the stranger, the mother, death itself.

You are the form that transforms itself forever,
that always towers up out of fate, alone,
that remains unacclaimed and unlamented,
as undescribed as a primeval forest.

You are the deep essence of all things,
which does not reveal the final secret of its being
and shows itself always as what it is not:
the land as ship and the ship as shore.

This poem is itself a hopeful projection, hopeful because it recognizes the God "who is the future" as ever-changing, and thus as
mysterious and paradoxical, showing itself "always as what it is not."
Because this projection does not assign fixed and immutable traits to
God, or even a fixed identity to God, it implies that the future itself is
open to ever new possibilities. God, the deep essence of all things, is
identified with morning, with the new day—the cock-crow, the dew,
the early matins, the maiden, the stranger, the mother—and therefore
with the death of the previous day and of all the days that are past,
spent, and exhausted.

Images of hope as self-projections.   If hopes are a projection of the
future, what enables them to be so? How do such projections work?
What makes them happen? The process, it seems to me, works something like this: As desires in response to felt deprivation begin to stir,
they stimulate feelings of anticipation: "Perhaps things could be different." "Maybe change is possible." But what are these "things," what
are these "changes"? In response to such questions, inner questionings
of which we may not even be aware, images of what is wanted or
desired begin to take form, at first indistinct and then more clearly.
Even though no promises have yet been made, we envision ourselves
being informed that we have been chosen for the position for which
we interviewed, and we may also—if we wish to make a further projection—envision ourselves being enthusiastically welcomed on the
first day of work, warmly introduced to the other workers, and plunging
into our work with equal enthusiasm. These are images of the anticipated event, some more immediate, some more distant. They usually
enter our minds without a great deal of conscious effort. If we find we
have to work hard to create them, this is a signal that we either do not

desire this outcome as much as we thought, or that we do not have much hope that it will in fact materialize.

Because these images involve us, creating a scene in which we ourselves are implicated, images of hope are *self*-projections. By hoping, we project *ourselves* into the future and envision our existence being different from what it is at present. The fact that hoping involves self-projections has inspired some psychotherapists to focus on their client's current self-images (their image of themselves as presently experienced) and their image of themselves as future-projection (what they see themselves becoming in the near and more distant future). By helping their clients to identify these two self-images, present and future, therapists enable them to find ways to close the gap that separates them, usually by assisting them in realizing the future self, enabling it to become more real and more present to the client. I will return to this point in the final chapter of this book.

For now, though, the important point is that our images of hope include self-projections. When we image the future, envisioning the not-yet, we place ourselves in this scene, for, after all, it is not some abstract or impersonal future that we are projecting and envisioning. It is *our* future, and thus our own involvement in the image can always be assumed. Even when we envision a future in which we are physically absent, as when we imagine a scene in which our families have gathered to mourn our own death, we have projected ourselves into this future, as we have envisioned ourselves as deceased and as witnessing the scene that stretches out before us.

Images of hope as catalysts for change. Because the future is unpredictable and has its own reality, our hopeful projections rarely fit the future with perfect accuracy. We may get the job we sought, but we may be told when we arrive that we were actually their second choice, that the first person to whom they offered the job turned it down. We may then be introduced to the other workers in a perfunctory way and they in turn offer a perfunctory welcome. Because our hopeful images of the future are rarely accurate in all details, we are often cautioned against engaging in such projections, as we may find ourselves being terribly disappointed. We are told instead to be "realistic." In some contexts, the word "projection" has come to mean something very different from what it means in the context of hope, due to the very fear that our projections may be wrong or seriously distorted. When television news programs "project" the winner of an election, they do so on the basis of hard evidence (exit polling and so forth) and are not so much "projecting" a future as reporting an established fact. The same is generally true of actuarial projections and projections of hunger and starvation in the world. To allay suspicions that these projections may be based more on hope or even wishful thinking than on fact, the constructors of such projections will often say that their projections are "conservative," that is, if they err, they err on the side of what is clearly known and established fact, rather than on the side of what is hoped for. This means that the photographic view of projection is being replaced by that of the social scientist, and that hope is being devalued in the process. It is increasingly difficult for hope to maintain itself in human society when it is hemmed in by those (often religionists) who would restrict the number and nature of the images we are allowed, and by those (often scientists) who prefer established facts to risky projections.

Thus, the more that hope is involved in a projection, the more likely the projection will violate or run counter to known or presumed facts. This does not mean, however, that such projections should be discouraged or suppressed, for, as Erikson has argued, hope is often the decisive element in *changing* the world of facts: "Hope not only maintains itself in the face of changed facts—it proves itself able to change facts, even as faith is said to move mountains."[15] If our projections are based only on what is certain, our calculus will be deprived of the life-changing potentialities of hope itself. Jack has tried to stop smoking so many times before. Why believe that this time it will be different? Hope's projections may not turn out to be accurate; they may prove to have been completely wrong. But they should not be discouraged or suppressed, for they are catalysts for change as they enable us to realize a future that is different from what it would have been had we not allowed ourselves to hope. As projectors of hope, we are in that very act becoming the agents of hope.

We should keep in mind that change itself is inevitable. The future will not be the same as the present, even as the present is not the same as the past. Basing itself on this known fact, hope chooses to anticipate the nature of the changes that may occur. It knows that such anticipations are risky and subject to error. Yet, future projections are in fact realities, as they have impact on the current state of affairs. This is why the capacity to hope was so vitally important to the prisoners in Nazi concentration camps during World War II. By projecting a future, hope alters the present. Physically, the prisoners were captives of the

15. Erik H. Erikson, "Human Strength and the Cycle of Generations," *Insight and Responsibility* (New York: W. W. Norton, 1964), 117.

Nazis, but inwardly they achieved a margin of freedom to the extent that they were able to hope. To project hopes is to achieve some degree of autonomy in the present. The margin of freedom that such projections effect may be slight, but it can be the difference between life and death.

Hopes as Envisionings of the Realizable

If hoping involves the perception that what is wanted will happen, it follows that our projected hopes will be envisionings of what is realizable. Hopes are not projections of what we believe to be impossibilities, as the very projection of impossibilities would not make for hope but for hopelessness and would therefore be grounds for despair. When we hope, we anticipate the realization of what is projected.

If so, this does not mean that hope only envisions *realistic* possibilities. To say that hope envisions the realizable does not mean that it is bound by the practical, the sensible, the proven, or the tried and true. In many situations, we have no way of knowing on the basis of prior experience what is or is not realizable. Sometimes, we realize more than previous experience would have indicated is possible. In other cases, we realize much less. So, hopes are not based on calculations of what is realistic on the basis of prior experience. Instead, they are based on the view that the future is open and that the future is to some degree amenable to our efforts to make a difference.

When we tell someone to be realistic, we often plunge a knife into hope itself, as such admonitions often create a spirit of quiet despair. Parents often tell their children to be realistic—about themselves, about their abilities and capacities, about their future prospects. Pastors often tell young couples who are about to be married to be realistic—about the problems they will inevitably face, about the dangers of relying on romantic love to see them through the crises of married life, and about the misplaced trust in marriage to effect change in their personalities, habits, attitudes, and behavior. Certainly, children and young couples need such admonitions, and, no doubt, parents and pastors are qualified to offer them. Yet, the adoption of a realistic approach can erode a hopeful approach to life, as it may cause us to settle for a less full and vital life than would in fact be accessible to us. As already noted, hopes change the world of facts. They enable our children to accomplish more than *we* ever thought possible, and they enable young couples to experience marriages that may in fact be far happier than those of the adults who are cautioning them not to expect more from marriage than they can realistically hope to experience.[16]

16. Also see the pastoral care case of Andy in Donald Capps, *Reframing: A New Method in Pastoral Care* (Minneapolis: Fortress Press, 1990), chap. 5.

The reversibility of loss.   But perhaps what is behind the thinking of those whose advice to us to be realistic is the belief that there are ways to assess in advance the possibilities for the realization of what we desire. If, for example, many of our deepest hopes emerge out of the experience of personal loss, one way to determine whether a given hope is realizable is to reflect on how the loss occurred and to arrive at a considered judgment as to whether this loss can be reversed, or whether it simply has to be "lived with." I know a man who wished he had never sold the 1948 Ford convertible that he owned when he was in college. When he retired a couple of years ago, he bought a 1948 Ford convertible and is in the process of restoring it to mint condition. It's not the same car, and he is no longer the dashing young man who traded his convertible for a family station wagon. But his sense of loss has been at least partially reversed.

This illustration shows that we have some measure of the realizability of a hope in the reversibility of a loss. The less reversible the loss, the less realizable the hope. One reason most of us remain hopeful even when the situation is very difficult and grim is that we can envision a loss being at least partially reversed. If we lose a well-paying job and are forced to take a lesser-paying one, we may console ourselves with the fact that, it we work hard, we stand a chance of a better paying job in the future. A minister always preached from a manuscript until his failing eyesight made this impossible. Now he preaches without a manuscript, and what his sermons lack in terms of tight systematic presentation is more than made up for in color and natural wit. And, of course, the sight of a blind person in the pulpit is its own inspiration.

On the other hand, there are situations in which our anticipation of the reversal of our loss is very weak. By definition, terminal illness is one in which there are little if any grounds for anticipating a reversal. Our hopes in such situations may therefore center less on the antic- ipation of such a reversal and more on how long one can expect to live, how painful it will be, how severe will be the physical and mental debilitation, and the extent to which the pain and debilitation can be moderated by pain-killing drugs and a positive mental attitude. If hope is to survive in situations where the loss is irreversible, our hopes may need to be recentered or redirected. This may involve focusing on other, realizable goals, such as surviving at least through the Christmas season, or getting one's financial affairs in order, or becoming rec- onciled with a particular family member, or resolving not to succumb to personal bitterness but to maintain one's good humor to the end.

Or, our focus may shift from hopes related to our present life on earth to hopes concerning the life to come. Most of us have the desire that death will not be final, and that whatever form our existence may take after we die, it will be more whole and complete than our earthly life has been. We have this desire, but we differ a great deal in our anticipation that this will in fact occur. For some of us, our anticipation of such an afterlife is very strong. For others, it is rather weak. Its strength or weakness is influenced by many factors but is related in part to whether we have found a way to image our future beyond the grave. Job imagined God setting a time to remember him sometime after his death (14:13), a time when God would recall and summon him. He was also impressed by the sight of a dead tree stump from which new leaves had sprouted because a spring flowed underneath. But he questioned whether this image of hope applied to himself, for, once dead, a human is cut off from all independent sources of life (14:7-10).

Persons for whom an afterlife is at best a faint hope are not necessarily unbelievers. Polls that have been conducted throughout the world over the past four decades always reveal fewer believers in an afterlife than believers in God. In some nations of the world, there is a 30- to 40-percent difference between the two beliefs. Thus, some believers in God do not anticipate a life with God beyond the grave, possibly because they are unable to imagine what such a life may be. This suggests a link between the projective feature of hope and envisioning what is realizable, as the images reinforce the hope. What images of life beyond the grave typically do for us is to enable us to envision the reversal of the ultimate loss resulting from personal death. It is not, as Freud suggested, that we anticipate compensation in the future life for frustrations experienced here, but that we envision the reversal of the loss that we sustain at death, the loss of life itself.

What is possible for me? The principle of reversibility is useful where the deprivation involves loss, but what about deprivations that have to do not with loss, but with the desire for something we have never before experienced or possessed? As with deprivations due to losses, we cannot have certain knowledge as to whether such hopes are realizable. If we could be certain that something we desire will come about, there would be no need for hope. As St. Paul puts it, "Now hope that is seen is not hope. For who hopes for what is seen?" (Rom. 8:24). On the other hand, we have already noted the problems with allowing what is "realistic" to determine whether a hope is entertained or not, for this is based on what we currently know, or believe that we know, and not on the fact that the future is fully capable of

surprising us. There are always more possibilities than a realistic assessment of our situation recognizes or acknowledges. The question
then becomes not "What is realistic to hope for?" but "What is possible
for me?" One reason we resent admonitions to be "realistic" is that
we suspect that they are based not on intimate knowledge of ourselves,
but instead on a knowledge of humanity in general or on some group
or category of humans with whom we are being identified on the basis
of age, gender, race, or cultural background. We feel that if the other
person really knew us, in our own unique individuality, he or she would
not be voicing these admonitions or would at least express them very
differently.

The question "What is possible *for me?*" points instead to the role
of self-knowledge in the formulation and realization of hopes. Based
on what we know about ourselves, we may anticipate that certain things
are possible for us and others are not. We weigh the possibilities that
are in front of us in light of our understanding of ourselves, our tem-
perament, our traits, our motivations, our values. What we envision to
be realizable is thus profoundly influenced by what we understand
ourselves to be.

We know, of course, that the realization of certain possibilities does
not depend entirely on us. But we also know that who we are has a
powerful influence on what we can anticipate in the future. If we
envision ourselves becoming medical doctors some day, but also know
that we do not have the personal motivation to endure years of medical
training, or that we hate science or cannot stand the sight of blood, it
should become clear to us, sooner or later, that the hope of becoming
a medical doctor is not a real possibility for us. On the other hand, if
we know that we do have the motivation to endure prolonged medical
training, and that we love science and do not hate the sight of blood,
the hope of becoming a medical doctor is a real possibility for us. It
is not a certainty, as there are many factors besides these that could
affect the outcome, some of which are entirely outside our control.
(Keats discovered while in medical training that he was incurably ill,
which is why he became a poet instead.) With hope, however, the
issue is not certainty but possibility, and genuine hope is based on
what is possible *for us.* The point is not that we should be realistic
about our chances for realizing this or that, but that we should make
an effort to know ourselves and to entertain those hopes that are not
contradicted by what we learn. Without self-knowledge, we are likely
to entertain hopes that will never be realized, and then we are more
not less likely to experience the future as closed. Self-knowledge enables us to envision the best of all possible worlds for us, not the best

of all possible worlds in general. The most hopeless situation of all is to be condemned to envision *for oneself* the innumerable possibilities that the future holds for all of us put together. As Biff, in Arthur Miller's *Death of a Salesman,* complained to his mother, "I just can't take hold, Mom, I can't take hold of some kind of life."[17]

Hopes Involve Risk

Because they involve desires that may or may not be realized, hopes are inherently risky. It is all too easy to idealize hopes, to declare that they are inherently good as they manifest a positive attitude toward the future. Yet, because the future is open, there is always the risk that our hopes will *not* be realized. Disappointment, demoralization, even feelings of devastation may follow. Given the risks involved, we sometimes keep our hopes to ourselves, so that if they do not materialize, we will not have the added humiliation of public failure. For much of the hoping we do, however, concealing hopes from others does not work because our hopes are revealed more by the way we live our lives than by what we say. A couple who have been dating for several months do not have to tell us in words that certain hopes are associated with this relationship. If, in time, we no longer see them together, we know without being told that certain hopes have not been fulfilled.

To hope, then, is to place ourselves at risk. We risk the failure of our hopes and the shame and humiliation that often accompany the failure of hopes. When our hopes fail, we take it very personally because in hoping we invest ourselves, putting our very existence on the line.

If one risk of hopes is that they set us up for possible failure, another danger is that they may direct us to unworthy goals or cause us to overlook other, more desirable objectives. We can become captive to certain hopes precisely because we judge them to be more realizable than others. Some hopes are realizable, but the price is too high. One may become the top salesperson in the firm—a long-desired goal— but find that the price in terms of shattered personal relationships, weakened personal integrity, and broken personal health was far too high. Or one finds that the achievement of professional success does not bring the anticipated personal satisfaction or financial security. There are also instances when the realization of some cherished hope leaves us confused or apathetic, as we no longer have the goal that previously energized us. Unfulfilled hopes cause despair, but fulfilled

17. Erik H. Erikson, *Identity: Youth and Crisis* (New York: W. W. Norton, 1968), 131.

hopes often cause depression, apathy, and boredom. People who discern that they are especially prone to such reactions in the wake of hope's fulfillment—people with self-knowledge—will often entertain more than one hope, or hopes that build on one another, so that when one hope is realized they have already oriented their lives toward another. As Erikson puts it, "It is in the nature of man's maturation that concrete hopes will, at a time when a hoped-for event or state comes to pass, prove to have been quietly superseded by a more advanced set of hopes."[18]

Balancing hope and love.   Another risk that hopes present is that we become so oriented toward their attainment that we neglect the satisfactions our present situation already affords. This is often used as an argument for curbing our desires and for being content with what we have. But a more useful perspective is to realize that our current situation is, in part, the fruit of various past hopes that have been fulfilled, and we should not therefore neglect their continuing meaning for us. We may need a hope-beyond-hope to sustain us through the period of depression or apathy that follows the realization of a given desire, but there are also times when our envisioning of still another hope causes us to overlook the satisfactions that previously realized desires afford.

Hope has a restless quality to it. By definition, it is oriented to the future. It should not be curbed or stifled, but it is not everything, and sometimes it needs to be balanced by other perceptions and experiences. When we experience satisfaction in our present reality, we allow love an equally significant place in our lives. Where hope is always oriented to the realizable, love is appreciation for what we already have. So, a discerning life—a life of wisdom—is based on our capacity to balance our hopes and our loves, and not to allow our lives to be dominated by one or the other.

Risks for others.   Still another risk in hopes is their consequences for others. There are times when our hopes, if realized, will make life more difficult for others, especially those who are dependent on us. A husband and father is offered a position with a new company in Denver and he takes it, leaving his secure but rather dull position in Syracuse for greater professional fulfillment. For reasons of their own, some members of the family may invest the move with hope: "The

18. Erik H. Erikson, "Human Strength and the Cycle of Generations," *Insight and Responsibility* (New York: W. W. Norton, 1964), 117.

teachers here in Syracuse keep reminding me how smart my older sister was. The teachers in Denver won't know anything about her." But others may find that their hopes are threatened by the move: "Just when I was making some really good friends in high school, Dad announces that we're picking up and moving."

Knowing that our hopes may carry risks for others, we may decide they are not worth the price that others may have to pay for them, and we resign ourselves to their unfulfillment. We may continue to harbor resentments against those who inhibited the realization of these hopes. Some people carry such resentments to their graves: "If only Jim had been more courageous and less practical." "If only I had trusted my own judgment instead of listening to Liz, with all her objections and 'what ifs.' " In turn, children of parents who sacrificed their own hopes for "the sake of the children" may carry through life the sense that they were the unwitting cause of a parent's disappointment or were made the scapegoat for a parent's inability to take the necessary personal risks involved.

Thus, as future projections that envision the realizable, hopes are risky and are typically experienced as such. Hopes can be exciting, scary, or unnerving. Unlike reveries, musings, and daydreams, hopes anticipate real changes, and because they do, we should not romanticize hope as if it were an utterly harmless activity. Hopes can have tremendously positive outcomes, but they are also responsible for harm. One test of our maturity as persons is our ability to hope in ways that do not put other individuals at unacceptable levels of risk. Other tests of our maturity are the willingness to accept higher levels of risk for ourselves than will be required of others, and our ability to make intentional, self-conscious efforts to minimize the costs of our hopes to others.

Hoping, then, is the perception that what is wanted will happen. It is fueled by desire and occurs in response to felt deprivation. Hopes are projections that envision the realizable and thus involve risk. Implicit in these understandings of hoping and hopes is a particular view of the self. It is a view of the self as fluid, as more process than entity. The self is not ascribed fixed traits or characteristics, nor is there an attempt to locate the self within moral discourse (i.e., to define what is the "good" self). In a very real way, the self here is understood more by what it lacks than by what it has or possesses, for, after all, it emerges from a sense of felt deprivation and is therefore identifiable by what it longs for rather than by what it can be said already to be or to consist of. The human self that is implied here is similar to

Moltmann's view of God's self as "I will be what I will be." Thus, to
the question "What is the self?" we do not respond with nouns but
with verbs: It is anticipating, desiring, risking. The self that hopes is
restless, like hope itself.

Yet, this does not mean that the hoping self is merely protean[19]—
ever-changing and therefore never identifiable—or that it is merely
amoral—incapable of lasting commitments—for, as we have seen, the
self that hopes is also a self that loves. We would not hope had we
not first been the object of another's love, and we would not hope had
we not returned her love. If hoping, then, emerges from a sense of felt
deprivation, the deprivation we feel can be traced, ultimately, to the
physical absence—and the internalized presence—of the one with
whom we were first fully yet anxiously in love. So it would not be
accurate to say that the hoping self is protean and amoral. Unlike the
protean self, the hoping self knows from whence it came, and unlike
the amoral self, it knows and accepts the constraints that love inevitably
places on its imaginings and aspirations.

19. See Robert Jay Lifton, *The Protean Self* (New York: Basic Books, 1993).

four

A WOMAN DARES TO HOPE

As an illustration of hope, the pastoral care case that follows is somewhat ambiguous, and valuable for that very reason. Strong glimmerings of hope are present, but these are set against a backdrop and history of a great deal of hopelessness. The counselee in this case has taken a major step—leaving her husband—an action that culminates months of deliberation and planning. But the decision itself is still too recent and its painfulness too raw for her to take any satisfaction in what she has done. Instead, it leaves her depressed and feeling guilty. Yet, her decision to leave her husband is an expression of hope as it reveals her desire to do something about her felt sense of deprivation, deprivation that made the last five years of her life seem like fifty. The decision also reveals that she projected a hope—that of achieving freedom from a destructive situation—and has taken a major step toward its realization in spite of risks to herself and others. She has acted to secure a new life for herself, not to restore what she had lost, so she is still feeling her way. Hope has been born and acted upon. Where will it lead?

The pastor in this case is the associate director of pastoral care and counseling in a general hospital. He spends roughly half his time in individual, marriage, and family counseling, both short- and long-term, and the other half in supervision of the hospital's Clinical Pastoral Education program. Here is his account of the counselee and the problem that brought her to him.

Rhoda is a twenty-six-year-old married woman who separated from her husband Matt two weeks ago. She converted to the Roman Catholic Church in order to marry him. A friend of a friend referred her for counseling. She and Matt have no children. Her situation is unusual in that Matt was injured in a motorcycle accident one year after they

were married and left quadriplegic. Since his treatment in a hospital
and rehabilitation center, they had been living with his parents. During
all this time she worked at a high-level secretarial position and is
financially independent. Matt is confined to a wheelchair and bed and
requires a great deal of daily care. His parents are middle-class people
who, with some assistance, have been able to afford a van equipped
so that he can be transported around fairly easily. Rhoda came to the
first counseling session accompanied by her mother, who waited in
the waiting room. The counselor describes her as "unremarkable
in appearance" and reports that she spoke rather freely about her
concerns.

During the first session, Rhoda related the history of her marriage
and what had happened to Matt in the motorcycle accident. It was not
completely clear to the counselor why she was seeking counseling,
except that she was going through some stress related to the separation
and that she seemed depressed. She gave some indication that Matt
and his parents supported the idea of counseling with the hope that
the counselor would persuade her to go back and live with him again.
She made it quite clear in the first session that she had no intention
of going back and that her decision to leave was one that she had
pondered and struggled with for a long time. The following verbatim
material is from the second session.

COUNSELOR: How have you been? (*after several minutes of silence*).

RHODA: About the same I guess. I do have a lot of guilt about
             leaving Matt, but I really don't see any alternative.

COUNSELOR: I think you said last week you had thought about this for
             a long time, and tried to talk with Matt.

RHODA: Yes, for several months I've known, it's just that I never
             could communicate very well with them, Matt or his
             parents. Before the accident he often put me down. This
             sounds awful to say but I think he always was self-
             centered.

COUNSELOR: What was your marriage like before the accident?

RHODA: Oh, I don't know. Sometimes I can hardly remember. The
             past five years seem like fifty. We dated in high school
             off and on until he went to college. People sort of as-
             sumed we would get married.

COUNSELOR: You kind of drifted into marriage.

RHODA: Uh huh, we enjoyed doing things together. We got along all right, I suppose.

COUNSELOR: You only had about a year of marriage before the accident?

RHODA: Something like that.

COUNSELOR: And then you were living with a quadriplegic and his parents.

RHODA: *(Thoughtfully:)* Nobody asked how I felt. I guess I was in shock. The first months when he was in the hospital and rehabilitation unit I was there every visiting hour. I learned how to take care of him and did it. They said it would get easier and it did as far as the actual doing it was concerned, but emotionally it got harder.

COUNSELOR: By leaving you finally acted on the emotional distance?

RHODA: I tried to talk to Matt and his parents. He'd get mad. I'd tell him, "I have to get away from here for a while," and he'd think I meant a day or two, and then I tried to tell him I wasn't coming back, but he just wouldn't hear me. His parents didn't either. Eventually his mother told me she would do all the daily care if I would stay there and be his companion. I taught her everything so I could leave. She didn't understand.

COUNSELOR: Nobody asked you how you felt, and when you finally tried to tell them, they didn't really hear you.

RHODA: I tried to tell Matt that I don't love him anymore; I guess I care about what happens to him.

COUNSELOR: There's really not much of a relationship left, except guilt. It doesn't seem you were very verbal with each other, and after the accident, there wasn't the possibility of doing things on a physical level either.

RHODA: Oh, this is really odd, but for some reason he can still do it, I mean perform sexually. It's really important to him.

COUNSELOR: Perhaps it's one of the few remaining ways he can feel like a man.

RHODA: I can see his feelings, it's just that it doesn't really mean anything to me. It never was that important to me, I guess.

COUNSELOR: It would be pretty impossible to just be a companion and friend-type person for him now.

RHODA: Yes.

COUNSELOR: Did he ever suggest that you leave him?

RHODA: No. He said he felt guilty, but he didn't want me to go. I think he was terrified I would, that's why he couldn't even talk about it. I haven't seen him in two weeks. I tried to call a couple of times. Once he hung up after a couple of minutes, another time his mother said he was sleeping.

COUNSELOR: Communication seems impossible. You're living with your parents now?

RHODA: Yes.

COUNSELOR: How do they relate to you?

RHODA: I think they understand. They don't express an opinion. I think my mother pampers me *(first smile of session)*.

COUNSELOR: You kind of like that.

RHODA: It's O.K. for now. Eventually I have to get out on my own. I left him with half the savings account, and he gets social security.

COUNSELOR: *(Nod and glance at clock.)*

RHODA: I don't know what else there is to talk about. I just feel so empty.

COUNSELOR: That's something you may need to talk more about, your emptiness, feeling dead.

RHODA: Yes, maybe.

COUNSELOR: Do you think it would be helpful to come back and talk next week?

RHODA: I suppose I could.

COUNSELOR: O.K. I'll see you next Thursday at 8 o'clock.

As it turned out, Rhoda did not come back to talk. Due to bad weather, she did not keep her next appointment and then did not reschedule. In his case report, the counselor said that he felt she came for counseling mainly to satisfy the pressure she was feeling to get some counseling so that her decision to leave her husband "would look less impulsive or self-centered." Nonetheless, he expressed the wish that she had not terminated counseling, because he had wanted to give more attention to her depression.

In his assessment of his counseling of Rhoda, the counselor emphasized his ethical contextualism, pointing out that "it was important for me to understand the context of Rhoda's decision to leave." He lifted up three contextual issues: The first was that Rhoda and Matt's marriage "was not particularly strong even before the accident." The second was that Matt "has almost no chance to have another relationship with a woman, so her leaving deprives him of both companionship and sexual contact with a female. Unlike most any other divorce decision, she is determining for him that he will be celibate for the rest of his life." The third contextual issue was that Rhoda "consented to the sacramental aspect of marriage practiced in the Catholic Church." He raised the question as to whether this makes her "duty to stay in the marriage more pronounced."

On the basis of this contextual inventory, he concludes that Rhoda's "decision to leave may well fall in the range of [ethically] acceptable alternatives, although it is by no means clearly the best alternative from a Christian standpoint." Quoting ethicist James Sellars, he questions whether Rhoda is demonstrating the "critical standards of excellence which [are] to be found in the Christian faith." But, even as he did not condemn her actions at the time of his counseling sessions with her, he says he does not condemn her now.

He does not allude to hope in his comments on the case. Nor did he or Rhoda use the word "hope" during the counseling sessions. Yet, this case is very much about hope, as hope is its central dynamic. Hope may be said to be the deep structure or depth dimension of this particular counseling case. While unspoken and unverbalized, hope is what was behind Rhoda's actions and is what currently sustains her, her depressive demeanor notwithstanding. Let us look at the case, then, viewing it through the lenses provided by the understandings of hoping and hopes presented in the previous chapter.

A WOMAN ENGAGED IN HOPING

We have seen that hoping is the perception that what is wanted will happen, a perception fueled by desire in response to felt deprivation. This applies to Rhoda and is very much what she is experiencing now. Her action in leaving Matt is the culmination of months of reflecting on the possibility that she might gain her freedom, that she might be able at last to live a life of her own choosing. After months of doubting and struggling with her conscience, she is now beginning to experience hopefulness, the sense that what she desires is now beginning to happen. She has left Matt and vows that she will never return to him. The past is over and the future has begun. She has acted out of the sense that her future is open, that a new life is unfolding before her.

As her conversation with the counselor reveals, she finds it difficult to communicate her newfound hope to another person. It seems she cannot express it very clearly or confidently even to herself, because the realization of its truth is so new. Yet, what also makes it difficult to communicate is the fact that to talk about her hopefulness, given the circumstances, seems callous and unfeeling toward Matt: "How can I be thinking about my hopes for the future when he is being consigned to a more miserable life?" The counselor alludes to this very problem both in the counseling session and in the case report. He makes the point to Rhoda that Matt has feelings and needs, and he wonders whether Rhoda is taking these sufficiently into account. She responds, "I can see his feelings, it's just that it doesn't mean anything to me." In the case report, he notes that Matt will probably be deprived forever of the love and care of a woman other than his mother.

The only time Rhoda seems to make even an indirect reference to her hope is when she notes, with quiet satisfaction, that she has been training Matt's mother to care for him so that she herself could eventually leave. If there is an edge of revengefulness in this comment— "Matt's mother never caught on to what I was really doing"—there is also a note of determination that she would do what was required in order to realize her hope of gaining her freedom.

Thus, sometime during the past months, Rhoda had begun to experience the sense that what she wanted might in fact be something that she could have. Deprivation gave rise to desire, and desire gave stimulus to hope, and this hope was strengthened and confirmed by the reaction she received from Matt and his parents. They did not understand how deeply deprived she felt, and their failure to understand this was further evidence of her emotional deprivation. Matt's pleadings certainly gave her pause, as they appealed directly to her sense of responsibility and played forcibly on her sense of guilt. In the end, however, these appeals were in vain, because the desire to overcome her sense of deprivation was too strong for it to be suppressed or renounced. Desire prevailed over these appeals to self-renunciation.

I am suggesting, therefore, that all of the elements of hoping are present in this case: There is a deep sense of deprivation that gives rise to desire that, in turn, gives rise to hope. The deprivation that she experienced was not primarily due to loss, because what she lacked was not something she once had, but something she had never really known, something having to do with personal freedom, personal independence, and the desire to be valued for herself. Because it was not based on an identifiable loss, her felt deprivation was difficult to communicate. The counselor attempted to relate her decision to leave Matt to loss, suggesting that the marriage was happier prior to his accident. But she challenged this interpretation, indicating that her sense of deprivation was far more related to what she had never experienced than to anything that she might have lost because of her husband's accident and disability. Marriage to Matt had never been especially fulfilling for her, as they had drifted into marriage, and he was too self-centered, even before the accident, to be concerned about her personal feelings or needs. So, reversing loss was not the desire behind her decision to leave. Her desire was for something different, a life more to her own choosing, a life that promised to be more self-fulfilling.

By all indications, her life with Matt consigned her to a closed future. This was not because of his disability, but because she felt herself to be a stranger in his parental home. As time went on, she felt herself deprived of life itself, five years seeming like fifty. Thus, by acting as she did, she made it clear that she was unwilling to consign the remainder of her life to what was, in effect, a state of hopelessness. She acted not out of revenge against Matt, but out of hope for herself.

HAVING HOPES MEANS
TAKING RISKS

As we have seen, a hope is a projection that envisions the realizable and thus involves risks. Rhoda's decision to leave Matt was an image that she had projected some months earlier. Because her own desires were involved, there was considerable self-investment in this projection. It had profound implications for her self-understanding, both as the individual she was (her present self-image) and the individual she saw herself becoming (her future self-image). She had resisted this particular image of her freedom from Matt and his family for several years, forcing it out of her mind even as she denied and renounced the desires that fueled it. But, as she appealed to Matt to hear and he was unwilling to do so, her image of hope took form and became clearer in her mind: "Yes, this is what must happen. It must happen this way." Then, Matt's mother's efforts to solve the problem by proposing a division of labor, herself assuming responsibility for Matt's physical care and Rhoda providing him wifely companionship (meeting his sexual needs?), enabled Rhoda to see that her vision of freedom was no idle fantasy, that it was in fact realizable for her. What had clouded this image from the outset was the fact of Matt's disability and his need for physical care. Until his mother made her proposal, Rhoda had believed that she was indispensable to Matt, that his survival depended on her. Now, her image of hope seemed realizable for her, for she could teach Matt's mother how to care for him and she herself would no longer be needed. Indeed, this arrangement would recognize the truth that she had long suppressed, that Matt's mother could—and would—meet all of Matt's needs except the sexual ones. It is little wonder that sex, for Rhoda, was "never that important to me."

The fact that Rhoda continued to feel guilty about what took place indicates that practical considerations—the physical care of Matt—were not the only impediments to the realization of her projected hope. As others had just assumed that she and Matt would get married, so she had just assumed they would stay married. His disability made it the more unthinkable that she might leave him some day. To leave him would be wrong, a violation of her conscience and a violation of her image of herself as a woman who stands by her husband when he needs her. There was the image of hope and, practically speaking, it was realizable. She knew this because other women had left their husbands and gone on to have fulfilling lives. But was it possible *for her,* for the self who is Rhoda? This was the crucial question, one that no one else could answer for her. In his analysis of the case, the counselor questioned whether she had chosen "the most excellent alternative from a Christian perspective." But she was not thinking about alternatives. She had an image of hope before her, and the question was whether she could truly project herself into it. The reason she was able, after much soul-searching, to see it as genuinely possible *for her* was that she took a searching look at herself, at what was becoming of her, and she was sufficiently disturbed by what she saw that she was able to marshal her inner resources toward the realization of her hope. She saw the person that Matt and his family were making of her, and she must have wondered why she had not protested years ago. She was feeling terribly deprived, as her past five years felt like fifty, and each day she returned from work to enter Matt's parents' home, the self that was hers was again taken captive. And now, quite simply, she wanted out.

I am suggesting, therefore, that Rhoda's image of hope was the leaving of Matt and his family, and that her struggle centered on the question of whether this image was possible for her. Since she did in fact leave him, we know how she answered this question, and we know how difficult it was to answer it in the way she did. Her depression is evidence of this. Yet, there is a corollary question that often arises when a momentous decision has been made and acted upon: "Was it really *I* who took the action taken? Was it truly *self*-initiated, or was it the action of a surrogate, even an imposter, acting on my behalf?" That she is adamant that she will not return, no matter how hard she might be pressured to do so, indicates that she is certain that the action was that of her true self. Still, she is having difficulty silencing the voice of guilt, which brings us to the fact that hope involves risk, always to self and often to others.

At this point, Rhoda isn't sure how things will turn out for her, and she realizes that she has taken a risk in leaving a situation that she at least clearly understood, placing herself instead in one of considerable ambiguity, its many possible consequences being as yet a great unknown. Will she be able to live without Matt and without the responsibility of caring for him? Will she be able to live with the fact that she has "walked out on him," that she will be confronted with the knowledge that others with whom she comes into contact will have difficulty understanding her action and will, moreover, view it as a sign of moral weakness, not of moral strength?

As she is financially independent, the greatest risks in Rhoda's case are psychological. She has relinquished her self-image as a wife who sacrifices herself, whatever the cost may be, before a new self-image is firmly in place. In the interim, her sense of self is seriously endangered, and this sense of self-endangerment is more responsible for her depression than her guilt, for underlying her present endangerment is a deep inner rage over the fact that her selfhood is now endangered. She feels anger toward Matt and his parents for what they did to her, but her rage goes deeper than what she feels toward them. It is a self-rage, an inner battle between two contesting selves, the one who tried to be responsible and self-giving for so many years and the one that is now coming to birth and whose shape and form is as yet unclear. This battle for her very soul leaves her feeling depleted, or, as she says, "I just feel so empty." No wonder, then, that she allows herself to be pampered by her mother, her original agent of hope. The counselor is right: Her depression should be addressed. But, we should also recognize that beneath her depression lies a firm fundament of hope: She mourns for the self that is dying inside, but she also yearns for the self that is coming to birth and ushering in the new day.

Rhoda's action in leaving Matt also places him at risk. As with Rhoda, the risk is psychological, as Matt has his mother to take care of his physical needs. The counselor has a point when he suggests that Matt's "sense of manhood" has already been dealt a severe blow because of the accident, and now Rhoda's leaving him exacerbates this still further. One is reminded here of the popular song, "Ruby," about a man severely wounded in war who watches helplessly as his wife leaves him in the evening and "takes her love to town." As she leaves the house, ignoring his plea to "turn around," he considers killing her or killing himself. Matt expresses his own rage by refusing to talk with Rhoda when she phones.

Acting on her hope for a new future for herself, Rhoda has certainly put Matt at psychological risk, but she has made the personal judgment that the gains for herself outweigh the risk to Matt. To help ensure this, and to demonstrate that she bears him no ill will, she has left him with half of the savings account, has taught his mother how to care for his physical needs, and has taken the initiative of getting in touch with him by phone. It may be that she could do more to mitigate the pain and humiliation that her leaving inflicts on him, but from what she reports she has done what she can to minimize the risk to Matt himself. We might even say that she has given Matt a potential gift in leaving him, the chance for him to develop a new self based on a new understanding of what it means to be a man. There is more to manhood than physical mobility and sexual performance, and Matt is now in a position to discover what this may be. The counselor may be right in noting that Rhoda has effectively deprived Matt of the love of a woman from this time forth, but since he seemed incapable of truly loving the woman he already had, it may be that her leaving him will enable him to discover what it truly means to love another.

Hopes, then, involve risk for self always and for others often. Yet, Rhoda's action is based on the conviction that she can no longer follow the path of the renunciation of her desires. She knows that what she has done carries great risk, and she needs no one to remind her that this is so. As noted in our earlier discussion of the risks involved in hoping, one test of our maturity is our ability to hope in ways that do not put other individuals at unacceptable levels of risk. I believe that Rhoda has met this test regarding Matt. Another test is the willingness to accept higher levels of risk for ourselves than are required of others, and our ability to make intentional, self-conscious efforts to minimize the costs of our hopes to others. Here, too, Rhoda has demonstrated such maturity. She has placed herself at the greatest risk of all, greater,

I would say, than the pain that she is causing her husband. When a woman closes the door behind her and walks out into a new world, she takes the ultimate risk of all, that the new world will be a carbon copy of the old and her act of courage will go for naught. This is the risk that Rhoda now confronts, and the future of hope itself hangs in the balance.

THE LIMITS OF MORAL COUNSELING

Pastors are preeminently agents of hope, and therefore they want to do everything they can to affirm persons in their hopes. At the same time, pastors are moralists, and, whether conscious of their moral attitudes or not, they usually introduce moral feeling, if not moral judgment, into their pastoral counseling. The counselor in this case is no exception. He wants to affirm Rhoda and wants to view her decision to leave Matt in the most positive and noncondemnatory way possible. But he also has some moral feelings about her leaving a disabled husband and is not at all certain that she has acted according to the "critical standards of excellence which [are] to be found in the Christian faith." While her decision to leave Matt "may well fall in the range of [ethically] acceptable alternatives," it is "by no means clearly the best alternative from a Christian standpoint." His feelings about what Rhoda has done were communicated during the session itself, as he questioned her about the impact of her actions on her husband, and these questions may well have been a reason that she did not return for a third session. If she came to the counseling session not only to satisfy Matt and his parents, who hoped the counselor would show her the error of her ways, but also to persuade him that her decision was neither "impulsive" nor "self-centered," he does not seem to provide her the assurance she desires that he considers her decision to have been anything but impulsive and self-centered. If she came for a pastoral blessing, he did not offer it—not, at least, in so many words.

In his analysis of the case, there is a strong moral tone in his assessment of Rhoda's decision. He notes that she is depriving Matt of a "relationship with a woman" and "sexual contact with a female," and "determining for him that he will be celibate for the rest of his life." This comes across as a moral indictment of Rhoda, as it makes her out to be a rather selfish person in spite of the fact that she has devoted a number of years of her life to selfless care of her husband under very demeaning circumstances. It may also reflect, however unintentionally, a condescending view of Rhoda and perhaps of women in general, as it suggests that women are more or less interchangeable and primarily sex objects. He is also concerned that she seems to have reneged on her wedding vows, vows that were the more serious by virtue of the fact that they were taken in a Catholic church and were therefore part of a holy sacrament. He asks, "Does this not make her duty to stay in the marriage more pronounced?" Perhaps so, but does this not neglect another "contextual" factor that she had converted to the Catholic Church in order to marry Matt? He also notes, "Since marriage vows explicitly state a covenant through 'sickness and health,' it would seem that Rhoda was reneging on the original promise which she made before God and humankind." Also, a point well taken. Yet, would not a contextualist assessment of her actions take extenuating circumstances into account, especially the fact that her marriage was condemning her to a life of hopelessness and despair?

When persons act on desires, especially desires that are not easily explainable to others (and perhaps even to themselves), they are likely to become the objects of moral suspicion. Even pastors who view themselves as agents of hope become numbered among those who have their suspicions, if not condemnations. The individual's attempt to explain or justify these actions are considered "rationalizations." Thus, concerning Rhoda's complaint that Matt and his parents were insensitive to that portion of the wedding vows which says that "a man is to leave his father and mother and cleave to his wife," the counselor felt this point was well taken, and yet, "It is of course possible that this is simply a rationalization for Rhoda to extricate herself from a difficult situation." In effect, Rhoda's attempt to explain and justify acting on her desires, desires that in this case arise out of a deep sense of personal deprivation, is devalued, if not discounted, as if it were merely self-serving and, therefore, inherently wrong.

Henrik Ibsen's play A Doll's House[1] involves a woman, Nora Helmer, who, like Rhoda, discovers that she does not love her husband Thorvald any longer and informs him that she is leaving him and the children. When he tells her she is acting disgracefully and that it is her "sacred duty" to stay with him and the children, she replied, "I have another duty, just as sacred. . . . My duty to myself." He answers, "Before everything else, you're a wife and a mother," to which she replies, "I don't believe that any longer. I believe that before everything else I'm a human being—just as much as you are . . . or at any rate I shall try

1. Henrik Ibsen, *A Doll's House and Other Plays,* trans. Peter Watts (New York: Penguin Books, 1965), 145–232.

to become one." He makes no direct answer to this, but says that her religion or at least her conscience should make clear to her that she cannot simply leave her husband and children. When she replies that neither her religion nor her conscience gives her any clear guidance in the matter, he suggests that she is ill, possibly out of her senses. When her determination to carry out her decision to leave him finally registers with him, he cries, "But to lose you—to lose you, Nora! No, no, I can't even imagine it. . . ." to which she replies, "That's just why it *must* happen." In the last scene of the play, he buries his head in his hands and hears the noise of a door slamming.

When *A Doll's House* was performed in Germany, the idea that Nora would leave her husband and children was so offensive that Ibsen was forced to write a different ending. In the sanitized ending, Thorvald compels Nora to look at her sleeping children. She finds herself unable to leave them, drops her traveling bag, and sinks to the ground as the curtain falls.

Nora's action in the original version of the play—the action of leaving home—is fueled by desires, desires for herself. The act of walking out at the end of the play is a painful but hopeful act. As she says to Thorvald, "Before everything else I'm a human being . . . or at any rate I shall try to become one." He cannot respond to this statement, not because he cannot hear it, but because it expresses a hope that he does not share for her and that excludes him, because it cannot be acted upon as long as she maintains her relationship with him. Thus threatened by her words, by the defiant but also determinedly hopeful tone in her voice, he resorts to several moral appeals, including the weight of her own conscience, her sacred duty to him and the children, and the requirements of her religion. When these appeals fail, he accuses her of suffering from emotional or mental illness and then offers what he considers some overwhelmingly compelling facts: the fact that she is indispensable to him and that what she plans to do is "unimaginable."

I cite Ibsen's play for the purpose of observing that some of the very appeals that Thorvald makes to Nora are the same points that the counselor makes in his analysis of the case of Rhoda. He, too, appeals to her religion (in this case, her religion by adoption); he, too, stresses her psychological distress (her depression); and he, too, emphasizes her indispensability to her husband (as without her he will lose what remains of his manhood). What has happened here is that the counselor, like Thorvald, has not heard the hopefulness in Rhoda's voice, but has only heard the words of self-doubt and the sighs of depression.

He does not hear them because, like Nora's words of hope to Thorvald, they are deeply threatening, as they indicate that she is determined to become a human being and to do it without the help of any man. She bears the counselor no ill will even as she bears her husband none. There just is not much for the two of them to talk about. When he asks her if she would like to come again and she says, "I suppose I could," she is signaling that she means to continue to do it her way, as her way is the way of hope. If I appear to be critical of the counselor here, it is not out of any sense that I—also a man—would have been any more "effective" than he. And it is only because we have the written case available to us to study, in hindsight as it were, that you and I are able to hear the still, small voice of hopefulness that murmurs beneath the heavy tones of depression that filled the counseling room that evening. Hope, after all, is a very subtle thing. It writes itself, so to speak, between the lines, and if expressed verbally, as in Nora's "That's just why it *must* happen," it strikes us as odd, as inappropriate, and is easily mistaken for something else—as impolite, inexcusable, even vindictive and cruel. This is especially true when the one who dares to hope is a woman.

HOPE, LOVE, AND SELF-OBLIGATION

In the past few years, more and more writers of pastoral care books have called upon pastors to affirm their role as moral counselors.[2] Often the point is made that pastors have bought into the value neutrality of "secular" psychotherapy and, in doing so, have abdicated their moral counselor role. I believe it is more often the case that pastors choose not to give priority to moral issues out of a concern that this will undermine their efforts to nurture and instill hope. The pastor in the case of the unplanned teenage pregnancy in chapter one commented briefly on the fact that what the young woman had done was wrong, but he was more concerned that she not repeat the same mistake than with pointing out her moral failure. The pastor in the case of the youth who was sexually active took a similar approach. He did not ignore the immorality of this behavior, but he stressed the danger of not doing something before it became impossible to change. In both cases, concern to nurture and instill hope took precedence over moral concerns. If moral counsel was not given primary emphasis, this was not

2. See Gaylord Noyce, *The Minister as Moral Counselor* (Nashville: Abingdon Press, 1989).

because the pastors were trying to be value neutral or took a lax view of sin, but because they viewed themselves first and foremost as agents of hope.

I believe that they had their priorities straight, that hope is the more important consideration in these cases. On the other hand, the case of Rhoda raises some important moral concerns that we simply cannot ignore. There are times when moral considerations play a crucial role in determining whether or not a particular hope can be a real possibility for us. After all, some of our desires are immoral. And here, I believe, we need to commend the counselor in the case of Rhoda for his willingness to address the moral issues the case presents.

Nora's action in the original version of Ibsen's play was fueled by desires that her husband considered immoral, a violation of her religion and of her conscience. But she responded by saying that neither her religion nor her conscience gave her any clear guidance in the matter. Assuming that Rhoda felt much the same way, what would we, as pastors, have said to her, had she come to us before leaving Matt and asked us whether we felt it was wrong for her to take such a step? What would be our response? How would we have advised her?

Here, Ibsen's play is very insightful and valuable to us, as it has Nora responding to Thorvald's appeal to her "sacred duty" as wife and mother by affirming her duty to herself: "I believe that before everything else I'm a human being . . . or at least I shall try to become one." Her sacred duty to herself was to become fully human, to become the self that she truly is. This is not merely an idea implanted by an "-ology" (e.g., psychology) or an "-ism" (e.g., feminism or individualism) or a personal or cultural pathology (e.g., narcissism), but a fundamental ethical principle.

In *Personal Destinies,* David L. Norton presents the argument that obligation to be ourselves has ethical priority over all other obligations. He discusses the "inner voice" or "daimon" to which we are obliged to be true, and uses language like "integrity" and "identity" to describe this inner voice. The great enemy of such integrity, he notes, "is not falsehood as such but—ironically—the attractiveness of foreign truths, truths that belong to others."

> If I happen to be uncertain just what my true work is, I shall be tractable to depictions of it by well-meaning others. When an individual allows herself to be deflected from her own true course, she fails in that first responsibility from which all other genuine responsibilities follow, and

whose fulfillment is the precondition of the least fulfillment of other
responsibilities.[3]

Thus, Nora's and Rhoda's highest obligation is to be true to themselves,
to try to become the human being each truly is. Their "sin" is not in
determining to become this human being, but in allowing themselves
to be reduced to something less than fully human and thus devalued
and demeaned.

On the other hand, in my earlier discussion of hope as envisioning
what is realizable for us, I noted that hope and love are often in conflict
with one another, that if we focus exclusively on hopes for the future,
we may fail to give appropriate attention to what we already have and
are. Then we overlook the importance of love in our lives, for love is
the appreciation of what we have already realized. One suspects that
this is what the alternative ending to A Doll's House is affirming. Nora
may not love Thorvald anymore, but surely she loves her own children,
and, with this alternative ending, love for children takes precedence
over hope for self. While this alternative ending comes across as emotional blackmail on Thorvald's part, as coercive and therefore false, it
might not be so if the scene were presented instead as a struggle within
Nora's own inner soul, between the self who loves her children and
the self who has hopes for herself.

This same inner conflict may also apply to the self in its own solitariness, for whereas hope emphasizes the self that we may yet become, self-love involves appreciation of the self that we already are.
Are Nora and Rhoda taking sufficient account of the fact that they are
already human beings in their present state, or are they disregarding
this fact in their restless quest to be more than they are? Their felt
deprivation suggests that this is not the case, that the question itself
is patently absurd. And yet, to the extent that this is not a meaningless
question, it is one that no one can answer for them. We can express
our opinions or offer advice, but, in the final analysis, their inner voice
is the only voice that really counts, and, for both, the answer the inner
voice gives is a quiet but resounding "no." In their present circumstances, their present experience of deprivation, they cannot take very
seriously the argument that they should love the self that they are and
not seek to be the self they hope to be.

Self-love, however, is one thing. What about one's love for others,
and the obligations that this places upon us to relinquish certain desires

3. David L. Norton, *Personal Destinies: A Philosophy of Ethical Individualism* (Princeton, N.J.: Princeton University Press, 1976), 9.

that may be hurtful and harmful to them? In the case of Rhoda, it is profoundly important that she says she does not love Matt anymore. This is important, as it frees her to look to the future, to give precedence to hope. A very helpful discussion in this regard is in Margaret Farley's book, *Personal Commitments,* in which she discusses the situations in which a "just love" may be released from its promises. These include: (1) when it truly becomes *impossible* to sustain the commitment-relationship; (2) when a *specific commitment-obligation* no longer fulfills the purposes of the larger commitment it was meant to serve; and (3) when another obligation comes into conflict with, and supersedes, the commitment-obligation in question.[4]

It might be argued that, in Rhoda's case, it would not be absolutely impossible for her to remain with Matt. Many women—and men—stay in marriages like this, so it would not be impossible for Rhoda to do the same. It might also be argued that the specific commitment-obligation of taking care of a quadriplegic husband does not threaten the purposes of the larger commitment it serves, the commitment that Rhoda and Matt made on their wedding day to love and cherish one another. In fact, to care for a disabled spouse offers an opportunity to demonstrate this love. Again, many women—and men—have stayed in marriages in which their spouses were physically or emotionally disabled precisely because caring for their spouses became the avenue through which they were able to express the larger purposes of the commitment-relationship. This is often, in fact, taken to be the essence of Christian love and is the more excellent way to which the counselor appeals when he says that Rhoda promised to love Matt "in sickness and in health."

But the third basis for release from a promise—when another obligation comes into conflict with and supersedes the commitment-obligation in question—is not nearly as easy to make a case against. Rhoda, like Nora, does not have obligations to other persons that conflict with her commitment-obligation to Matt; rather, she has an obligation to herself, and this obligation conflicts with her commitment-obligation to Matt. Thus, on the one hand, Farley notes that "some self-sacrifice is morally required if we assume a commitment-obligation." There are several reasons why this is so:

> We live, for example, in a finite world, where not every claim can be met and not every need fulfilled. It is not just the claims of others on

---

4. Margaret Farley, *Personal Commitments: Beginning, Keeping, Changing* (San Francisco: Harper & Row, 1986), 84.

us that can conflict. Our own needs and the needs of those to whom
we are committed also sometimes compete. But part of why we make
a commitment is to clarify boundaries beyond which we will not assert
our own claims. (p. 104)

Farley also points out that "we are not whole and harmonious within
ourselves," and therefore our willingness not to assert our own claims
may conflict with the counterdesire to press our claims: "But, again,
part of why we make the commitment is to assure the one to whom
we give our word that we will not revoke it just because conflicting
desires arise within us" (p. 104).

Yet, on the other hand, Farley recognizes that, if commitment includes self-sacrifice, there must be limits to the sacrifice that is required
or even morally allowed. She agrees with Ibsen's Nora that affirming
oneself as a human person like other persons is not just desirable, it
is a moral obligation. Thus, we have a moral obligation not to relate
to another person in a way that is truly "destructive of ourselves as
persons," and such destruction is more likely to occur in a situation
where "a disproportionate burden of sacrifice is lain on one person
in a commitment-relationship" (p. 107).

In the final analysis, the individual must be the judge as to whether
the situation is self-destructive. We cannot make this judgment for the
other. But we can at least offer our view that one is being dehumanized,
destroyed as a person, if one is being deprived of the very capacity to
hope. As Farley points out, "We may not sacrifice in a final sense our
autonomy," for to do so is to accept the destruction of ourselves as
persons. And how do we protect our autonomy? By refusing to relinquish our capacity to hope. Hope, Farley says, is "our way of being
free in relation to the future" (pp. 106, 57).

Thus, based on the ethical views of Norton and of Farley, we may
say with considerable confidence that Rhoda has in fact demonstrated
"the critical standards of excellence that [are] to be found in the
Christian faith." I doubt that many of us male pastors would be inspired
to hug Rhoda at the end of the session and dare to say to her, "Rhoda,
you have done the right thing, and you can be proud of how you have
handled a very difficult situation." Yet, our failure to do so may well
reveal how far removed our own thinking has become from the more
radical perspective of the Gospels, as reflected, for example, in Jesus'
unflinching defense of his disciples when, in their hunger, they plucked
ears of grain on the sabbath, as he said to those who raised moral
objections to their behavior: "But if you had known what this means,

'I desire mercy and not sacrifice,' you would not have condemned the guiltless" (Matt. 12:7). Or, if this response is deemed too mild, there are other pronouncements of his that are even more supportive of a woman who dares to entertain hopes for herself. Julia Kasdorf, a poet who grew up in a Mennonite community in Pennsylvania, thinks of how different her mother's life would have been had she taken the "mean words of Jesus" to heart.[5]

> *The Mean Words of Jesus*
>
> In the home movies that run endlessly
> through my head, Grandpa offers Dad
> a new car if he'll quit school at sixteen
> to help run the farm. And Dad turns him down.
> Then the other Grandpa offers Mom
> a store-bought dress if she'll stay home
> from college to take care of her mother.
> She doesn't want a dress that much,
> but stays, and one of his cows fetches enough
> to pay tuition at a nursing school nearby.
> When her mother finally dies, Mom's home again
> for six months, cooking and cleaning, giving
> birth to me while my father works miles away.
> This is the part I cannot stand to see
> another time. Here I edit the scenes
> and reverse all their consequences. Here
> my mother must turn to her father
> at the last minute when the music swells
> unbearably as in the last scene of *Casablanca,*
> and in that soft, trembling light,
> the mean words of Jesus must fly
> from her lips: Who is my mother?
> or better yet: Let the dead bury the dead.
> Here she must announce, "I can't reproduce
> her cream sauce or spotless windows;
> let the strawberries rot on the vine
> if no one will pick them." Here she'll remember
> her mother's high school diploma, framed
> and stern as a clock above the cookstove,
> earned while younger sisters dropped out
> to work in a bakery, take in laundry,
> scrub rich people's floors, and their mother
> grew sicker in body and soul.

5. Julia Kasdorf, *Sleeping Preacher* (Pittsburgh: Univ. of Pittsburgh Press, 1992), 10.

five

THE THREE MAJOR
THREATS TO HOPE

I n the pastoral care cases presented in chapter one, each of the pastors was aware that hopefulness is not easy to achieve, that one must put some effort into it. All were aware that we confront strong pressures to succumb to hopelessness, and that maintaining a hopeful attitude toward life involves more than being optimistic or engaging in positive thinking. In our exploration into the experience of hoping in chapter three, we saw that hope is kept alive through desire, and we are painfully aware that it is all too easy, when confronted with the realities of life, to relinquish our desire, to resign ourselves to a state of desirelessness.

The fact that a hopeful attitude requires effort to maintain indicates that hope has its adversaries, that there are influences or forces in our lives that threaten hope. Hope is threatened by contrary attitudes to which all of us are susceptible, whether we are victims of a harsh objective world or simply faced with the ordinary challenges and frustrations of life. This chapter describes three attitudes that, once internalized and well established, pose an especially powerful threat to the maintenance of a hopeful attitude toward life. These are the attitudes of despair, apathy, and shame.

Because these attitudes save us from a life of casual optimism, these adversaries of hope should not be considered absolutely harmful to hope. As those who have experienced the loss of hope and its subsequent recovery have often pointed out, it was in their struggle against one of hope's adversaries that they came to a more mature understanding of hope and a deeper appreciation of its role in their lives. So, despair, apathy, and shame are not absolute evils. They often are the means by which hope, its very survival threatened, is enabled to grow and mature. But neither can we view these tests of hope as mere skirmishes. They are fully capable, singly or together, of destroying a hopeful attitude toward life, undoing what was done for us in our infancy by a caring other.

Despair is chief among the threats to hope, and therefore we give it particular prominence here. But apathy and shame are also serious threats to hope. The pastors whose cases were reported in chapter one testified to this. These pastors were so concerned to help the person in crisis sustain an attitude of hope because they knew how fragile hopefulness can sometimes be, and how easy it is to succumb to despair, to apathy, and to an immobilizing sense of shame. It is all too tempting for us to endorse hope and to talk about what a good thing it is to maintain a hopeful attitude toward life, while ignoring the forces that undermine it. If pastors view themselves as agents of hope, they need to be aware of, and to know something about, the attitudes that undermine and destroy hope, leaving hopelessness in their wake.

As in our discussion of the origins and experience of hope, I will be drawing primarily here on the writings of psychologists. I am aware that religious thinkers have also written on these topics; for example, Søren Kierkegaard on the subject of despair and Jürgen Moltmann on the topic of apathy.[1] (Significantly, with the exception of some occasional comments, no equally major religious thinker has written on the topic of shame.) Yet, my concern here is to explore these three attitudes from the perspective of the self that undergoes them, and, for this, it is altogether appropriate to center on the work of contemporary psychologists, for whom the self and its vicissitudes is of primary interest and concern. We begin with what is usually considered the archenemy of hope, the attitude of despair.

DESPAIR: THE CLOSING OF THE PERSONAL FUTURE

Viktor Frankl calls despair "suffering without meaning."[2] This definition captures the felt meaninglessness of a life of despair, but it is somewhat

---

1. Søren Kierkegaard, *Sickness Unto Death: A Christian Psychological Exposition for Upbuilding and Awakening,* trans. Howard V. Hong and Edna H. Hong (Princeton: Princeton University Press, 1980). Also Jürgen Moltmann, "Hope and the Apathetic Person," lecture at the Center for Ethics and Social Policy, Graduate Theological Union, Berkeley, California, 1974. Discussed by W. H. Capps in *Hope Against Hope: Moltmann to Merton in One Decade* (Philadelphia: Fortress Press, 1976), 133–34.

2. Viktor Frankl, *Man's Search for Meaning: An Introduction to Logotherapy,* trans. Ilse Lasch (New York: Washington Square Press, 1963), 104–5.

too broad and general for our purposes here. A definition of despair that relates more directly to our earlier discussion of hope is that despair is the perception that what is wanted will *not* happen, the sense that what is realizable for others is not realizable for me, in spite of the fact that I very much desire it. In this view, despair contrasts starkly with our previous discussion of the process of hoping and the entertainment of hopes. Unlike hoping, which involves the perception that what one desires will happen, despair involves the opposite perception: "I have desires, but there is no reason to have them, as they will never come to pass for me." Also, unlike hopes, which involve the envisioning of what is realizable for me, despair takes the opposite view: "Of course, what I want is theoretically possible, as it is possible for others, but, for reasons that have to do with *my* personal life and *my* personal circumstances, these things are an impossibility for me."

Psychologists who work with despairing persons have noticed that their despair is strongly related to their perception of time and, more specifically, the sense that time is not for but against them. In discussing the crisis of "integrity versus despair" that older adults especially experience, Erikson says that "despair expresses the feeling that the time is now short, too short for the attempt to start another life and to try out alternate roads to integrity."[3] Here, time is against us because there is not enough of it.

Another sense of time often associated with despair is what Erikson calls "time forfeited."[4] This is the despair that comes with looking back on periods in one's life, or perhaps the whole of one's life, and realizing that there were years, even decades, that were essentially wasted or misdirected. There were years spent in the wrong career, with the wrong spouse, with the wrong set of values or goals. Reflection on time forfeited contributes to despair because it kindles the desire to live those years very differently. Yet, this desire, one senses, cannot be fulfilled. We perceive that we cannot go back in time, that we cannot "do it over again." Erikson suggests that the sense of despair is so great that it gets projected outward. Despair, he says, "is often hidden behind a show of disgust, a misanthropy, or a chronic contemptuous displeasure with particular institutions and particular people."[5] What gets hidden in this projection is one's self-contempt, one's disgust for oneself.

Besides being projected outward in the form of disgust for the world around us, despair is also self-directed, turned inward. When this

3. Erik H. Erikson, *Identity: Youth and Crisis* (New York: W. W. Norton, 1968), 140.
4. Erik H. Erikson, *The Life Cycle Completed* (New York: W. W. Norton, 1982), 63.
5. Erikson, *Identity: Youth and Crisis*, 140.

occurs, one form that it takes is depression. A clinician who has written extensively about despair turned inward in the form of depression is Frederick Towne Melges, who, in his book *Time and the Inner Future,*[6] explores depression in relation to hope and hopelessness. For persons suffering from depression, "the future seems blocked. The severely depressed patient may give up trying to pursue anything in the future" (p. 173). The major causes of depression are hopelessness and unresolved grief, both of which create the sense of a blocked future. The depressive's experience of the future as blocked differs from psychotic loss of control of the future and neurotic dread of the future. In psychotic loss of control, the images of the future are fragmented and confused with past images; in acute schizophrenia, for example, time sequences are commonly jumbled. A severe depressive disorder, by contrast, may involve difficulty in concentrating because the patient cannot think as quickly as before, but she is usually able to keep track of time sequences and to distinguish past, present, and future.

Severe depressive disorders may also be distinguished from the neurotic dread of the future: "One of the prominent characteristics of neurotic anxiety is uncertainty about the personal future. This uncertainty of images and plans is different from the hopeless giving up of a severe depressive disorder. That is, the neurotically anxious patient is still striving; he has not given up hope even though he has many conflicts and uncertainties as he enters his future" (p. 174). Thus, the major difference between the neurotic who dreads the future and the depressed individual for whom the future is blocked is that the latter feels hopeless. This hopelessness "is characterized by a disjunction between future images and plans of action. The patient believes that his plans of action are insufficient for meeting future goals. The reasons for this may be an incapacity for carrying out plans of action, perfectionistic or unrealistic goals, or both" (p. 174). Thus, hopelessness is the consequence of a serious disjuncture between future images (projections) and plans of action, and once hopelessness sets in, it becomes a vicious cycle, since it forecloses consideration of alternative plans of action. The future images, what we would call hopes, are not abandoned, but they are considered unrealizable, as one lacks the means to bring them about.

The disjuncture between plans and goals (or future images) may take different forms of hopelessness, depending on how one habitually

---

6. Frederick Townes Melges, *Time and the Inner Future* (New York: John Wiley and Sons, 1982).

anticipates that outcomes will occur. In Melges's view, these anticipations are influenced by three central beliefs. The first is the degree to which the individual believes that skills, on the one hand, or chance, on the other, may be expected to influence future outcomes. The second is the degree to which loyalty to others versus exploitation of others is expected to effect the desired outcome. The third is whether the desired outcome is anticipated in the short run or in the long run. The individual who is most prone to becoming depressed and thus hopeless is oriented toward skill rather than chance, to loyalty instead of exploitation, and to the long term rather than the short run. Such persons "are often viewed as 'solid citizens' who are dedicated workers, nonmanipulative with others, and conscientiously committed to long-term goals" (pp. 180–81). They believe that outcomes are determined largely by their own skilled actions rather than by chance or luck: "While this feeling of self-efficacy is important for self-esteem for most people, it is a rigid and inflexible belief in those persons vulnerable to depressive hopelessness" (p. 181). Such persons also tend to be loyal and trusting toward others and believe that they can make relationships work well by being dedicated and committed. They are often attached to a "dominant other" and have few important relationships besides this other person. They live mainly to meet the expectations of this other person, and they become deeply depressed when the other appears disloyal or exploitative. They also believe in the value of long-term goals and are known to neglect outcomes in the present and near future because they are driven toward accomplishing a dominant goal.

These orientations toward skill, loyalty, and long-term goals produce a "narrow" view of one's personal future. It is not that the normal future-time perspective is foreshortened, but that it is limited in breadth, like a very long and very narrow tunnel. Hopes are associated with our own actions, they are based on expectations relating to one dominant individual, and they are long-term. Because the future time perspective is so narrowly conceived, it is vulnerable to blockage, and, since we are not accustomed to envisioning a range of goals associated with a range of personal relationships, it is difficult to form alternative plans when this happens.

Hopelessness becomes a "downward spiral" when we realize that our plans of action are no longer effective for meeting our goals, and yet we still cling to them. As these goals involve maintaining an important relationship with another person or an important long-range achievement, and usually both, the end of the relationship or conclusive evidence that the long-range goal will not be achieved may be the event that triggers hopelessness, which then continues as a downward spiral as we remain attached to this goal. If "the person clings to his future images, such as his former relationship and goals, long after he knows that it is impossible to reach or sustain them, the gap between his plans and his future images widens and he becomes increasingly hopeless. As the hopelessness deepens, he often gives up trying to execute his plans and becomes inactive" (pp. 183–84).

In Melges's view, the major trigger of hopelessness is a loss of some kind, usually a loss of skill, of a loyal relationship or of the long-term future. The loss of skill can be caused by skills becoming outmoded, lack of youthful energy, physical illness, initial signs of organic brain disease, or being trapped in a situation that demands accomplishing a continuing goal for which we are inadequately prepared. The loss of a loyal relationship may be overt, as with death, separation, or infidelity, but it may also be subtle, as when the relationship does not live up to mutual expectations of support, trust, and loyalty. Typically, a feeling of betrayal results, but it is difficult to relinquish the goal of maintaining the relationship, even though it seems hopeless. The loss of a long-term goal may occur when it becomes evident that the dominant goal of our life will not be realized, or when we are diagnosed as terminally ill: "When a person is customarily oriented toward the long term future, the prospect of losing it often robs the present and near future of zest and meaning, making life seem even more hopeless" (pp. 184–85).

Melges asks why the depressed individual clings so tenaciously to goals that are unlikely to be realized. Why isn't there a switch to alternative, realizable goals? One reason is the tendency to persist in behavior that was previously rewarded long after rewards are no longer forthcoming. This is especially common in cases involving reward, or nonreward, for skilled behavior. While rewards attributable to luck are not expected to continue, rewards owing to skill are expected to continue as long as our skills are intact. Thus, because depression-prone persons place great emphasis on skill rather than luck to secure their goals in life, they are less able to adapt when rewards are no longer forthcoming. If skills were successful before, it is difficult to imagine that they will not be successful again. Also, persons oriented toward long-term goals are more likely to disregard negative feedback from present outcomes than are persons who are oriented toward short-term goals.

What is the ultimate result of such downward spirals of hopelessness? As the hopelessness worsens, the future time perspective foreshortens and there is an increase in ideas about ending one's life. When the future time perspective, already narrow, now becomes foreshortened, the risk of suicide is at its highest, especially when it seems to be the only alternative way to escape from the hopeless situation. The foreshortening of the future, together with its narrow focus, tends to close off consideration of alternative courses of action (or new images of hope).

For Melges and his colleagues at Duke University Medical Center, therapeutic work with individuals who have become hopeless and deeply despairing involves helping them replace their intense skill-orientation with a more whimsical attitude toward life. It also involves helping them focus on goals that are realizable in the near rather than the distant future. Also, where the loss of a significant relationship is involved, a wide array of relationships with other persons is encouraged. Development of an array of relationships is a way for the individual to restore a damaged sense of self resulting from the experience of disloyalty or betrayal. These initiatives, which address the primary, self-inflicted causes of hopelessness, are designed to arrest the downward spiral of hopelessness by "unfreezing the future." As Melges puts it, "By making the patient aware of the wealth of options that can bring pleasure and satisfaction in the present and near future, the patient begins to realize that his plans of action can be meaningfully connected with his future images. By restructuring the expectations underlying hope, hopelessness is combatted" (p. 193).

In short, a basic cause of depressive hopelessness is the tendency to focus on long-term goals to the neglect of short-term and more immediately realizable goals. As the biblical proverb puts it, "Hope deferred makes the heart sick, but a desire fulfilled is a tree of life" (Prov. 13:12). Depression is able to take root when there is a very long and very narrow time perception. In such a time perspective, neither the realization of short-term hopes nor the enjoyment of the fruits of short-term hopes previously realized is considered important or vital. Then, as the long-term goal is deferred or indefinitely delayed, or its realization begins to appear doubtful, the downward spiral of hopelessness begins. One suspects that had Jacob known in advance that it would take fourteen years for him to realize his hope of gaining the hand of Rachel in marriage, he may well have succumbed to hopelessness; that he did not know this until the first seven years had elapsed may have been key to his ability to wait for seven more years. Alternatively, had Laban informed Jacob after the first seven years that he could only have Leah, that Rachel would be forever denied him, we can be certain that Jacob would have given in to hopelessness and despair, as he would have incontrovertible evidence that his skill had nothing to do with realizing his deepest hope, and that he was the victim of betrayal and deceit.

Despair, then, may take essentially two forms: It may be projected outward in the form of *disgust* directed against other persons or institutions, or it may be deeply internalized in the form of *depression.* What makes it so difficult to combat is that it feeds on itself in a downward spiral of hopelessness. It involves the perception that the future, already narrowed, is foreshortened, either because it is too late to start over, or because the future is blocked.

Thus, the feature of hoping that is most affected by despair is the perception that what is wanted will happen, and the aspect of a specific hope or hopes that is most vulnerable in despair is the envisioning of the realizable. The despairing person has had very strong desires and has made a hopeful projection upon them. These desires may derive from an equally strong sense of personal deprivation, and because the hoped-for outcome was both so singleminded and so self-invested, considerable risk was involved. But now this projection appears more than dubious, and, as a consequence, life becomes hopeless. The risk in hope is largely born in this case by the one who has dared to hope, and the painfulness of knowing that the hoped-for outcome will not be realized is all the greater because we thought that we possessed the skills to bring it about. We believed it to be possible because we had the requisite skills to make it happen.

This means that persons most susceptible to despair are those of us who project very clear and concrete images of hope, and who have strong confidence in our own ability to realize what is hoped for. In envisioning and working toward the desired outcome, we place ourselves at much greater risk than we place others, as we are not exploitative by nature. At the same time, we are left very much alone when our hope is not realized as our singleminded pursuit of what was wanted has left us bereft of personal relationships that could soften the blow and provide solace. We have been victimized by our belief that only one hoped-for outcome would give our life meaning.

In despair, therefore, we place a great deal of blame on ourselves for the failure of our hopes to materialize. It is our deficiency, the inadequacy of our own skills and abilities, which is primarily, even exclusively, responsible for the frustration of our hopes. Moreover, we are the ones who will suffer the most for the failure of our hopes, because our hopes did not place others at risk or even involve reliance on others for the fulfillment of these hopes. We were careful, even scrupulous, not to make our hopes a difficulty for others. Thus, even in situations where our hopes involved a relationship and not, for example, a personal career goal, the fact that the relationship did not turn out as we had hoped is very much our own fault, for had we possessed better "interpersonal skills," the relationship, we firmly believe, would have had a much better chance of making it. The very fact that we may have been too singleminded in our pursuit of this relationship, or too solicitous of the other to the exclusion of concern for ourself, may simply reinforce our perception that had we possessed better interpersonal skills, the relationship would not have ended so badly: "I wanted it too much," "I tried too hard," and so on. In other words, we are quite easy on the other as we blame and chastise ourselves. And the fact that we may simply have been a victim of bad luck would never cross our minds.

What pastors may do to help those who are despairing in this way is to enable them to perceive that meaning may be found in other, as yet unimagined hopes, especially hopes that are more immediate and less distant. They may also assist the despairing individual to see that hopes need not depend solely or exclusively on the skill of the one who hopes, that many hopes are realized through the fortuitous and providential through no effort of our own. They can encourage the despairing one to depend more upon *less* significant others, even on persons previously considered peripheral to one's life, persons who touch one's life at its margins: The friendly waitress who always has a kind word when serving breakfast; the coworker who has not seemed all that important to one's primary goals but who, on reflection, has been unstintingly supportive and has never asked for anything in return; the sister or brother who always provided a listening ear when the two of us were growing up but from whom one has drifted in one's adult years precisely because she or he did not figure much in one's dominant goals in life. In their own ways, pastors can do what Melges and his colleagues do at Duke University Medical Center. While Melges and his colleagues have special skills in this regard, Melges is also quick to acknowledge that there is no mystique in what they do as they seek to help despairing persons refocus their lives. Encouraging a more whimsical view of life, challenging the other to focus on short-term goals, and inviting the other to depend on a wider range of acquaintances than before: This is something that pastors can do and often have done without being consciously aware of the fact that they are thereby acting as agents of hope. Also, because pastors are themselves often numbered among the *less* significant others in their parishioners' lives, they can become, for a time, the person on whom a parishioner leans until other more committed relationships are formed. In time, the pastor will become expendable, no longer needed, but there will be other despairing souls, others who have been so singleminded in their long-term goals and committed relationships that they, too, need the distracting, disarming agency of the pastor in their lives. We should not for a moment minimize the significance for these persons of the pastor's role in this regard, and we should especially not overlook the enabling power of a pastor's encouragement of a more whimsical view of life. Such a view of life may, as Melges suggests, recognize the role that luck—good or bad—often plays in human life, but it may also recognize that the grace of God has more to do with keeping our hopes alive than any skills we may possess. After all, it was not our skills, but the benevolence of another, that secured our first and all subsequent feedings in the early months of life when we were most vulnerable to despair. *"Good luck," vs. "It was God's will" "Bad luck."*

APATHY: STATE OF DESIRELESSNESS

In discussing the effects of despair on hope, we have focused primarily on the depressed self. As we turn to our consideration of the effects of apathy on hope, we will be concerned with two types of selves, the acedic self and the sociopathic personality. Both suffer from apathy, but for very different reasons. We begin with the acedic self.

The Acedic Self

A second major threat to hope is apathy, which is basically the state of desirelessness together with a strong element of "not caring" about what is happening around us, to us, or within us. In an article entitled "Acedia: The Decline of Desire as the Ultimate Life Crisis,"[7] Bert Kaplan, then professor of psychology at the University of California at Santa Cruz, focused on acedia, the fourth of the deadly sins, which emerged into Western consciousness through the writings of the desert fathers of the fourth century. His discussion of acedia or apathy is most relevant

7. Bert Kaplan, "Acedia: The Decline of Desire as the Ultimate Life Crisis," in Donald Capps, Walter H. Capps, and Gerald Bradford, eds., *Encounter With Erikson: Historical Interpretation and Religious Biography* (Missoula, Montana: Scholars Press, 1977).

for us here, as it centers on the issue of desire and desirelessness and thus concerns the second characteristic of the hoping process, the fact that hoping is fueled by desire.

Acedia is described by the early fathers "as a state resulting from the isolation and loneliness of the hermitage in the desert, a fatigue attributable to the conditions of withdrawal and fasting of the Christian retreat" (p. 389). It was reflected in malaise, lassitude, laxness, and apathy. Noting that the word "acedia" comes from the Greek term translated as "not caring state," Kaplan sees it as "both a failure to find the world and its activities interesting, and a religious hopelessness" (p. 389).

Kaplan suggests that acedia is "a good starting place for a discussion of the category Desire, the relation of Desire to its objects, its precarious situation in the world, the circumstances of its decline and finally the possibilities of its restoration" (p. 390). He is critical of modern psychologists who speak frequently about "needs," but treat need as "something" rather than "the absence of something," and who talk about the "satisfaction" of a need, as if it were "a certain quantity of energy to be got rid of" (p. 390). To view need in this way is to neglect the fact that desire is a state of privation, the experience of the absence of that which is desired. As Sartre puts it, "Desire is the presence of an absence" (p. 390).

Noting that we are by nature desiring beings, since we are always experiencing the presence of an absence, Kaplan is intrigued by acedia or apathy because it describes a condition that is the very antithesis of human nature. How is it that individuals become desireless, and what is it like to be without desire? Kaplan believes that desirelessness can be traced to early childhood, when we first have experience of the world as "indifferent or hostile to desire" (p. 392). He points out:

> For Desire [the] question of good "object relations" is crucial. Almost the sole criteria for psychological health is whether or not our objects are good. If we like them, want them, find them interesting, our success in acquiring them or possessing them is secondary. Desire's relationship to its objects is so close that not to welcome them as good is sickness and is the sign of a mixed-up psyche. The confusion that what seems "so lovely fair that my senses ache at thee" is in fact corrupt and foul is such a basic crack in the world that it can be understood as psychosis. Melanie Klein speaks of the "paranoid position" and the "depressive position" to indicate the seriousness of the disturbance that it creates. (pp. 391–92)

Such experiences of disillusionment concerning one's objects of desire owing to the discovery that they are not "good" but "bad" is an especially devastating blow to desire, and it is not at all surprising that a condition of desirelessness might result. But Kaplan is also interested in the desirelessness that results from the withdrawal of "good" objects for reasons that seem altogether appropriate and without malice. The weaning process is exemplary of this, and it creates something of the same confusion as the experience of a good object proving bad: "The world that feeds and provides care and shelter for the babe in the womb and at its mother's breast unfortunately turns into a hostile one to the weaned child. In varying degrees its good objects are at least partially withdrawn and provided only on a conditional basis" (p. 392). Yet, while many children do experience great severity, privation, and harshness in early life, Kaplan believes that "the full seriousness of weaning is ordinarily encountered, in this country and in this period, by the young adult who has recently left his or her family, that most womb-like of human institutions, and has 'come into the world' " (p. 392). Students report that the sense of being weaned from family care develops over a period of years and that it is experienced partly as a function of their own desire for independence and freedom: "Nevertheless, the full force of the fact of being alone in an indifferent world is a good deal more than they have bargained for. The crisis of this period of life may be regarded as a re-experiencing of the anxieties of the earlier period of weaning, but this time without the support of the family" (p. 392).

What happens to desire in the world of "the weaned person"? Kaplan believes that the normal circumstance is for desire to become even stronger. In the world of the weaned person, when the objects of desire are lost, absent, difficult to reach, or in the possession of someone else, desire takes the form of searching and hunting:

> One might call it the world of the lean and hungry, where desire is intense and the hunt is urgent. Despite the suffering and frustration and the empty landscape, it is a moment when desire and the world are both strong. . . . In this world there is no doubt about the goodness of the object sought, the problem desire faces is its absence. (p. 394)

In this world of the lean and hungry, "hope becomes the medium or form in which desire is kept intact. The absence is suffered but in a basic way the individual's relation to the world is intact and perhaps even strengthened. The good object is also intact and believed in, even though it is nowhere in view" (p. 394).

Yet, it is also possible that the weaned person will come to the conclusion that the "good object" is nowhere to be found, no matter how much one may search and hunt for it. This is not necessarily a prescription for desirelessness, for if one's hunting is unsuccessful, one may try to construct a good object out of one's need much as one might build a house to keep one sheltered, and one may give up the active search for the good object and live by cherishing in memory the goodness one once knew. These redirections of the original desire are typical ways in which we cope with the loss of the world that provided care and shelter from birth until the weaning process comes to its culmination in young adulthood (p. 394).

But there are some for whom these redirections of desire toward construction of a new good object and remembrance of the old does not occur, or does not suffice, and even among those who are able to so redirect their desires, there are periods of bleakness when "nothing of significance seems to be happening." This bleakness is captured in Beckett's *Waiting for Godot,* where "the terminus of desire is contemplated, described, considered, and perhaps anticipated," where there is "a confrontation with desire's decline and disappearance" (p. 395). Before desire itself disappears, however, it typically takes "that intensified form we call suffering." Suffering in this context may be understood "as the absence of desire's objects when desire is at its strongest and most needful" (p. 395). Thus, suffering can be taken as a sign that desire is strong and intense, even if suffused with a great sense of hopelessness. On the other hand, suffering may instead come "to have a positive aspect and itself become the desired object" (p. 395). As Kaplan points out, there are persons who make a career of their suffering, and if they do not enjoy it, they at least have all of their interest centered in it: "In this respect suffering may be said to have become the object of their desire" (p. 396). This occurs, however, only when desire for good objects is itself endangered or lost, for if suffering becomes the object of one's desire, this is a tacit acknowledgment that desire, even in the redirected forms described above, is no longer viable.

If, for some, suffering becomes the object of desire and a basis for living, for others the only alternative when desire is endangered is indifference. For Kaplan, "the true crisis of life is the confrontation with the prospect of Indifference" (p. 397), and the transition "from the most intense and acute suffering to the 'not caring state' of Acedia is one of the two most radical transformations possible in life" (p. 398), the other being the transition from "the non-being to the being of the self as a New Birth" (p. 399).

While he devotes most of his essay to the circumstances that lead to the loss of desire, Kaplan does address the restoration of desire. He suggests that psychoanalytic thinking addresses the restoration of desire by emphasizing the "education of desire," viewing the repeated experience of loss and recovery as a learning experience that prompts us to limit desire's "greed" by becoming more reasonable, while simultaneously developing a certain limited confidence "that lost objects will sometimes return." Psychoanalytic thinking also emphasizes that our desires' own activities can influence the situation and that desire "can actually create out of its own efforts objects of value" (p. 400). What psychoanalysis does, in effect, is to chasten our desires, to challenge their insatiability, and to educate us to the truth that the world is actually filled with objects that are worthy of our desire and that we are worthy of them in return. Life need not be an all-or-nothing or a one-or-nothing thing. While we cannot have all that we want, and often cannot have the one thing we most desire, there is a great plurality of desirable objects in the world, many of which are accessible, many of which are good and worthy of our desire.

Kaplan also notes, however, that Christian thought, especially when under the influence of Platonism, has tended to press not for the "education" of desire but for its "elevation." The "elevation" of desire involves recognizing that the problem with desiring objects is that they are only objects and the nourishment they provide is both insufficient and temporary. Thus:

> If desire is to be recovered it must be on the basis of the discovery of that which is worthy to be desired without reservation. Desire must find its destination in the Divine. This does not mean the abandonment of all mundane objects although in Christian monasticism and asceticism it took this form. It does involve loving these objects in a different way. It involves a loosening of ties to particular loved objects and the emergence of a relationship to the world taken as a whole and to the reality of the creation of that world. (p. 400)

While Kaplan suggests that the psychoanalytic approach seems "to be a mild, almost feeble climax to the career of Desire," he does not condemn it. Nor would I, as I believe its program of the "education" of desire can be a very useful antidote to the very danger he cites in reference to the Christian "elevation" of desire approach, namely, the potential abandonment of all mundane objects. Against the ascetic extremes of the Christian approach, the psychoanalytic approach recommends investment of desire in these mundane objects, even to the point of creating objects of value to replace those that have been lost or withdrawn.

On the other hand, there is another Christian approach to desire that Kaplan overlooks, and one that in my judgment is more deserving of our attention and commitment than the "elevation" approach. We find it in various places, but perhaps most notably in Chaucer's "The Parson's Tale."[8] While Kaplan alludes briefly to Chaucer's tale, he does not adequately explore its own program for the "education" of desire. What Chaucer recommends is the cultivation of virtues or certain inner strengths that enable one to sustain desire, and thus to maintain hope, even when there are few objective grounds for doing so. These inner strengths offer an alternative to the suffering that accompanies desire and to allowing suffering to become one's central desire in life. If psychoanalytic thinking advocates the "education" of desire and the Christian approach of which Kaplan speaks advocates the "elevation" of desire, the Christian approach that Chaucer's Parson advocates may be said to "energize" desire from within.

The Parson describes the acedic self in the following way: "He does all things with annoyance, and with rawness, slackness, and excuses, and with idleness and lack of desire" (p. 560). He also notes that acedia has a close relationship to asceticism, for "this foul sin of acedia is . . . a great enemy of the livelihood of the body, for it takes no provision against temporal necessity, for it wastes and despoils, and destroys all temporal goods through carelessness" (p. 560). Thus, for the Parson, a major cause of acedia is the ascetic tradition's emphasis on the life hereafter and the resulting devaluation of life in the here-and-now. Confidence that long-term desires have already been met leads to the devaluation of life in the here and now, as reflected in the neglect of "the livelihood of the body." Immediate and short-term desires have no real significance. At best, they are necessary evils and, at worst, they are not entertained at all. Tasks associated with the here-and-now are avoided and ignored, left for others to perform. Even when performed, they are not invested with desire.

To combat this devaluation of temporal life, the Parson warns that "heaven is given to them that labor, and not to idle folk" (p. 563). Moreover, the failure to invest in temporal life leaves one open for despair, for "now enters 'wan hope," which is despair of the mercy of God, and comes sometimes of too extravagant sorrows and sometimes of too great dread: for the victim imagines that he has done so much

---

8. Geoffrey Chaucer, "The Parson's Tale," in *Canterbury Tales* (New York: Avenel Books, 1985), 512–95. All quotations are taken from this edition.

sin that it will avail him not to repent and forego sin" (p. 561). Now, one begins to feel that she has forfeited the future hope of a blessed life in the hereafter, and the fear that this engenders may drive her into permanent despair.

On the other hand, the Parson suggests that despairing of one's future hope may also be the catalyst to turn one's life around, forcing one to take steps that are genuinely therapeutic. To initiate this turn-around, the Parson recommends that one reflect on the great dangers of despair, for, as the example of Judas, the betrayer of Jesus, reveals, there is no crime one is incapable of committing when one has aban-doned hope. He also encourages reflecting on the promises and sac-rifice of Christ, which offer assurance that God's mercy is sufficiently large to embrace the worst of sinners, even those who have despaired of this very mercy. Yet, these reflections are merely the first step in the recovery of hopefulness. Now, it becomes extremely important that certain inner strengths are cultivated against apathy and the loss of desire. Foremost among them is *fortitude,* or the despising of the annoyances that inhibit the performance of good and valuable tasks, which "enhances and reinforces the soul, even as acedia abates and makes it feeble." Other supportive strengths include *courage,* which enables individuals "to undertake hard and grievous things, by their own will, wisely and reasonably"; *diligence,* the ability to complete worthy tasks that one begins; and *constancy,* or stability in courage (pp. 564–65).

The common feature of these inner strengths or virtues is that they focus on the immediate future and involve commitment to good and useful projects in the here-and-now, challenging the idea that all that matters is life beyond the grave. They also encourage one to do what Kaplan says the psychoanalytic tradition encourages, namely, to dis-cover that desires' own activities can influence the situation and can actually create out of their own effects objects of value. Yet, the psy-choanalytic thinking seems "feeble" here because it says little about the inner strengths that may be cultivated to instill and maintain desire. This is why Erikson's view that psychotherapy has the implicit goal of engendering such inner strengths is such an important contribution to psychoanalytic thinking, especially because this is not the imposition of a new agenda upon psychoanalytic practice but a recognition of what in fact has been one of its primary objectives.[9] In the essay in

9. Erik H. Erikson, "Human Strength and the Cycle of Generations," *Insight and Responsibility* (New York: W. W. Norton, 1964), 111–12.

which he called for greater explicit attention to the "inner strengths,"
he acknowledges:

> Some of this process we call "ego-synthesis," and we gradually accu-
> mulate new observations under this heading. But we know that this
> process too, in some [persons] in some moments and on some occa-
> sions, is endowed with a total quality which we might term "animated"
> or "spirited." This I certainly will not try to classify. But I will submit
> that, without acknowledging its existence, we cannot maintain any true
> perspective regarding the best moments of [one's] balance—nor the
> deepest of [one's] tragedy.[10]

Here, Erikson introduces the language of the spirit into psychoanalytic
discourse, and, as we have already seen, hope is the strength that he
nominates as of central importance in the life of the inner spirit.

It is also noteworthy, in light of Chaucer's emphasis on the cultivation
of inner strengths that sustain desire, that Erikson would turn to Old
English for the word—and its meaning—that best captures what he
is saying here. The word is "virtue," but the Latin meaning, with its
emphasis on virility, is not right, as "we would, of course, hesitate to
consider manliness the official virtue of the universe, especially since
it dawns on us that womanhood may be forced to bear the larger share
in saving humanity from man's climactic and catastrophic aspirations."[11] Rather,

> Old English gave a special meaning to the word "virtue" which does
> admirably. It meant *inherent strength* or *active quality,* and was used,
> for example, for the undiminished potency of well preserved medicines
> and liquors. Virtue and spirit once had interchangeable meanings—and
> not only in the virtue that endowed liquid spirits. Our question, then,
> is: what "virtue goes out" of a human being when he loses the strength
> we have in mind, and "by virtue of" what strength does man acquire
> that animated or spirited quality without which his moralities become
> mere moralism and his ethics feeble goodness?[12]

Such virtues, as Chaucer's Parson points out, uphold and sustain desire,
especially at that juncture when desire is in process of redirection. So,
to Kaplan's two approaches to the restoration of desire—the *education*
and the *elevation* of desire—we may add a third, the *energizing* of

10. Ibid., 112.
11. Ibid., 113.
12. Ibid.

Add energizing (Erikson)
to Education and elevation (Kaplan)

desire, and affirm that it has affinities with both psychoanalytic thinking and Christian tradition.

As noted above, Kaplan suggests that those who are most susceptible to the eventual loss of desire are young adults, especially those who have difficulty redirecting their desire toward new "good objects." There is also some evidence to suggest that men are more susceptible to apathy, the state of desirelessness, than women. In a study of Christian laity's attitudes toward the deadly sins, I found that 18 percent of the laymen and only 7 percent of the laywomen considered apathy the sin with which they most personally identified. Also, when respondents were asked to indicate whether they considered a given deadly sin to be more characteristic of men, or women, or of both genders equally, the men responded as follows: 48 percent said that apathy is predominantly male, 45 percent said it is gender neutral, and only 8 percent said it is predominantly female. The women responded this way: 60 percent believed it is gender neutral, 35 percent said it is predominantly male, and 5 percent said it is predominantly female. Thus, not only is apathy considered more characteristic of men than of women, but men are even more inclined to this view than women are.[13]

A survey of clergy showed that they held similar views regarding apathy as more characteristic of men than of women: 54 percent said it is gender neutral, 44 percent said it is more characteristic of men, and 2 percent said it is predominant among women. However, when clergy were asked which sin they personally identified with the most, only 3 percent identified with apathy, in spite of the fact that 85 percent of the clergy in the sample were men.[14] This may mean that clergymen are simply not as subject to apathy as their lay counterparts, although it could also mean that some clergymen are unaware of the fact that they are suffering from apathy. If pastors are agents of hope, apathy is the spiritual malady that is most threatening to this professional self-understanding. Thus, a member of the clergy may find apathy especially difficult to acknowledge, even to oneself. Further study is needed, however, to determine whether clergymen's apathy is being underrepresented, and, if so, the possible reasons for this (e.g., have clergymen been so involved in the pastoral care of others that they have neglected the cultivation of the spiritual virtues in their own lives?).

The same question may be asked regarding why men are likely to be more apathetic than women. One possible explanation is that men

13. Donald Capps, "The Deadly Sins and Saving Virtues: How They Are Viewed by Laity," *Pastoral Psychology* 37 (1989): 229–53.
14. Donald Capps, "The Deadly Sins and Saving Virtues: How They Are Viewed by Clergy," *Pastoral Psychology* 40 (1992): 209–33.

are more likely than women to direct their desires toward long-term objectives and to give less attention to the more immediate. If so, this is a type of this-worldly asceticism, as the long-term objective is not hope in the life hereafter, as it was for monks, but long-term hopes associated with life in this world. Support for this interpretation can be found in the fact that middle-aged men looking forward to retirement often become apathetic, as anything that stands between them and their anticipated retirement seems rather meaningless. They may engage in more immediate goals and projects, but these carry little significance and generate little enthusiasm. The danger is that apathy can become a permanent attitude, so that when the long-awaited retirement does come, it, too, becomes a meaningless exercise, involving little desire or self-investment.

In short, the element of hoping that is missing in apathy as experienced by the acedic self is that of desire. One lacks desire, however, not because one no longer has confidence that what is wanted will happen, but because the hoped-for event is so far removed from one's daily life that it has little compelling power or influence. In the meantime, the activities of day-to-day existence seem far removed from this ultimate objective, and the ultimate objective depends very little on what one does in one's daily activities, whatever they may be. Thus, like the despairing, the problem is that one focuses on the very long term, but the difference is that the despairing have given up the quest for the long-term goal while the acedic self sees no meaningful connection between short-term activities and long-term goals. The long-term goal is realizable, but short-term activities appear to have little relevance to it. I will get my B.A. degree whether I work for it or not. I will become my father's successor as manager of the family business when he eventually retires or dies; in the meantime, there isn't much incentive to apply myself to here-and-now tasks.

Recognizing the problem, Chaucer wanted his listeners to appreciate that the two—long-term objectives and short-term activities—are not necessarily as disconnected as they may appear, and he wanted them to see that it is in fact possible to lose the assured long-term objective if one does not devote oneself to the here-and-now. There is, in fact, considerable truth in this observation, for apathy in the short run can eventually create apathy in the long run as well, for apathy can become an attitude or disposition, an addiction, as it were, and we may well find ourselves losing interest in our long-term hopes, even in those whose realization is assured. The here-and-now, then, becomes the locus for the development and cultivation of inner strengths such as fortitude, diligence, and constancy. It may not be the actual outcome of our short-term accomplishments that most matters, but the fact that, through them, we develop inner strengths that assume a life of their own and that, independently of outcomes and achievements, sustain desire and thereby keep us eternally hopeful. What we have done, in other words, is to redirect our capacity for suffering in the absence of the desired object into inner strengths of fortitude, diligence, constancy, and courage. Pastors, especially those responsible for youths who are going through the "weaning" process (e.g., campus ministers), can become agents of hope by helping these younger persons redirect their inner sufferings—which are often more painful than anything they will ever again experience in life—toward the cultivation of inner strengths that may seem insignificant to them now but will prove in time to have been absolutely essential to the formation and maintenance of an eternally hopeful self.

The Sociopathic Personality

Another type of apathetic individual—suffering from a state of desire-lessness—is one who has no long-term hopes at all. These are not persons who despair of attaining a long-term goal, or acedic persons who invest in long-term goals to the neglect of the mundane here-and-now, but persons who have no realizable hopes beyond the most immediate present. For this second type of apathetic personality, even short-term desires are difficult if not impossible to entertain because there are no long-term aspirations or desires to which these more immediate desires are related.

Melges's discussion of hopelessness in antisocial personalities sheds some light on this type of apathy.[15] While not all persons who suffer from this form of apathy are antisocial personalities (or socio-paths), the sociopath reveals the difference between this and the acedic form of apathy.

As Melges notes, we tend to focus on sociopaths' impulsive hedonism and reckless seeking of pleasure and miss their particular kind of hopelessness. In contrast to the depressed individual who becomes disillusioned about the long-term future, the sociopath, beginning in childhood, has never had much hope for the long-term future and is therefore "geared primarily to getting immediate gratification in the present and near future."[16] Thus, sociopaths experience hopelessness

---

15. Melges, *Time and the Inner Future,* 187–90.
16. Ibid., 187.

when their orientation to the present meets with repeated frustrations, especially when they feel forced to consider the long-term consequences of their current activities.

In contrast to the depressed personality, the antisocial personality believes primarily in (1) chance rather than skill; (2) exploitation of other people, not reliance on loyalty to others, as a means of bringing about desired outcomes; and (3) the present and short-term future rather than the long-term future. These beliefs reinforce one another, causing a spiral of hopelessness. Thus, "his risky and impulsive behavior aimed at exploiting others often breeds hostility from others; this aggravates his distrust of long term commitments and further prompts him to seek whatever rewards he can find in the present through impulsive acts that exploit others."[17]

The impulsivity of sociopathic persons betrays their apathy. They become involved in what is happening around them not because they are genuinely invested in it, but because these activities do not require long-term investments. As Melges points out, many of the actions of sociopaths, such as their involvement in violence, are comparable to a "pick-up" game in a neighborhood park; that is, somebody starts the action and the others just join in. The actions are considered temporary, and one believes, rightly or wrongly, that they can be terminated at will, leaving no adverse effects. They are taken because they either offer immediate rewards or provide relief from tension or boredom. In either case, they reflect no enduring or long-range goals.

The impulsive actions of the sociopath, of course, receive the most media attention, especially when they are vicious, as in the case of the brutal beating of the Central Park jogger in New York City several years ago. However, sociopaths are not characterized primarily by their impulsive actions, but by their chronic state of hopelessness. As Melges points out, "The sociopath has long since given up hope of striving for continuing and long-term goals and, instead, habitually seeks goals and opportunities available in the present."[18] While their action system is impulsive, their attitudinal system is one of apathy and callous indifference to life, including their own.

Melges' therapeutic recommendations for the sociopath are the reverse of those for the depressive personality. They involve (1) building skills rather than reliance on chance; (2) forming loyal bonds to replace the manipulation of others; and (3) extending awareness into the distant future instead of focusing only on the present and near future. The

17. Ibid., 187–88.
18. Ibid., 189.

primary therapeutic goal with sociopathic personalities is to break their spiral of hopelessness, but this cannot be done merely by encouraging them to consider the long-range consequences of their actions, for their own awareness of these consequences has contributed to their sense of hopelessness. As Melges puts it:

> Paradoxically, sociopathic sprees of impulsive behavior often occur when the sociopath feels forced to consider long-range consequences. That is, when his present-oriented, exploitive behavior meets with repeated frustrations and control from authority figures, forcing him to at least look at long-range consequences of his behavior, he then may become doubly hopeless—hopeless about the present as well as the future.[19]

Awareness of the consequences of one's actions is therefore insufficient. It needs to be supported by the building of skills and the forming of loyal bonds, and these, of course, require opportunity, time, and patience.

We who are older, middle-class, and employed may not see ourselves in Melges's description of the sociopathic personality. The young, underclass, unemployed male is undoubtedly our prototype of the sociopathic personality, and therefore Melges's description of this form of apathy may seem irrelevant to us, except to the extent that we have a pastoral concern for those who fit this description. Yet, a closer look at ourselves reveals more similarities with the sociopath—at least as far as apathy is concerned—than we may want to acknowledge. Consider the tendency of sociopathic personalities to get involved in what is happening around them, not because it has compelling interest for them, but because no long-term investment is required or demanded. Many of our own actions, as professionals, are comparable to a "pick-up" game of basketball in a neighborhood park: Somebody starts the action and the others just join in. These activities are considered temporary, and we believe that we may disengage from them whenever we might choose to do so. Nor do we entertain the thought that they may have adverse affects. Routinely scheduled committee meetings and group projects that are long on planning but short on actual results are obvious examples. We believe that meaningless committee meetings are harmless, having no deleterious effects, but that is not necessarily true. They can sap our mental, physical, and even spiritual energy and contribute to our sense of apathy.

19. Ibid.

The work life of middle-class professionals also tends to follow the same alternation of impulsive behavior and apathetic inaction of the sociopath. Suddenly, and without much warning or forethought, we become quite agitated about a problem in our workplace, and we can hardly contain our frustration. We may suddenly lash out in anger, prompting a coworker to ask the same question the public asks of the sociopath: "Whatever got into him?" In stark contrast to these occasional impulsive outbursts, there is the more chronic mood that prevails from day to day, from week to week, of lethargy, listlessness, and sluggishness, because no long-term aspirations can be thought about, much less worked toward. The immediate is all-consuming.

While we do not count ourselves sociopaths, we are no strangers to the same apathetic attitudes, and this means that we may not be strangers to the spiral of hopelessness that sociopathic personalities experience. Many religious professionals have long since given up hope of striving for continuing and long-term goals. We may make invidious comparisons between ourselves and those acedic personalities who were so invested in the life hereafter that they were unable to engage in the here-and-now, yet, in many respects, we have replaced the acedic form of apathy with the sociopathic form, having substituted the apathy of long-term assurances with the apathy of a controlling present.

Regarding specific hopes, the Christian ascetic model was designed to eliminate uncertainty concerning one's ultimate future through the "elevation" of desire. In this approach, the risk inherent in hope has been removed, replaced by the conviction that the outcome is perfectly knowable in advance. But difficulties in sustaining such an elevated desire created doubts about the inevitability of this anticipated future. Thus, a sense of risk, and therefore the need for courage, fortitude, diligence, and constancy, may revive as one begins to have serious doubts about the projected outcome being possible *for oneself*—in which case the acedic self has the opportunity to become a person whose life is lived on the basis of hope and not of entitlements, possibilities and not certainties. In marked contrast, sociopathic personalities make no projections and have long since given up the idea that possibilities that exist for others may also exist for themselves. They live a life that involves considerable risk, both for self and others, as it is based on chance and not skill. Yet, the risks have little to do with hope. The one risk that the sociopathic personality does not take is that of hope, as this requires the same human strengths demanded of the acedic self, but which sociopathic persons do not believe they can marshal—strengths of fortitude, courage, diligence, and constancy. Yet, by envisioning short-term hopes and developing skills for realizing them, the sociopathic personality can create and nurture such strengths and thereby make them available for longer-term hopes. Thus, for both the acedic self and the sociopathic personality, there is much to be said for the point of view developed by Chaucer in "The Parson's Tale," that desire can be energized by the development of inner strengths or virtues that enable one to accept the risks involved in the entertaining of hopes.

Our all-too-brief analyses of the acedic self and the sociopathic personality indicate that apathy is a condition to which pastors (especially male pastors) may be vulnerable. If so, three possible approaches for dealing with apathy have been identified: the *education* of desire wherein desire is taught to redirect itself and, if necessary, to scale down its aspirations; the *elevation* of desire wherein one focuses on the One who alone is able to satisfy and nourish; and the *energizing* of desire through the cultivation of such inner strengths or virtues as fortitude, courage, diligence, and constancy.

One senses that most of us may be vulnerable to apathy, not, however, because we have neglected all of these approaches, but because we have depended on one of them to the exclusion of the others, perhaps because it served us well in the past (for example, when we were in the throes of being weaned from our families). Thus, it may be that self-care, as well as the pastoral care of others, requires an individual to realize when a shift from one approach to another is needed. Each approach has proven to be a valuable strategy for confronting apathy, but whether one or another proves effective for us depends on our personal circumstances at any given time or period in life. We know from Augustine's *Confessions,* for example, that salvation came for him when desire previously focused on earthly "objects"—each of which was, in its own way, a "good" object—found its destination instead in the Divine. Based on his own personal experience, Augustine advocated what Kaplan says the elevation model is all about, namely, the "loosening of ties to particular loved objects and the emergence of a relationship to the world taken as a whole and to the reality of the creation of that world."[20]

20. Kaplan, "Acedia," 400. See also James E. Dittes, "Augustine: Search for a Fail-Safe God to Trust," in *The Hunger of the Heart: Reflections on the Confessions of Augustine,* ed. Donald Capps and James E. Dittes (West Lafayette, Indiana: Society for the Scientific Study of Religion Monograph Series, No. 8, 1990), 255–64; ibid., Eugene TeSelle, "Augustine as Client and as Theorist," in *The Hunger of the Heart,* 203–16.

On the other hand, Chaucer's Parson points out that such "elevation" of desire may itself give rise to apathy, for it is difficult to maintain an exclusive desire for the Divine. For those who have tried to live as if God were the only good object worthy of desiring, Chaucer recommends renewed investment in the affairs of mundane, secular existence, and contends that it will be necessary to develop certain inner strengths to energize desire for the "good objects" that comprise the everyday world, for these good objects will necessarily prove insufficient, inadequate, or elusive. When, however, one is faced not just with the inadequacy of good objects but their obvious failure or even their transformation into "bad objects," it may then be time to adopt the psychoanalytic approach which advocates learning from desire's disappointments and betrayal and saving desire itself by reducing it to more modest, less grandiose proportions, accepting the limitations under which desire necessarily operates. This is not a prescription for mere resignation, however, because the scaling down of desire is intended to rekindle a spirit of hopefulness, the willingness to risk hoping again.

In short, all three approaches may prove necessary for the combatting of apathy, and personal circumstances may dictate which one is more needed at any given time or juncture in life. What we especially learn about hope when we view it from the perspective of apathy, however, is the fact that hopes are themselves risky—always risky for self and often risky for the others we involve in our hopes—and that apathy often results from the fact that our approach to life has become too safe, too absent of risk. Even the risk-taking of the sociopath is symptomatic of the absence of the true risk-taking that hopes involve, for the risks here are mainly those of being consigned to a life characterized by more of the same, not a life in which one seeks and welcomes genuine novelty. And the acedic self, who may be rather certain of what the future holds, at least in general terms, risks even less than the sociopath. Boredom and indifference are characteristics of apathy, in both its acedic and sociopathic forms, and the fact that risks are not taken by apathetic selves is surely not because love constrains them, but because they have ceased to love: no love for the other, no love for self, and no love for the world of nearly infinite possibility. Perhaps the only way for apathetic selves to find hope again is to rekindle the fires of love that have long since been extinguished, for love is the ultimate source of all desire.

SHAME: THE HUMILIATION OF DASHED HOPES

Shame is a very complex feature of human life, and not all of its aspects have direct bearing on our subject of hoping. But there is one important sense in which shame is very directly related to the experience of hoping. This is the fact that shame is very often our most immediate and deeply felt reaction to the failure of our hopes to materialize. When our hopes do not turn out as we anticipated or expected, we may feel guilt, holding ourselves responsible for their failure to come true ("I didn't adequately prepare for the interview"), but the deeper, more persisting and more painful feeling that failed hopes evokes in us is shame. When our hopes fail to come about, we have feelings that are typically associated with shame: We may feel exposed, an easy target for the ridicule or derision of others ("She actually thought they would hire her over all those other people who had much better credentials than hers"). We may feel embarrassed, even humiliated, and have a powerful sense that others pity us ("Poor soul, he wanted that promotion so badly"). And we feel that the failure of our hopes to materialize is a direct and total indictment of us. We may feel utterly stupid for having entertained such a hope, and the disappointment we feel may translate into a total, pervasive sense of worthlessness: "I am just no good."

Thus, a third major threat to hope is shame, the painful realization that events have in fact turned out very differently from what was hoped for and confidently expected. While similar in some respects to despair, as both concern the failure of hopes to materialize, shame differs from despair in one important respect. Whereas the despairing person anticipates that what is wanted is not likely to come to pass, shame is the painful, after-the-fact realization that what was wanted did not happen, in spite of the fact that it was fully expected to. Shame is also the painful discovery that the future image we projected was a misprojection, a false or mistaken image. Since hope's projections involve self-projection, we feel deeply the shame that accompanies the realization that we have made a serious misprojection, since it means that we have misprojected ourselves, that we have been the victims of self-illusion or of self-misunderstanding.

What makes shame painful is the fact that we were so oblivious to the possibility that matters would not turn out as anticipated. Having fully entered into the hoping process, and having perceived that what is wanted will happen, we now feel foolish, stupid, or naive: "It didn't ever occur to me that she would reject my proposal of marriage. How could I have so badly misjudged her feelings toward me? How could I not even have known that she was dating someone else?" What these shame experiences reveal is the risk inherent in hopes, especially the risk to oneself.

Sometimes, the shame we feel over dashed or denied hopes has partly to do with the fact that others knew about the hopes we had entertained. We may have talked openly about the proposal of marriage that would surely be accepted. Or, our hopes are evident from our behavior or even the way we have been living our lives. When a couple divorces within months of getting married, we assume that there were expectations of a long future together and that these have now been proven wrong. We experience shame whether other people knew about our confident expectations or not, but our shame is compounded when we have reason to believe that others know. Even though others may be sympathetic and assure us that we had every reason to be confident, this does not eliminate the shame we feel or the pain that goes with it.

The realization that our hopes have not come true may have a profoundly negative impact on our willingness to entertain other hopes and thus undermine our hopeful attitude toward life. Such experiences may create doubts about ourselves and about our ability to "read" situations accurately. While we may continue to entertain as many hopes as before, we may be much more cautious in the future, warning ourselves not to take anything for granted. Such self-constraints may enable us to be less naive the next time around, but they may also turn hoping into a grim and calculating business without its former tingle of excitement and keen anticipation.

Why do these misjudgments evoke shame and not guilt? As various interpreters of these two emotions have pointed out, guilt is associated with wrongdoing whereas shame is associated with failure. As Gerhart Piers points out: "Whereas guilt is generated whenever a boundary . . . is touched or transgressed, shame occurs when a goal . . . is not being reached. It thus indicates a real 'shortcoming.' Guilt anxiety accompanies transgression; shame, failure."[21] Helen Merrell Lynd also notes that, because shame involves a sense of personal failure, it is

defined as a wound to one's self-esteem, a painful feeling or sense of degradation excited by the consciousness of having done something unworthy of one's previous idea of one's own excellence. It is, also, a

21. Gerhart Piers and Milton B. Singer (Springfield, Illinois: Charles C. Thomas, 1953), 11.

peculiarly painful feeling of being in a situation that incurs the scorn or contempt of others. The awareness of self is central in both conceptions, but in the second the feeling or action of the others is also a part of shame. There is no legal reference as in guilt, no question of a failure to pay a debt, and less implication of the violation of a prescribed code.[22]

Misprojection of our own personal failure is not a punishable offense. In fact, the pain of realizing that we have been wrong, stupid, or naive, that we have assumed too much, is usually considered punishment enough. Further shaming, as when friends chastise us for being stupid or naive, adds insult to injury, and the original shame is injury enough. Furthermore, the injury is not easily healed, as it is an injury to our very selves, which accounts for the fact that shame, originally an emotion produced by a devastating experience, may become an enduring attitude regarding ourselves. Some of us feel shameful even when we have no objective grounds for feeling this way about ourselves. Shame has become a chronic attitude with us, one that is especially damaging because it is self-directed.

In her discussion of shame as *self*-involving, Lynd points to the relationship of shame and hope. Noting that shame is an experience that affects and is affected by the whole self, she says that

> one is overtaken by shame because one's whole life has been a preparation for putting one in this situation. One finds oneself in a situation in which hopes and purposes are invested and in which anxiety about one's own adequacy may also be felt. In shame the inadequacy becomes manifest, the anxiety is realized.[23]

Thus, what makes hopes potentially shame-producing is that we have invested ourselves in them. We often fail to realize how deep this self-investment is until we are suddenly confronted with the failure of the hoped-for outcome to occur. We may not realize, for example, how invested we were in our graduate work until we are informed that we have failed the qualifying examinations. We may not be aware of how much we are invested in the success of the church we have been serving until the bishop tells us that he believes the church might do better under new leadership. Before these events, we may have been wondering if we were perhaps too good for the graduate program we were enrolled in, or whether our talents were being wasted in a small

22. Helen Merrell Lynd, *On Shame and the Search for Identity* (New York: Science Editions, 1961), 23–24.
23. Ibid., 49–50.

and contentious congregation. It never occurred to us that the faculty might think *we* were not good enough for *their* program, or that the bishop could possibly think that the problems in the congregation had anything to do with *our* leadership.

Such shame experiences make us painfully aware of the depth of our self-investment in enterprises in which we have failed, as least as viewed by those who have the prerogative of making such judgments. Such experiences may also reveal that precious little sense of self remains once our projected future lies in ruins, for much of our sense of self is tied up in our anticipation of the realization of future hopes. As Lynd notes:

> An experience of shame of the sort I am attempting to describe can't be modified by addition, or wiped out by subtraction, or exorcised by expiation. It is not an isolated act that can be detached from the self. . . . Its focus is not a separate act, but revelation of the whole self. The thing that has been exposed is what I am.[24]

Shame, Hope, and the Bipolar Self

Why do we misproject the future and thereby make ourselves vulnerable to shame? Some of the reasons for this have to do with the world we live in and with the fact that other people are unpredictable and that social institutions, even those that seem to have our best interests at heart, are undependable. Yet, the fact that failed hopes cause us to condemn *ourselves* ("How could *I* have been so stupid?" "How could *I* have so badly misjudged the situation?") indicates that we usually recognize ourselves to be partly responsible. Heinz Kohut's concept of the bipolar self helps to explain our own complicity in such misprojections. Kohut sees the human self as bipolar, with one pole being the exhibitionistic, ambitious or *grandiose* self that emerges in infancy, and the other being the values- or goal-oriented or *idealizing* self that emerges in later childhood. He claims that "the sense of the continuity of the self, the sense of our being the same person throughout life [emanates] from the abiding specific *relationship* in which the constituents of the self stand to each other."[25]

Either the grandiose or the idealizing self may be the focus of shame, depending on the circumstances. For example, a patient arrives at a

24. Ibid., 50.
25. Heinz Kohut, *The Restoration of the Self* (New York: International Universities Press, 1977), 179–80.

therapy session flooded with shame because of a faux pas that he committed at a social gathering:

> He had told a joke which turned out to be out of place, he had talked too much about himself in company, he had been inappropriately dressed, etc. When examined in detail, the painfulness of many of these situations can be understood by recognizing that a rejection occurred, suddenly and unexpectedly, just at the moment when the patient was most vulnerable to it, i.e., at the very moment when he had expected to shine and was anticipating acclaim in his fantasies.[26]

In such cases, it is the grandiose self—the self that sought acclaim—that experiences the shame.

On the other hand, it is the idealizing self that experiences shame when our values or goals are rejected or disconfirmed, as when a student who is confident of his intellectual ability unexpectedly receives a low grade on a research paper, or a woman who is confident of her ability to make accurate character assessments realizes that the man she is involved with is not the person she believed him to be.

Whether it is the grandiose or the idealizing self that experiences the shame, the effect is the same: The relationship in which the constituents of the self stand to each other has been disrupted, and, at least temporarily, the self that was not directly shamed becomes more assertive as the self that *was* shamed becomes more passive and demoralized. If the grandiose self has suffered rejection, as in the case of the party goer, his first reaction may be to raise his grandiosity up another notch, as his "mind returns again and again to the painful moment, in the attempt to eradicate the reality of the incident by magical means, i.e., to undo it."[27] But, realizing that he does not have the power to eradicate the event by magical means—this is a grandiosity that few of us allow ourselves to be taken in by—the next reaction is typically for the idealizing self to assert itself as he now becomes self-critical. The idealizing self criticizes the grandiose self's judgment for telling an inappropriate joke, for talking too much, and for not giving prudent and sober thought to dress codes.

On the other hand, if it was the idealizing self that suffered the shame, as in the case of the unexpectedly low grade, then the grandiose self asserts itself, plotting ways to gain revenge against the professor,

26. Heinz Kohut, *The Analysis of the Self* (New York: International Universities Press, 1971), 230–31.
27. Ibid., 231.

to humiliate him in class, or to prove him wrong in the future: "When I receive the Pulitzer Prize one day, I'll remind that old fool of the grade he gave me in English Lit, assuming he hasn't already died of senility." Thus, the equilibrium that existed between the two selves has been disrupted by the shame experience, and they are no longer functioning as a unit.

Kohut speaks of the "cohesive self," describing it as "an independent center of initiative" that points to a future and has a destiny, and he contends that what most threatens the self as a center of independent initiative is its disintegration or fragmentation.[28] However, as fragmentation is a severe form of self-pathology, a far more common experience is self-depletion, which is found among those who on the surface appear to be living productive lives but who are empty inside. Kohut observed such self-depletion in patients who described "subtly experienced, yet pervasive feelings of emptiness and depression." Such patients had the impression that they were not fully real, or at least that their emotions were dulled, and they were doing their work without zest, seeking routines to carry them along because they lacked initiative.[29] The connecting link between shame and self-depletion is "the dejection of defeat," the failure to achieve one's ambitions and ideals, and the realization that one may not be able to remedy the failure in the time and with the energies still at one's disposal. Kohut calls this a "nameless shame" and says that it is most commonly found among persons in late middle age, although it is certainly not exclusive to them.

In short, Kohut's analysis suggests that we make ourselves vulnerable to shame experiences in which our expectations are shattered because we are "set up" by our grandiose and idealizing selves. Our grandiose self seeks acclaim and recognition, and our idealizing self sets high standards for personal achievement. Were it not for these internal pressures to shine and excel, we would not even dare to project future hopes. We wouldn't risk ourselves. So, for hope to occur at all, they are very much needed. Yet, our grandiose and idealizing selves also set us up for shame experiences in which we fail to receive the expected acclaim or to live up to our personal standards of excellence or achievement. Like the patient who commits a faux pas at a party, or the student who receives a low grade on a research paper, we are unprepared for shame experiences because our grandiose and idealizing selves did not anticipate this eventuality. They led us to believe that we had nothing to worry about, that what we expected to happen would surely happen.

28. Kohut, *The Restoration of the Self,* 94–95.
29. Kohut, *The Analysis of the Self,* 16.

Anyone is vulnerable to such experiences of misprojections of what will happen, not just those with an excessively high opinion of themselves. Persons who are normally stable and realistic about their abilities can get caught up in their successes and they begin to entertain aspirations, either of acclaim or achievement, that they might not otherwise consider possible *for them*. Thus, we are all potential victims of shame. Because we all possess a grandiose and an idealizing self, we are capable not only of experiencing personal failure but also of failing to anticipate such failure in advance.

Defensive Strategies against Shame

To defend itself against the depletion that may result from shame experiences, the self typically takes countermeasures. In his delineation of the defending strategies we erect against shame, Gershen Kaufman identifies two that are especially relevant to hope. One is *striving for power*. As Kaufman explains:

> The striving for power is a direct attempt to compensate for the sense of defectiveness that underlies shame. In selecting for power, the individual sets about gaining maximum control either over others or over himself in whatever situations are encountered. To the degree that one is successful in gaining power, particularly over others, one becomes less vulnerable to further shame.[30]

One way that power is maintained and further shaming of ourselves is avoided is by shaming others: "What, you haven't finished that report yet? What's wrong with you?" Or, "You are the dumbest group of students I have had in thirty years of teaching." By shaming others, we are able to reduce the possibility that we will be the objects of shame. Striving for power, however, turns what were previously events that allowed for spontaneity and the unpredictable into events that are carefully controlled, choreographed down to the smallest detail. It is very difficult for hope to survive in this context, for hope flourishes where there is possibility, not the certainty that derives from exercising total or absolute control over one's environment. Also, as there are inevitable limits to anyone's ability to control the objective world, shame can return with a vengeance. One may be able to maintain tight control over one's subordinates and yet be vulnerable to unexpected shaming

---

30. Gershen Kaufman, *Shame: The Power of Caring,* 2d rev. ed. (Cambridge, Mass.: Schenkman Books, 1985), 76.

from one's superiors. Or, as in Ibsen's *A Doll's House,* the one over
whom one exercised power may simply choose to walk out. As Thorvald
discovered, there is no defense against the shame of being decisively
rejected. His only hope lay in the possibility that Ibsen, the one who
created him, might be pressured by public opinion to rewrite the
ending. But, in the real world, such magic does not occur.

A second defensive strategy having particular bearing on hope is
striving for perfection. Like power-seeking, the quest after perfection
is a striving against shame, an attempt to counter the sense of failure
that shame evokes: "If I can become perfect, I will no longer be vulnerable to shame." Kaufman says that we resort to perfectionism because we feel that "the only means of escaping from the prison that
is shame is to erase all signs that might point to its presence."[31] The
problem with this strategy is that it is bound to fail, and many possibilities for life will be sacrificed in the process:

> The quest for perfection itself is self-limiting and hopelessly doomed
> both to fail and to plunge the individual back into the very mire of
> defectiveness from which he so longed to escape. One can never attain
> that perfection, and awareness of failure to do so reawakens that already-
> present sense of shame. . . . No matter how well one actually does, it
> could have been better.[32]

Striving for power is the solution to shame to which the grandiose
self is most prone, while striving for perfection has particular appeal
to the idealizing self. As the grandiose self views it, the solution is
more grandiosity, reflected in greater ambition and acquisition of power. For the idealizing self, the solution is more idealization, reflected
in the highest ideal of all, the quest for self-perfection. In each case,
the assumption is that future shame experiences can be avoided because nothing is being left to chance. Everything will be controlled
and carefully choreographed, and all possible contingencies will be
anticipated and planned for in advance. Projections are being made,
not, however, on the basis of hope, but from the fear of failure. We
are not so much anticipating possibilities as forestalling them, which
is why Kaufman contends that these defensive strategies are self-
limiting.

Thus, shame, especially if it becomes chronic, is a threat to hope
because it undermines the premise on which our hopes are based,

31. Ibid., 78.
32. Ibid., 78–79.

namely, our ability to anticipate what may happen and especially what is possible *for us.* Previous shame experiences cause us to have self-doubts about our ability to perceive what stands a good chance of happening in our lives, and thus they undercut the confidence that is essential to hoping: "If you were wrong once, you can be wrong again." We may continue to entertain specific hopes, but these are now more subject to calculation and not infused with an easy confidence. They are no longer expressions of our self-autonomy, but of our self-defensiveness. Now, fully and painfully aware that hopes involve risk, we seek ways to minimize the risk in advance. We resort to defensive strategies that cut out the very heart of hope as the fear of future failure causes us to temper our desires. It is not that we become desireless, as in apathy, but that we limit our desires to what is virtually assured, and we may not even be aware of the fact that what we once desired for ourselves has been given up and relinquished. When reminded of the fact that we once entertained desires that we no longer permit ourselves, we are surprised that anyone remembers, for we have forgotten what it was that we formerly desired. Which is to say that shame produces in us a strong disposition to forget, both to forget the experiences that caused us the shame and the desires that caused us to have such experiences in the first place. Some years ago, I expressed this need to forget in the form of an aphorism: "Amnesia is to shame as rationalization is to guilt."[33] But what I did not adequately perceive at the time is the fact that the desires that led to the experience of shame are also susceptible to amnesia. It is not just that we try to put the shame experience itself out of mind, but that we also try to forget, to dissociate ourselves, from the very desires that resulted in our being shamed. Many such desires were altogether good and worthy of our continuing investment.

While some of the techniques used by psychotherapists who work with shame-bound counselees involve more time or counseling expertise than we pastors typically possess, there are several things that we may do to help such individuals. In *The Psychology of Shame,*[34] Gershen Kaufman devotes a substantial part of the book to psychotherapeutic interventions that he has employed with considerable effectiveness with shame-bound counselees. These include (1) using the therapeutic relationship itself to provide what these persons have

33. Donald Capps, "Parabolic Events in Augustine's Autobiography," *Theology Today* 40 (1983): 260–72. Quote is on p. 268.
34. Gershen Kaufman, *The Psychology of Shame: Theory and Treatment of Shame-Based Syndromes* (New York: Springer Publishing Company, 1989).

lacked in their lives (such as security, identification, and reparenting);
(2) returning internalized shame to its interpersonal origins (e.g., by
helping the counselee recover early scenes of shame, by making shame-
binds conscious, and by identifying "inner voices" that are associated
with experiences of shame); and (3) initiating and sustaining the restoration process (e.g., by helping the counselee create new scenes
and scripts, to reown disowned parts of the self and to disinternalize
bad inner voices, and achieve equal power in their families of origin)
[pp. 159–245].

Given time and competency constraints, pastors are not in a position
to work this extensively with a counselee. However, Kaufman's discussion of the general goal of therapy with shame-bound persons is
very relevant to pastoral ministry and has significance well beyond the
counseling relationship. This occurs in a section of his book entitled
"Self-Affirmation: From Shame to Pride." Here, he suggests that "central
to the resolution of shame is the development of a self-affirming capacity with the client. The self must learn to affirm the self from within"
(p. 224). This capacity to affirm oneself "translates into having esteem
for self, valuing of self, respect for self, pride in self" (p. 225). Pride,
however, has always been suspect because it is associated with conceit,
and we "are generally socialized to avoid the appearance of conceit,
arrogance, or superiority. In an effort to banish these particular qualities
from children and adults, pride itself has become bound by shame"
(p. 225). Yet, pride is "enjoyment over accomplishment" while the
source of conceit, arrogance, and superiority is contempt, which "el-
evates the self above others." The failure to distinguish between pride
and attitudes of contempt "has resulted in universal shaming of expressions of honest pride" (p. 225).

Kaufman encourages therapists to foster their counselees' sense of
pride by teaching them how to develop an inner source of pride in
self. One method he employs is to instruct counselees to keep a "pride"
list by writing down the "small" events in any day that make them
genuinely proud. The events noted and recorded can be tangible accomplishments or simply situations that were handled "well enough."
The purpose of this exercise is to teach clients that they can be proud
not just of actual achievements but of who they are and how they live
their lives, of "the self they truly are" (p. 225). It is a tool for cultivating
"not just a sense of pride, but an inner source of pride."

While the development of an inner source of pride as a means to
counter shame is Kaufman's major focus, he also emphasizes that "the
capacity to affirm oneself has multiple sources," pride being just one

of these. Self-affirmation also derives "from actively embracing all of the disparate aspects of one's being," including those that were previously disowned because one was bound by shame: "Nurturance of self and forgiveness of self walk hand-in-hand with genuine pride in self. Together, these form a new, self-affirming identity" (p. 225).

In *The Depleted Self,*[35] I used the story of Jesus and the "woman of the city" who anointed his feet with alabaster ointment to make the point that he affirmed her self-affirmation by praising her bold decision to come into the house where he and his friends were gathered and thereby risk rejection and ridicule. Disregarding the criticisms of his host and other guests who suggested that if he were a real prophet he would have been able to discern that she was a bad woman, he said to her, "Your faith has saved you; go in peace" (Luke 7:50). I suggest that what he was calling her "faith" was her "self-affirmation." The case of Rhoda presented in chapter four may be interpreted in much the same way, that is, as a woman who, having become frustrated and weary of her shame-bound existence, took her first significant step toward self-affirmation. Jesus' affirmation, "Your faith has saved you; go in peace" applies to her as well. Is this not a model for pastoral care of those whose lives have been in captivity to shame?

In *Shame: The Exposed Self,*[36] Michael Lewis suggests another contributor to the restoration process that has particular relevance for pastors. This is the proposal that confession can be of particular value for those who are shame-bound. While we normally associate confession with guilt, he recommends its use by those who suffer from shame. What confession does is to enable "the self as the 'confessee' to look upon the self as the object rather than the subject" (p. 132). As the self that is "looked upon" in confession is the self that is the source of the shame, one thereby "moves from" the shameful self and disengages from it. To illustrate how this works, Lewis cites the example of a man who, on meeting a former fiancée after an interval of ten years had passed, was able to accept her recollections of what a disagreeable person he had been. These charges were easy for him to accept because it was "as if we were talking about someone else. It was as if we both were looking at me from a distance" (p. 132). Lewis suggests, "A similar shift of the self to the position of the other is exactly what occurs during confession." Thus, it is not that the shame-bound person is confessing to have done something wrong—that is, committed a sinful or immoral act—but rather that what is being confessed

35. Donald Capps, *The Depleted Self: Sin in a Narcissistic Age* (Minneapolis: Fortress Press, 1993), 162–63.
36. Michael Lewis, *Shame: The Exposed Self* (New York: The Free Press, 1992).

is the fact that one feels shame about some aspect of one's self. The act of confessing "allows one to dissipate some of the intensity of the devalued self through regaining value by a positive action" (that is, the confession itself) (p. 132).

Lewis believes that one reason such confession is effective is because "we may be witnessing the reenactment of the original shame-inducing events" (p. 135). This belief is supported by the fact that confessions are usually made to individuals to whom one typically assigns reasonably high status in a society, and are therefore identified in some way as authority figures. Thus:

> To the extent that the confession reenacts the parent-child relationship, the confession will be able to reduce shame through forgiveness and love. If, as I believe, prototypic shame is caused by the withdrawal of love, which is caused by violation of standards, then love through confession banishes the shame. Confession, then, is a reenactment of the original source of shame. Through it, we are able to dissipate our shame and restore our intrapsychic life to balance. (p. 135)

In *Life Cycle Theory and Pastoral Care,* I discussed the case of a woman who was near death and requested a visit not from her own pastor but from her son's pastor. In the course of the conversation, she made the observation that "life—it's arguments, feuds, and all. It's all so silly when you think about it." She then proceeded to relate how, years earlier, she had engineered her reelection as president of the church women's society by circulating false rumors about another candidate's moral character. It is clear that she felt guilty about her behavior, as what she had done was morally wrong, but there was a deep sense of shame as well, as her behavior in this instance contradicted the image she held of herself as a woman of Christian integrity. What she had done demeaned herself even more than it demeaned the woman who was victim of her character assassination.[37] While it did not occur to the pastor that her confession might be one of shame, it is possible that it was nonetheless restorative, as it enabled her to distance herself from the "self" who was capable of behaving so shamefully, and to experience forgiveness of her shameful self.

Lewis concludes his discussion of the potentially positive role that confession can play in the restoration of shame-bound selves by relating the increase of narcissistic disorders (which are shame rather than

---

37. Donald Capps, *Life Cycle Theory and Pastoral Care* (Philadelphia: Fortress Press, 1983), 94–96.

guilt-based) to the decline of the confessor's role in contemporary society:

> If shame cannot be forgiven because no social structure exists within the culture that allows it to be forgiven, the experience of shame becomes especially dangerous and people will seek to avoid it. To this extent, the role of confession within a society is significant; indeed, its loss (associated with the decline of religion) is likely to be related to the rise of narcissistic disorders.[38]

On the other hand, the very fact that pastors are no longer officially involved in the practice of confession may make them ideal candidates for the more informal and occasional role of "confessor" that shame-bound persons find helpful to them. As Lewis points out, confessions of shame to loved ones and friends often place an emotional burden upon them, especially if they have themselves been hurt by the events being alluded to by the confessing one. Pastors can be more effective in the role of confessor because they, by virtue of their sympathetic but disinterested perspective, assist the "distancing" process to occur. In this way, the confessor role becomes a constituent part of the pastor's agency of hope, for hope is revived as we are able to dissipate our shame.

In this chapter, I have discussed three major threats to the maintenance of a hopeful attitude in life. Each in its own way relates to the feeling that what is wanted will happen, the central feature of the experience of hoping. Despair occurs when we have reason to believe that what we desire so much to come about is not likely to occur after all. We will not, for example, survive the illness that holds us in its deadly grip. Apathy occurs when we no longer invest desire in anything that is happening to us, and it usually results from the fact that the future is already determined. Thus, the son of parents who went to Harvard and anticipate that he will follow in their footsteps may be as apathetic as an inner-city youth who believes that the only future for him is a life of drugs and violence. Shame occurs when what we confidently expected to happen does not occur and we are faced with the painful realization that we put our trust and confidence in a reality that was not there.

What can be so devastating about these threats to hope is not only that they make us more reluctant to entertain specific hopes (we assume that what is possible for others is impossible for us) but that we

---

38. *Shame: The Exposed Self,* 136.

allow them to affect our basic sense of who we are, our very selfhood. As hopes involve self-projections—projecting ourselves into the future as though it, in a sense, already exists—the effect of these threats to hope is that we are more reluctant so to project ourselves, and therefore our very selfhood is diminished. It is the nature of the self that it links our past to our present and our present to our future. Those who have little sense of these connections (e.g., those who suffer from severe brain damage) can be said to lack this essential characteristic of self-hood. If, however, we find ourselves unable or reluctant to project ourselves into the future because of the danger that we will misap-prehend it, then a vital feature of our selfhood will be severely un-derdeveloped. It is necessary for us to be able to project ourselves into the future, and this means being able both to envision what is possible for us and to risk the possibility that our envisionings may prove to have been wrong or misguided. The despairing self, the apathetic self, and the shameful self all share a reluctance to project themselves into the future—short-term or long-term, it doesn't matter. As a result, they become less than fully vital and living selves, for true selfhood is not something we possess, as if it were comprised of fixed characteristics or accomplishments, but is the vision we have of ourselves, the one we envision ourselves to be. Thus, the capacity to hope is the core of human selfhood, and this is why despair, apathy, and shame are so destructive of the human self, especially when these three enemies of hope take on a life or existence of their own.

six

THE THREE MAJOR ALLIES OF HOPE

In identifying despair, apathy, and shame as threats to hope, I have emphasized how each of these can become a prevailing life-attitude, a controlling disposition in the way we engage or fail to engage the world. It is the fact that they can assume a life of their own that makes them so destructive of hope. Surely, all of us have our moments of despair, our apathetic moods, our experiences of shame. We would not be human if we didn't. These moments, moods, and experiences are directly related to hopes that we have entertained for ourselves or for others who are important to us, and are therefore associated in our minds with hopes that did not materialize. Therefore, the danger they pose for us is, in part, that we will not entertain hopes that are real possibilities for us. We will assume instead that while they are possible for others, they are impossible for us. We may be wrong about this, but we may never know this because we have not permitted ourselves to make such hopes our very own by projecting ourselves into them. In retrospect, we may tell ourselves that we could probably have attained this particular goal or aspiration if we had had more courage, more self-confidence, more willingness to risk, and our retrospective view may well be right.

The even greater danger, however, is that these experiences of despair, apathy, and shame will cause us to view the experience of hoping itself with such terror, to associate hoping with such strong feelings of suffering and pain that we begin to dissociate ourselves from the very experience of hoping. Now, it is not that we fail to entertain specific hopes that may well be realizable for us, but that we disengage from hoping itself.

This is not a hypothetical situation. In fact, it may be far more common than we realize. No doubt, every reader of this book knows

137

someone who may accurately and without malice be described as a hopeless person, a person who has totally disengaged from the experience of hoping. This person may or may not use the language we typically associate with this condition: "What's the use?" or "What good would it do?" or "What difference would it possibly make?" This person may or may not be consciously aware of being one who has disengaged from the hoping experience, and those of us who know this person may not always be able to discern the degree to which he or she has so disengaged, for such disengagement can be masked, such as by hiding it behind a controlling or sardonic demeanor.

The question this raises for pastors who seek to be agents of hope is whether there are other life-attitudes or dispositions that counter these enemies of hoping. If despair, apathy, and shame can take on a life of *their* own, are there comparable life-attitudes or dispositions that align themselves with the hopeful self, existing independently of specific hopes and supporting a hopeful view of life in spite of unrealized and dashed hopes? Are there dispositional conditions for the maintenance of a hopeful self?

If despair, apathy, and shame are life-attitudes that threaten hope, attitudes that undergird it are trust, patience, and modesty. I see trust as providing the necessary conditions for hope, patience as playing a crucial role in sustaining hope, and modesty as helping us to put our hopes into perspective, that is, by not allowing ourselves to be overly dominated by them. In my discussion of each, I will indicate how they counteract the negative effects of the attitudes discussed in the previous chapter.

TRUST: CONDITIONS FOR HOPE

The Reliable Other

The most general meaning of trust is that it is a confident expectation, anticipation, or hope for the future. This understanding of trust establishes a relationship between trust and hope. Other, more specific meanings of trust throw additional light on this relationship. One is that trust is a firm belief or confidence in the honesty, integrity, relationship, or justice of another person or thing. Erik Erikson emphasizes this understanding of trust in his discussion of the "basic trust versus basic mistrust" stage of infancy, as he suggests that the "general state of trust" found among infants indicates "that one has learned to rely on the sameness and continuity of the outer providers."[1]

1. Erik H. Erikson, *Childhood and Society,* 2d rev. ed. (New York: W. W. Norton, 1963), 248.

Key to the trustworthiness of the infant's providers is their reliability. It is not the other's honesty, integrity, justice, or any other moral quality, but the other's dependability that matters. Such reliability is communicated by the mothering person as she employs a consistent and predictable pattern of caring for the infant. A deep, abiding belief in the trustworthiness of the other develops from such reliability. Trust is more than a vague feeling or a random idea. It is a firm conviction, a tacit belief in the reliability of the other, a belief that requires little conscious thought or reflection, as it is based on the way things are. This is why betrayals of trust are so difficult to accept, for they disconfirm what we assumed about the other, an assumption that we saw no reason to question or to doubt. If we have to talk ourselves into trust, if we have to marshal evidence in support of it, we can be sure that it is not trust. Trust is knowing that the other can be relied upon, that no matter what the circumstances, the other will not fail us.

In *A Rumor of Angels,* Peter Berger suggests that it is the mothering person who first communicates to the child that the world itself is dependable and thus worthy of trust. He describes the following scenario:

> A child wakes up in the night, perhaps from a bad dream, and finds himself surrounded by darkness, alone, beset by nameless threats. At such a moment the contours of trusted reality are blurred or invisible, and in the terror of incipient chaos the child cries out for his mother. It is hardly an exaggeration to say that, at this moment, the mother is being invoked as a high priestess of protective order. It is she (and, in many cases, she alone) who has the power to banish the chaos and to restore the benign shape of the world. And, of course, any good mother will do just that. She will take the child and cradle him in the timeless gesture of the Magna Mater who became our Madonna. She will turn on a lamp, perhaps, which will encircle the scene with a warm glow of reassuring light. She will speak or sing to the child, and the content of this communication will invariably be the same—"Don't be afraid—everything is in order, everything is all right." If all goes well, the child will be reassured, his trust in reality recovered, and in this trust he will return to sleep.[2]

Berger notes that in her role as "a high priestess of protective order" the mother represents not only the order of this or that society but of order as such, "the underlying order of the universe that it makes sense

2. Peter L. Berger, *A Rumor of Angels* (Garden City, N.Y.: Doubleday Anchor, 1970), 54–55.

to trust. . . . 'Everything is in order, everything is all right—this is the basic formula of maternal and parental reassurance. Not just this particular anxiety, not just this particular pain—but everything is all right. The formula can, without in any way violating it, be translated into a statement of cosmic scope—'Have trust in being.' "[3] Thus, as Erikson has also often noted, it is the reliability of the mothering person that communicates to the infant that she inhabits a world which is inherently trustworthy. As Freud tells of the consolation offered by a dramatist to his hero who is facing a self-inflicted death, "We cannot fall out of this world."[4]

So, trust involves the tacit, unquestioning belief in the reliability of another—whether mother, father, friend, wife, husband, lover, daughter, son, or mentor. Of course, this other person will fail and disappoint us, will frustrate and upset us. Trust does not depend on the other living up to our every expectation or meeting our every need. Yet, reliability is the sine qua non of trust. Without it there can be no trust, because the other's unreliability causes us to give conscious thought to whether or not there is reason for trust. Once we move from a tacit belief in the other's reliability to the weighing of evidence, pro and con, the trust itself has become eroded. If such weighing of evidence continues, it is not long before trust itself has dissipated and is replaced with a sense of mistrust: "I can no longer count on you." The "order" of which Berger speaks has fissured, opening the possibility of disorder, even chaos.

Noting that he has chosen to use the word "trust" instead of Therese Benedek's word "confidence" to capture the first existential crisis of life in infancy, Erikson explains why: "If I prefer the word 'trust,' it is because there is more naivete and more mutuality in it: an infant can be said to be trusting where it would go too far to say that he has confidence."[5] In other words, confidence is something that we have, whereas trust is a state of being. As a state of being and not a quality that we possess, the naivete and mutuality that characterizes trust in infancy remain essential properties of trust throughout our adult lives. We may develop confidence in others, but confidence cannot take the place of trust, for trust has to do with the assurance that everything is and will be all right, that there is an underlying order to all things, that we cannot fall out of this world.

3. Ibid., 55.
4. Sigmund Freud, Civilization and Its Discontents, trans. James Strachey (New York: W. W. Norton, 1962), 12.
5. Erikson, Childhood and Society, 247–48.

This means that the reliability of the other is associated with her own being and not only with what she is able to accomplish in our behalf. When she caresses her child in the middle of the night, reassuring him that everything is all right and there is nothing to fear, such reassurance is based not on what she is able to do to prove that everything is all right, but on her very presence—her body, her voice—which is inherently reassuring. The mother is reliable by virtue of the fact that she is herself. Reliability is not what one does, but what one is. Whether or not she should go in to comfort her child was never an issue. She came because she is the one who comes.

The Caretaker

Another meaning of trust involves the act of entrusting something of value to us into the hand of another person or institution. Here, trust means to give something over to the care of another: entrusting our children to the care of teachers and schools, or entrusting our lives to the care of doctors and hospitals. Thus, entrusting focuses on the trusted other, on her capacity to take care of what has been entrusted to her. Here, the reliability of the other *does* have to do with the other's capabilities and not only with the other's being as such. We have certain expectations of the other and we anticipate that she will not disappoint us. However, we cannot control what the other does with what is of value to us, for this is precisely the point: We have relinquished control over its fate or future by entrusting it to the care of the other.

Entrusting is a voluntary act. If we give someone or something over to another under duress or coercion, this is not an act of trust. Trusting someone else with someone or something of value to us is an expression of our autonomy, an act of our own choosing. *We* are the ones who do it. In a moving eulogy preached at the graveside ceremony on the occasion of his nine-year-old son's death, Friedrich Schleiermacher tells the company of relatives and friends gathered around that he is now handing his son over to God, entrusting him to God's care.[6] The act of giving the child over is deeply painful, but the father is neither hesitant nor grudging. He is comforted by the knowledge that his son is with God, the only one who has the capacity to care for him. This act of giving Nathanael over to God is neither pro-forma nor an

6. Albert L. Blackwell, "Schleiermacher's Sermon at Nathanael's Grave," *Journal of Religion* 57 (1977): 64–75. Republished in *Pastoral Psychology* 26 (1977): 23–36. I have discussed this eulogy in *Pastoral Counseling and Preaching* (Philadelphia: Westminster Press, 1980), 142–51.

expression of pious sentiment. For the boy's father, the ancient formula, "God has given, God has taken," is a way of affirming that everything is in order, that everything will be all right, that those who are gathered to mourn the death of Nathanael needn't fear for his well-being, because he has been entrusted by his parents into God's loving care.

Thus, like the theme of the reliable other, the theme of the caretaking other points beyond the immediate situation and affirms that the universe itself is grounded in trust. If the former theme stresses the reliability of the universal order of things, the latter emphasizes that this order is oriented toward caretaking. The theme of the caretaking other places greater emphasis on the capabilities of the other, on our confidence in the other's intention to take good care of what we have entrusted to the other. The act of entrusting is therefore not as simple and naive as is trust in the reliable other. As we have the sense that we are engaging in a voluntary act, making a conscious choice, so do we also have the conviction that the universal order is voluntarily disposed to care. If God is one who gives and also takes, God is one who decides, acts, and exercises personal autonomy. God demonstrated this autonomy in entrusting this child to the care of the human parents who named him Nathanael. Now these human parents are exhibiting the same God-given capacity to entrust their Nathanael to the One who gave him to them in the first place.

Trust versus Fear

Berger's example of the mother who reassures her child that everything is all right suggests that the need for trust arises due to fear. The child suddenly awakens in fear, perhaps even terror, and cries out. The mother appears and assures him that there is nothing to fear, that he is safe, that whatever appeared to threaten him has gone away and will not return. By implication, then, religion—which offers assurance on the cosmic scale—is a defense against fear. In *The Varieties of Religious Experience*,[7] William James notes that Christian theology has traditionally argued that our "lower nature," that part of our dual nature that inhibits us from living more consistently and confidently in our "higher nature," is wilfulness or rebellion. But modern mind-curers dispute this traditional theological view, contending that what inhibits our living in our higher natures is fear, and this, in James's view,

7. William James, *The Varieties of Religious Experience* (New York: Mentor Books, 1958).

"is what gives such an entirely new religious turn to their per-
suasion" (p. 90).

In exploring the issue of fear, James quotes from a sermon by an
English preacher, Mr. Voysey, who makes a direct connection between
fear and trust:

> It is the experience of myriads of trustful souls, that this sense of God's
> unfailing presence with them in their going out and in their coming in,
> and by night and day, is a source of absolute repose and confident
> calmness. It drives away all fear of what may befall them. That nearness
> of God is a constant security against terror and anxiety. (p. 219)

Voysey goes on to say that these persons are not at all assured of
physical safety, nor do they "deem themselves protected by a love
which is denied to others," but, when injury does befall them, they are
"content to bear it because the Lord is their keeper," and therefore,
"the injury is no calamity at all." He concludes:

> Thus and thus only is the trustful man protected and shielded from harm.
> And I for one—by no means a thick-skinned or hard-nerved man—am
> absolutely satisfied with this arrangement, and do not wish for any other
> kind of immunity from danger and catastrophe. Quite as sensitive to
> pain as the most highly strung organism, I yet feel that the worst of it
> is conquered, and the sting taken out of it altogether, by the thought
> that God is our loving and sleepless keeper, and that nothing can hurt
> us. . . . (p. 219)

The similarity between Voysey's image of God as "our loving and sleep-
less keeper" and the mother in Berger's scenario is a striking one.
When we entrust our very self to God, we are able to quiet the fears
and terror of life with equanimity and courage.

James also describes his own overwhelming sense of "panic fear"
and reveals how he was able to bring himself out of it:

> Whilst in this state of philosophic pessimism and general depression
> of spirits about my prospects, I went one evening into a dressing-room
> in the twilight to procure some article that was there; when suddenly
> there fell upon me without any warning, just as if it came out of the
> darkness, a horrible fear of my own existence. (p. 135)

At that moment, "there arose in my mind the image of an epileptic
patient whom I had seen in the asylum, a black-haired youth with
greenish skin, entirely idiotic, who used to sit all day on one of the

benches, or rather shelves against the wall, with his knees drawn up against his chin, and the coarse gray undershirt, which was his only garment, drawn over them enclosing his entire figure." The image was horrifying to James: "This image and my fear entered into a species of combination with each other. *That shape am I,* I felt, potentially. Nothing that I possess can defend me against that fate, if the hour for it should strike for me as it struck for him. There was such a horror of him, and such a perception of my own merely momentary discrepancy from him, that it was if something hitherto solid within my breast gave way entirely and I became a mass of quivering fear." The effect of this experience was devastating: "After this the universe was changed for me altogether. I awoke morning after morning with a horrible dread at the pit of my stomach, and with a sense of the insecurity of life that I never knew before. . . . It gradually faded, but for months I was unable to go out into the dark alone" (pp. 135–36).

What enabled James to keep his sanity, to escape from total despair? He continues: "The fear was so invasive and powerful that if I had not clung to scripture-texts like 'The eternal God is my refuge,' etc., 'Come unto me, all ye that labor and are heavy-laden,' etc., 'I am the resurrection and the life,' etc., I think I should have grown really insane" (p. 136). These scripture verses emphasize trust in God, and they encourage the entrusting of oneself to God. Thus, in the midst of his fear of self-disintegration, James clung to biblical assurances that he had grounds for trust and reason for hope.

Trust, Despair, and Hope

Fear, then, is the experience that threatens our natural disposition to trust and our willingness to entrust ourselves and that which is dear to us to another. Against those who have preached that it is our rebelliousness that breaks trust with the reliable other, James contends, rather, that the problem is fear. The source of fear can be outside of us as the world is not a uniformly safe place to be. It may also be due to the fact that the person or persons on whom we must rely are unreliable or even abusive. In such cases, the world is a fearful place to be because the very ones whose task it is to protect us are the ones who instead pose the greatest threat. The source of fear may also be inside us, in the dreams we conjure up at night and in our paranoias that bear little relation to the real world as they misjudge both the ways in which the external world does in fact threaten us and the degrees to which the external world is benevolently disposed to us. How does

such fear relate to hope? What does hope have to do with fear? As I
now want to show, trust is the necessary condition for hopefulness
precisely because it relativizes our fears, enabling us to risk ourselves
to an uncertain future.

The meanings of trust explored above indicate that trust is the
necessary condition for hope. Hope does not appear ex nihilo, it is
not created from nothing. For it to occur, there must be certain pre-
conditions for it. In order to hope, we must first have experience of
trust. Unless we have belief in the reliability of another and assurance
that we can entrust ourselves to her, we are unable to hope, as hope
is based on the assurance that a certain reciprocity exists between
ourselves and the world "out there," that what we desire is congruent
with what the other desires. Trust in the reliability of the other and
assurance that we may entrust ourselves to her are the basis for our
conviction that what we desire mirrors what the other desires too. If
we yearn to be loved and cared for, there is an "other" who yearns to
love and care for us. In fact, we have the presumption that the other's
desire anticipated and preceded ours.

On the other hand, basic hopefulness, a hopeful attitude toward
life, does not depend solely on the existence or presence of a *human*
other whose desires mirror ours. It is perhaps through this human other
that trust initially develops, yet this experience of trust is a reflection
of the larger cosmic order, and this order is "in effect" at all times,
whether or not there is an immediate human manifestation of it. Thus,
our original experience of the reliability and trustworthiness of another
creates in us a hopeful attitude toward life itself, which, in turn, enables
us to be hopeful even when we are, humanly speaking, entirely alone.
It is enough for us to know that the universe is trustworthy, and, on
this basis, many if not most of our hopes are entertained.

The ability to entrust something of value to us is especially important
for entertaining specific hopes. Winnicott's notion of the transitional
sphere enables us to see why this is so. Observation of infants indicates
that they are at first reluctant to hand over a valued object to an adult
for safekeeping. When this reluctance is finally overcome and the object
is voluntarily given over, a major advance has occurred, since the
conditions have been met for the emergence of the second stage of
hoping in which autonomy plays a significant part. "Trusting in" is
thus the most basic condition for hope, while "entrusting to" is the
secondary condition; and yet, it is no less essential for hope, as it
introduces the element of choice and choosing which is vital for entertaining specific hopes.

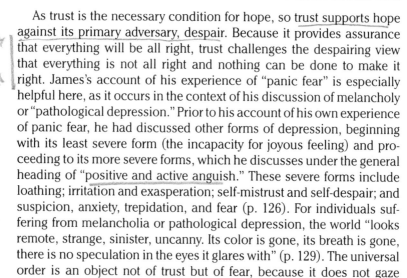

As trust is the necessary condition for hope, so trust supports hope against its primary adversary, despair. Because it provides assurance that everything will be all right, trust challenges the despairing view that everything is not all right and nothing can be done to make it right. James's account of his experience of "panic fear" is especially helpful here, as it occurs in the context of his discussion of melancholy or "pathological depression." Prior to his account of his own experience of panic fear, he had discussed other forms of depression, beginning with its least severe form (the incapacity for joyous feeling) and proceeding to its more severe forms, which he discusses under the general heading of "positive and active anguish." These severe forms include loathing; irritation and exasperation; self-mistrust and self-despair; and suspicion, anxiety, trepidation, and fear (p. 126). For individuals suffering from melancholia or pathological depression, the world "looks remote, strange, sinister, uncanny. Its color is gone, its breath is gone, there is no speculation in the eyes it glares with" (p. 129). The universal order is an object not of trust but of fear, because it does not gaze upon us in loving regard, but glares *at* us, generating a horrible fear of our very existence.

Against the view that melancholiacs are simply misguided in perceiving the universe in this untrusting fashion, James cautions against dismissing their vision of things too easily and suggests we consider instead the fact that the

> normal process of life contains moments as bad as any of those which insane melancholy is filled with, moments in which radical evil gets its innings and takes its solid turn. The lunatic's visions of horror are all drawn from the material of daily fact. Our civilization is founded on the shambles, and every individual existence goes out in a lonely spasm of helpless agony. (p. 138)

Consider, says James, the prehistoric reptiles that look so helpless and benign as museum specimens: "Yet there is no tooth in any one of those museum-skulls that did not daily through long years hold fast to the body of some fated living victim struggling in despair" (p. 138).

Such evidences of evil in the universal order of things, and thus of our grounds for despair, cannot be ignored as if such evil did not exist. Christians, and also Buddhists, do not ignore it, but focus on means of deliverance or liberation from it. Bunyan and Tolstoy are two Christians who, having tasted despair, found reason to hope again: "They had drunk too deeply of the cup of bitterness even to forget its taste," but "each of them realized a good which broke the effective edge of his sadness" (p. 155). Tolstoy "does well to talk of it *as that by which men live;* for that is exactly what it is, a stimulus, a faith, a force that re-infuses the positive willingness to live" (p. 155).

For Bunyan, his perception of this world as evil remains strong, but precisely because of this, he finds it essential to be able to entrust himself and those he values to God. The most difficult task is to leave his family behind, knowing that they will suffer in his absence:

> The parting with my wife and my poor children hath often been to me as the pulling of my flesh from my bones, especially my poor blind child who lay nearer my heart than all I had besides. Poor child, thought I, what sorrow art thou like to have for thy portion in this world! Thou must be beaten, must beg, suffer hunger, cold, nakedness, and a thousand calamities, though I cannot now endure that the wind should blow upon thee. But yet I must venture you all with God, though it goeth to the quick to leave you. (p. 156)

As James notes, Bunyan's tone here has more of the "hue of resolution" than the "full flood of ecstatic liberation." Yet his point is that Tolstoy and Bunyan are more trusting than despairing. Conscious that he has forfeited much of his life in literary pursuits and thus has reason for despair, Tolstoy is confident that it is not too late for him to begin anew. Aware that he is dying and is faced with despair, Bunyan entrusts himself and those whom he loves to God. His hope is expressed in his resolution to "venture you all with God."

So, fear is the threatening experience to which religion must give response, for otherwise we are left to despair. Religion counsels us to trust in Being and to entrust ourselves and that which we value to God. From such trust, hope is born. That the selfsame experience may engender both fear and hope is attested in this wonderful line from the Christmas hymn, "O Little Town of Bethlehem": "The hopes and fears of all the years are met in thee tonight." Like Bethlehem, the human self is torn between despair and trust, fear and hope. For James, there are grounds for both. Yet, what weighs in favor of trust, and so of hopefulness, is that trust is an act of our own choosing, whereas despair is resignation to having no choice at all. As Gerald Dworkin puts it, "What makes a life *ours* is that it is shaped by our choices."[8] The hopeful person dares to risk, to make what Bunyan calls "a venture."

8. Gerald Dworkin, *The Theory and Practice of Autonomy* (New York: Cambridge University Press, 1988), 81.

PATIENCE: KEEPING HOPES
ALIVE

If trust provides the necessary conditions for hope, patience is concerned with keeping hopes alive. Dictionaries indicate that patience has two meanings: It is the will or ability to wait or endure without complaint; and it is steadiness, endurance, or perseverance in performing a task. At first glance, the first meaning appears the most relevant to hope, as it concerns our ability to wait for an expected outcome. Because hope involves future projections, patience as the capacity to wait seems especially germane to hope. Furthermore, the idea that patience means to wait *without complaint* has great appeal as well, as it stipulates the proper way to wait for one's hopes to materialize. One is to wait in an uncomplaining manner, accepting and serene.

The second meaning stands in considerable tension with the first, and appears less relevant to hope. In my view, however, this second meaning is actually more relevant, for it implies that the patient one is not sitting idly by, waiting for some expected outcome to happen, but instead is self-involved in the outcome. As we saw earlier, hopes are future projections that, by their very nature, are self-projections as well, and this means that one is necessarily involved, proactively, in the hoped-for outcome. This does not mean that one is attempting to accelerate the timetable, to force events to occur before their appointed time, for that is what happens when we become impatient. Yet it does mean that we are determined to do what is in our power to see that the hope itself is realized. Patience is what we develop by engaging in difficult tasks without giving up. This inner capacity or virtue—call it steadiness, endurance, perseverance—keeps hopes alive. And whether or not we complain in our perseverance is really beside the point.

Writing in "this forty-ninth year of my life," Adrienne Rich begins her poem "Integrity" with the declaration:[9]

> A wild patience has taken me this far
> as if I had to bring to shore
> a boat with a spasmodic outboard motor
> old sweaters, nets, spray-mottled books
> tossed in the prow

9. Adrienne Rich, *The Fact of a Doorframe: Poems Selected and New 1950–1984* (New York: W. W. Norton, 1984), 273–74.

some kind of sun burning my shoulder-blades.
Splashing the oarlocks. Burning through.
Your fore-arms can get scalded, licked with pain
in a sun blotted like unspoken anger
behind a casual mist.

Rich's "wild patience" has nothing remotely to do with passivity, or even with waiting without complaint. It has everything to do with steadiness, endurance, or perseverance. It is the patience itself that has "taken me this far." Without it, she would not by anywhere close to the goal, the desired outcome. This "wild patience" is precisely not the sort of passive-acceptance-of-whatever-happens that we saw in Mary, the hospital patient we encountered in chapter one. Rich speaks here of determination, of standing up to the heat and the pain, of not allowing one's will to be broken. This is a patience that has nothing whatever to do with avoiding complaint, for, after all, it is fueled by an unspoken anger. It endures—not passively, though, but with a vengeance.

That good patience is wild—undomesticated—takes nothing away from the fact that patience stands in opposition to the attempt to accelerate the timetable of life (while working passionately within the limits the timetable sets for us). As David Elkind points out in *The Hurried Child,* impatience—trying to force events to occur before their appointed time—is very much the hallmark of our time:

> The pressure to grow up fast, to achieve early in the area of sports, academics, and social interaction, is very great in middle-class America. There is no room today for the "late bloomers," the children who come into their own later in life rather than earlier. . . . Children have to achieve success early or they are regarded as losers. It has gone so far that many parents refuse to have their children repeat or be retained in kindergarten—despite all the evidence that this is the best possible time to retain a child. "But," the parents say, "how can we tell our friends that our son failed kindergarten?"[10]

There is also the widespread suspicion that if we wait patiently for what we desire, we may be left waiting forever. This is what seems to happen to the main characters in *Waiting for Godot.* They wait all evening and into the night for Godot to come, only to be informed that Godot will come tomorrow instead. As the play draws to a close, they

10. David Elkind, *The Hurried Child* (Reading, Mass.: Addison-Wesley, 1981), 17.

have decided to come back tomorrow, and if Godot comes they will be saved, and if he doesn't, they will hang themselves. Is there any reason to believe that Godot is more likely to come tomorrow than today? Is patience warranted?

The traditional Christian view, articulated by the author of the book of James, is that patience is what sustains us as we wait for our hopes to be realized. As the farmer waits for the precious fruit of the earth, being patient over it until it receives the early and the late rain, so "you also must be patient. Strengthen your hearts, for the coming of the Lord is near" (5:7-8). Then, in what appears to be a misunderstanding of the book of Job, the author notes, "You have heard of the endurance of Job, and you have seen the purpose of the Lord, how the Lord is compassionate and merciful" (5:11). The fact that Job was a very angry individual has led some to challenge the idea of "the patience of Job," claiming that he was anything but patient. Yet, perhaps it is fortunate that the tradition has ascribed patience to him, as this means that patience has nothing to do with serenity, self-composure, or equanimity. Patience is steadfastness, the ability to continue to hope even as we are sorely tempted to give it up.

Does this mean that we must jettison the idea that patience means waiting "without complaint"? Surely, Job's complaints are legendary, and no one, including God, was spared of them. But, again, it is fortunate that the author of James chose Job for his example of patience, because the very fact that Job was a complainer means that we must distinguish between complaints concerning the losses and sufferings he endured and complaints related to the hope for deliverance. About the former, Job complains long and loud. Concerning his hopes, however, he is willing and able to wait until the proverbial cows come home. Immediately after complaining about God's siege tactics against him (19:6-12), and against his friends for desertion (19:13-20), he expresses hope that his redeemer "will rise on the dust— after, that is, my skin is peeled off!" (19:25-26). In other words, he indicates that he is willing to wait until he is long dead for his good name to be restored.[11] Thus, he certainly complains, but not about the time it may take for his hopes eventually to be realized.

But why is it important that we not complain about hopes being long in fulfillment? If I understand the author of James correctly, this is because such complaining may have a negative influence on the hope itself. If we complain about the waiting, it won't be long before

11. Translations from the book of Job are from Norman C. Habel's commentary, *The Book of Job* (Philadelphia: Westminster Press, 1985).

we will be complaining about the hope itself. We may begin to believe the hope is not worth waiting for and give it up entirely. This is what the author of James is afraid has already begun to happen, and it is why he assures his readers that the Lord will come again. The other side of Job's steadfastness is the Lord's purposefulness. The Lord will come because the Lord reciprocates our desires. What matters is that once envisioned and entertained, our hopes are kept alive. It is too easy to let them die and not even be aware of their passing.

Patience versus Frustration

If fear is the experience that creates the need for trust, I suggest that *frustration* is the experience that creates the need for patience. Acedic selves are frustrated by the fact that the future is so far removed from the present, and sociopathic personalities are frustrated by the fact that they are imprisoned in the immediate and unable to project themselves into the future. But, basic to apathy is the experience of frustration, and patience is the human capacity that enables us to endure it. The main reason we abandon long-term hopes is that we cannot endure the frustration involved. Patience is the assurance that the hoped-for outcome is worth the frustration and therefore keeps us steadfast in our hope.

Various developmental theorists such as Erikson and Winnicott have noted the positive value of frustration, provided that it is not so severe that it destroys the child's autonomy and initiative. If not too severe, frustration enables us to develop the necessary patience to entertain and work toward longer-term goals. In his study of the child-rearing practices of the Dakota Sioux, Erikson tells how the children were nursed by their mothers until they were about three years of age, and were then abruptly, even ruthlessly, weaned. After such a long period of indulgence, sudden, unanticipated weaning was calculated to make the child angry, and the angrier the better, for "Good fortune hunters . . . could be recognized by the strength of their infantile fury."[12] Erikson also notes the frustrations experienced by school-age children as they struggle to become adept at manipulating the tools of their trade and to become literate and informed.[13] Excessive frustration during this critical stage of development may cause them to despair of ever becoming productive members of their society, but manageable frustrations are a stimulus to further achievements and to the entertaining of longer-range goals.

12. Erikson, *Childhood and Society*, 137.
13. Ibid., 259–60.

In a similar way, Winnicott, noting that "frustration belongs to sat-isfaction-seeking," discusses the positive effects of an increasing ca-pacity for tolerance of frustration.[14] His concept of the "good enough" mother incorporates the idea that if she were too good, the child would not experience frustrations necessary to positive growth.[15] Also, one reason that a child resorts to a transitional object is that she is frustrated, perhaps because things have not gone her way. Such recourse to transitional objects means that hoping, as expressed in the act of reaching out to "another," is a direct outcome of frustration. In other words, mothers *must* frustrate their children. Otherwise, the child will not be sufficiently motivated to move beyond the symbiotic relationship of mother and child and thus to engage the world where long-range hopes ultimately lie.

The question is how frustration can be kept within the limits that enable it to be a catalyst for longer-range hoping and not a source of hopelessness. The answer is whether or not the frustrations contribute to the development of an attitude of patience. As patience develops into an enduring attitude, it, in turn, enables us to keep our sense of frustration at manageable levels so that we do not abandon our hopes. Patience also enables us to *redirect* our frustrations toward the reali-zation of our hopes. This seems to be what the author of the book of James wants his readers to understand. Like them, he is obviously frustrated. Before his celebrated appeal for patience, he gives vent to this frustration, noting that the rich get away with murder. He lashes out at the fat cats of his day: "You have lived on the earth in luxury and in pleasure; you have fattened your hearts in a day of slaughter. You have condemned and murdered the righteous one, who does not resist you" (5:5-6). He longs for the day when these callous and self-serving people will experience the miseries that are surely coming upon them (5:1), and he tells them to start weeping and howling, for that day is surely drawing nigh. These diatribes against the evil people of his day are worthy of Job himself! He makes no effort to conceal his frustration that their day of judgment has not yet come, but his frustration is not so overwhelming that he cannot continue to hope. What tempers and redirects it is the fact that he has also cultivated the inner strength of patience: not passivity, but a "wild patience" that is fueled by the same outspoken anger and aggression that fuels his frustration. Without patience, his frustration would be unbearable; with it, his frustration actually helps to keep his hopes alive.

14. D. W. Winnicott, *Playing and Reality* (New York: Penguin Books, 1982), 95.
15. Ibid., 11–12.

Patience, Apathy, and Hope

As Elkind notes, patience is not a very popular idea these days. One reason for this is that we have trivialized it by identifying it with complacency and inertia and contrasting it with anger, aggression, and indignation. Thus, we have aligned it with the very apathy that real patience so vigorously opposes. As the "I Gotta Be Patient" case in chapter one reveals, what the patient termed her attitude of "patience" was, in the pastor's judgment, a reflection of apathy. There was too little desire, too much passivity and listlessness in her "patience." Real patience is far more proactive, much more tenacious and spirited. When we are subject to acedia owing to our investment in very long-term goals, it is patience that enables us to continue to engage in valuable tasks and recognize their relevance to our long-term hopes. The steadiness, endurance, and perseverance of patience is very much like Chaucer's list of inner strengths or virtues that combat acedic apathy: fortitude, courage, diligence, and constancy. When we are subject to sociopathic apathy, the apathy of the controlling present, it is patience that enables us to envision something beyond the immediate present and to dedicate ourselves to its realization. Of course we are frustrated; like Jonah, "enough to die." But frustration can serve one of two masters—apathy or hope—and patience says, "Choose hope, for to choose hope is to choose life itself."

Perhaps the way for us to rehabilitate this vitally important human strength is to attach certain adjectives to the word, as Adrienne Rich has done, with her "wild patience." No one could mistake "wild" patience for passivity, complacency, or inertia, for one can hardly miss the fact that it has to do, instead, with the marshalling of inner resources in preparation for a long, protracted struggle. If "wild" patience does not say it right for us, however, then we must supply another adjective that does. It is vitally important that we do so, for how we say it will inevitably influence how we live it.

That patience has been demeaned and trivialized, and thus allowed to serve apathy instead of hope, has something to do with our tendency as a society to prefer immediate gains to long-range hopes and to view as foolish those who would devote their lives to hopes that cannot reasonably be realized in their own lifetime. As Dag Hammarskjöld observes in *Markings:*

> It makes one's heart ache when one sees that a man has staked his soul upon some end, the hopeless imperfection and futility of which is immediately obvious to everyone but himself. But isn't this, after all, merely

a matter of degree? Isn't the pathetic grandeur of human existence in some way bound up with the eternal disproportion in this world, where self-delusion is necessary to life, between the honesty of the striving and the nullity of the results? That we all—everyone of us—take ourselves seriously is not *merely* ridiculous.[16]

Who is to say when the line of futility has been crossed? Who can know in advance how far a wild patience may take us? In her poem "The Five Stages of Grief," an ironical comment on Elizabeth Kübler-Ross's famous theory of the stages of dying, Linda Pasten describes hope as "a signpost pointing straight in the air" and notes that "Hope was my uncle's middle name, he died of it."[17] Yes, hopes may be exercises in futility and they may take us far—to nowhere. But apathy *is* futility, so the better course is not to avoid long-term hoping, but to throw ourselves into such hopes with some kind of patience. Name it what you will—"wild," "tenacious," "tough"—or call it by some other name—"fortitude," "courage," "diligence," or "constancy." As Winston Churchill is said to have observed, "Success is going from one failure to another to another." Not giving up—this is the essence of patience, and it is what we can do for ourselves as we wait for the world out there to prove that our waiting was not in vain.

MODESTY: LETTING GO OF FAILED HOPES AND OF THE SELF WHO ENVISIONED THEM

We have seen that trust enables us to hope and patience enables us to sustain hopes in the face of frustration. What about situations in which our hopes have not materialized, when the job we coveted went to someone else, when the person we hoped to marry rejected us, when the financial security that eluded us throughout our working lives is now in our retirement a practical impossibility? What about hopes that have failed?

In the previous chapter, we saw that failed hopes evoke feelings associated with shame. Failed hopes cause embarrassment and humiliation as we feel the disapproval and condemnation of an unsympathetic public or the well-intentioned sympathy of friends. Because these experiences of failure are so self-involving, they leave us feeling

16. Dag Hammarskjöld, *Markings,* trans. Leif Sjöberg and W. H. Auden (New York: Ballantine Books, 1964), 8.
17. Linda Pasten, *The Five Stages of Grief* (New York: W. W. Norton, 1978), 61–62.

empty and depleted. A common reaction to the shame our failed expectations produce in us is to employ defensive strategies designed to forestall future shame experiences. What these strategies do is to turn up our grandiose and idealizing selves another notch, as striving for power and for perfection are even more grandiose and idealizing. So, these defenses are little more than attempts to compensate for our failure instead of coming to terms with it, and they are inherently self-defeating.

This brings us to the subject of modesty, our third ally of hope. In his two articles on hoping, Paul Pruyser writes about the roles of modesty and humility in hope and often discusses the two together. Thus, in his 1964 article "Phenomenology and Dynamics of Hoping,"[18] he says that the hoping person's attitude "is one of modesty and humility before the nature of reality" (p. 89). In the same article, he adopts Gabriel Marcel's word "chastity" and suggests that the "chastity and humility of hoping can be seen for the relation between hoping and its global object. Hoping is not predicting that such and such will happen, nor is it claiming that such and such must happen. It is entirely outside the sphere of rights and certainties. If the things hoped for do not happen, there may be disappointment, but there is no urge to take revenge" (p. 89). The modesty (or chastity) and humility in hoping arise from the fact that hopes are not predictions, nor are they assertions of rights. Also, they are about possibilities, not certainties. Given hopes' uncertainties, the appropriate attitude for us to take when we hope is one of modesty and humility.

In exploring the fact that hopes are not certainties, Pruyser employs Marcel's distinction between hoping on the one hand and both certainty and doubt on the other. Marcel contends that in the phrases "I am sure" and "I doubt" there is always an aggressive undertone, as the speaker "sets himself apart as different from somebody else. . . . My certainty stands over and against someone else's doubt; my doubt over and against someone else's certainty." Thus, both doubt and certainty are part of an "argumentative dialogue." In contrast, "When a speaker says 'I hope' he stands beyond argument. He is now making a self-reference, not a statement about external things and circumstances" (pp. 88–89). It seems appropriate, then, to say that the person who hopes has an attitude of modesty and humility, as these are congruent with the fact that he is not making an argument but speaking of himself: "It is *I* who hope."

18. Paul W. Pruyser, "Phenomenology and Dynamics of Hoping," *Journal for the Scientific Study of Religion* 3 (1964).

Pruyser also employs Marcel's distinction between hoping and optimism to make much the same point. He notes that people who are
optimistic "take some distance from reality so as to minimize or at-
tenuate the obstacles that separate them from their goals."[19] Thus,
optimism centers on external things and circumstances, "outside the
intimacy of the self."[20] Optimists are also rather aggressive in stating
the correctness of their views: "They reason rather competitively 'If you
could only see things as clearly as I do . . . ,' and boast thereby of
their greater acumen, if not ultimate wisdom."[21] In contrast to optimists,
"Persons who hope . . . remain part of the scheme of things and do
not aggressively place themselves above others. Their attitude is one
of modesty, both toward other people and toward the vast power and
often unfathomable design of reality."[22] Because those who hope remain part of the scheme of things and do not attempt to stand outside
of reality itself, they have "a degree of modesty vis-à-vis the power and
workings of nature or the cosmos" and "some feeling of commonality,
if not communion, with other people."[23]

While elements of both humility and modesty are present in the
hopeful person's stance, Pruyser, while not discounting the role of
humility in hoping, stresses modesty over humility,[24] viewing modesty
as a more accurate description of the attitude the hopeful person takes
toward other people and toward the vast power and often unfathomable
design of reality. So, I have chosen to emphasize modesty as a major
ally of hope. This makes particular sense in light of the fact that, in
our schema here, it is being paired with shame. While modesty is
sometimes considered a synonym for humility (i.e., as unassuming or
humble behavior), one meaning of modesty has little to do with humility. This is the idea of modesty as expressive of moderation or the
avoidance of excesses or extremes. This understanding of modesty
retains the sense that when we hope, we remain situated within the
real world and do not try to distance ourselves from it. Also, because
hoping is self-referential, a statement about ourselves, the use of this
understanding of modesty suggests that, in hoping, we try to avoid the
self-deception that occurs when we take leave of the real world and
enter a fantasy world. The issue here is not so much the need to be

19. Paul W. Pruyser, "Maintaining Hope in Adversity," *Pastoral Psychology* 35
(1986): 122.
20. "Phenomenology and Dynamics of Hoping," 89.
21. "Maintaining Hope in Adversity," 122.
22. Ibid.
23. Ibid.
24. Ibid.

humble about ourselves, but the need to address the matter of what is possible or realizable in a spirit of moderation: neither resignation on the one hand nor demandingness on the other.

Modesty versus Failure

Modesty is also relevant to the problem of failed hopes, as it is an appropriate reaction to their failure to materialize and a positive alternative to shame. When our hopes fail, shame results precisely because hopes are self-referential. If it was *I* who hoped, then it is *I* who must acknowledge the failure and accept the fact that it is *I* who failed. While extenuating circumstances are always present, it is rarely possible for us to externalize the experience entirely, to accept no personal responsibility for the failure of our hopes to materialize.

On the other hand, Pruyser's discussion of hoping indicates that when we hope we recognize the fact that we are participants in the world and subject to its power and workings. If we did not hope, we might not fully appreciate this fact. Because we do, we know how true it is, especially when our hopes fail to materialize in spite of our concerted, even heroic efforts to bring them about. By recognizing our place in the world and accepting the fact that our hopes are vulnerable to events and circumstances beyond our power to control, an attitude of modesty regarding ourselves can emerge, and, paradoxically, such an attitude fortifies us against shame, because it enables us to see that the failure of our hopes is no reason for us to feel humiliated or ashamed. To be ashamed by the failure of our hopes is to claim greater power to direct the course of our lives than we actually possess.

Thus, the very lesson that failed hopes have to teach us is that our power to influence and control events is necessarily limited, as we are not omniscient beings who are able to anticipate everything that may or may not happen in the future. What we learn from the experience of failed hopes is that our own power to anticipate, influence, and control the events and experiences of our lives has its limits. We will continue to hope in spite of this knowledge, but we will be impressed by the risk involved in hoping and therefore appropriately modest about our power to influence the course and outcome of our lives. Both the grandiose and the idealized selves are chastened by failed hopes and are replaced not by the shameful self, which takes the failure much too personally, but by the modest self, which is characterized by its capacity to maintain a hopeful attitude toward life because it does not hold itself so totally responsible for what has taken place. It takes

two—the self and some segment of the world—to make a success
and to make a failure. To believe that we are alone accountable for
either is the essence of immodesty.

In his article "Forms and Transformations of Narcissism,"[25] Heinz
Kohut identifies the "attitudes and achievements of the personality"
that are reflective of a well-integrated self, one that is not susceptible
to excessive grandiosity on the one hand or an excessive idealizing
self on the other. The attitudes and achievements that are especially
relevant to our interest in the relationship between modesty and hope
are the capacity to contemplate our own impermanence, a sense of
humor, and wisdom. For Kohut, these three attitudes make a cluster
of their own, as together they "form a new psychological constellation
which goes beyond the several emotional and cognitive attributes of
which it is made up" (pp. 121–22).

The capacity to acknowledge the finiteness of one's own existence
is rooted in the conviction that the impermanence of a thing—person
or object—does not detract from its worth. Our own impermanence
is especially difficult to accept, but what is gained from such acceptance is "a valid conception" of the time frame within which we live
and hope and of the necessary limits that our transiency places on
our desires and their realization. Acceptance of our impermanence
means being able to relinquish our "narcissistic insistence on the
omnipotence of the wish" (p. 118). As Kohut points out, such acceptance will not result in hopelessness if we transfer our desire for
permanence onto the cosmos, finding consolation and comfort in the
fact of *its* permanence, timelessness, and limitlessness. As we saw
earlier, this is precisely what Keats, confronting his own impermanence, was able to do: "Bright star, would I were steadfast as thou art."

Kohut admits that it may seem "a long way from the acceptance of
one's transience and the quasi-religious solemnity of a cosmic narcissism to another uniquely human acquisition: the capacity for humor.
And yet, the two phenomena have much in common" (p. 120). Humor
is an acceptance of one's finitude and limits; yet, at the same time,
humor, as Freud put it, is also "the victorious assertion of invulnera-
bility." Like the transfer of our desires for permanence onto the universe
itself, humor enables us to suspend the limits of everyday life, not by
ignoring them, but by making ourselves invulnerable to their ability to
inflict psychological pain.

25. Heinz Kohut, "Forms and Transformations of Narcissism," in Charles B. Strozier,
ed., *Self Psychology and the Humanities* (New York: W. W. Norton, 1985), 97–123.

Kohut acknowledges that these two achievements are often expressed in ways that are not authentic: "If a person is unable to be serious and employs humor excessively, or if he is unwilling to face the pains and labors of everyday living and moves along continuously with his head in the clouds, we will be suspicious of both the clown and the saint, and we will most likely be right in surmising that neither the humor nor the otherworldliness are genuine" (p. 120). On the other hand, if a person "is capable of responding with humor to the recognition of those unalterable realities which oppose the assertions of the narcissistic self, and if he can truly attain that quiet, superior stance which enables him to contemplate his own end philosophically, we will assume that a transformation of his narcissism has indeed taken place" (p. 120). Acceptance of one's impermanence and a sense of humor about oneself achieve the transfer of desires and aspirations once invested in "the cherished self" to "supraindividual ideals" and to "the cosmic world" with which one now identifies one's ultimate future: "The profoundest forms of humor and cosmic narcissism therefore do not present a picture of grandiosity and elation but that of a quiet inner triumph with an admixture of undenied melancholy" (p. 121).

Kohut regards the acceptance of one's impermanence and a sense of humor about oneself as achievements. He reserves the word "attitude" to characterize wisdom, which is "a stable attitude of the personality toward life and the world" (p. 122). Wisdom is more than a cognitive achievement, as it is "not the result of an isolated intellectual process but is the victorious outcome of the lifework of the total personality in acquiring broadly based knowledge and in transforming archaic modes of narcissism into ideals, humor, and a sense of supraindividual participation in the world" (p. 122). Wisdom involves the creative expansion of the ideals that were formed in youth and the transformation of the humor of one's years of maturity "into a sense of proportion, a touch of irony toward the achievements of individual existence," including one's own wisdom (pp. 122–23). So, accompanying the clown and the saint and encompassing them both is the person of wisdom, who adds to the humor of the clown and the ideals of the saint the sense of proportion that ensures that neither humor nor ideals become excessive or pretentious.

Such a sense of proportion is beautifully expressed in Psalm 131, a psalm that ends on a note of hope precisely because it begins on a note of modesty:

> O Lord, my heart is not lifted up,
>   my eyes are not raised too high;
> I do not occupy myself with things
>   too great and too marvelous for me.
> But I have calmed and quieted my soul,
>   like a child quieted at its mother's breast;
> like a child that is quieted is my soul.

> O Israel, hope in the Lord
>   from this time forth and forevermore.

Here modesty creates the conditions for being at peace with the world and at peace with oneself, possessed of a sense of proportion about oneself and one's achievements that Kohut calls wisdom.

Modesty, Shame, and Hope

The "sense of proportion" that makes wisdom a stable attitude of the personality toward the world is modesty, the absence of excesses and pretensions. This means that modesty is not simply a matter of personal demeanor, but is a fundamental attitude toward life and integral to "the lifework of the total personality." Thus, what we can hope for is subject to the limitations placed upon us by our impermanence and the constraints of the world of things and circumstances, but it is also subject to the lifework of our total personality and to the values and ideals that this represents. This is to say that, given who *I* am and what *I* have become over the years, certain hopes are simply unthinkable. Ambitions and achievements are important, but not at the expense of ideals and of my sense of supraindividual participation in the cosmos. Transformed narcissists—individuals who view themselves with a sense of proportion and moderation—know that this way of thinking has its personal costs. But they would have it no other way.

These three expressions of the transformation of our narcissistic self together represent a coming to terms with life's disappointments and failures. Coming to terms with our disappointments and failures means that they are not allowed to define who we are and are not permitted to control us. As far as our hopes are concerned, we view them all—those that have been realized, those that are pending, and those that have failed—with a sense of proportion. The elation of realized hopes, and the shame of unrealized hopes: Both are swallowed up in the attitude that encompasses and transcends them both, that

Parents hope and failures.

of modesty, which is better known for what it is not than for what it is: the lack of excesses and pretensions about ourselves.

Modesty is not a call for scaling hopes back or down, or for entertaining mediocre and trivial hopes. On the contrary, in helping us to achieve a cohesive self that is competent to engage the external world, modesty enables us to *expand* the horizon of our hopes in ways commensurate with our total lifework. This means that modesty is the basis for a hopeful, self-sustaining approach to life. Such modesty simply comes with the cautionary note that hopes are not facts, but are concerned to change facts, and some facts, try as we might, are impervious to change.

The three strong allies of hope are trust, patience, and modesty. It is tempting to add, "And the greatest of these is trust," for without trust, we would not dare hope at all. Yet, more important than prioritizing these allies of hope is recognition of the fact that they are mutually supportive. Because we trust, we are able to exercise greater patience. Because our attitude is one of modesty, we are conscious of the necessity of trust. These, then, are not discrete virtues, but are a system of dispositions that support and enhance one another. Most importantly, the three of them together assume a life of their own and sustain the hopeful self even as specific hopes may go unrealized.

All of us know individuals who have met with frustration and failure and who have every reason to fear the future. Yet they remain hopeful in spite of this. I submit that if we were to probe beneath the surface of their lives, we would find there a deep fundament of trust, a history of tough patience, and a modest sense of themselves in the face of the powerful reality that surrounds them. Such individuals have made their share of mistakes in life, and their failures are ample evidence that they are far from omnipotent and omniscient. Indeed, we may be struck by how oblivious they are to matters of power and control, and there is a kind of childlike disregard for what looms ahead. They are quite willing to entertain hopes that you and I may consider ill-advised or futile, and they do so without calculating the potential cost to themselves if their hopes should fail. From their point of view, the costs are, in a sense, rather minimal, for there is precious little danger that they will become discouraged or demoralized, that they will succumb to despair, apathy, or a debilitating sense of shame. Instead, they will take frustration and failure in stride. As for fear? What is there to fear if God is their reliable Other—one whom they have no reason not to trust—and the caretaker of all that they hold dear? The hopeful self is sustained not because all or even most desires are met, but

because the risking has revealed to them, time and time again, that
God is their reliable Other. As Denise Levertov expresses it in her poem
entitled "Suspended":[26]

> I had grasped God's garment in the void
> but my hand slipped
> on the rich silk of it.
> The "everlasting arms" my sister loved to remember
> must have upheld my leaden weight
> from falling, even so,
> for though I claw at empty air and feel
> nothing, no embrace,
> I have not plummeted.

Because we cannot fall out of this world, there is no reason for us not
to hope, again and again and again.

---

26. Denise Levertov, *Evening Train* (New York: New Directions Press, 1992), 119. Her
sister was apparently recalling Deut. 33:27: "The eternal God is your dwelling place,
and underneath are the everlasting arms" (RSV).

seven

HOPE AND THE REFRAMING OF TIME

The life-attitudes of trust, patience, and modesty are formed and sustained through the myriad of relationships and experiences we have in life. Yet, for most persons, their relationship to the pastor is not among the more sustaining of such relationships. The more significant formative relationships are those we had with parents and brothers and sisters while we were growing up, and the more significant supportive relationships are those we currently have with spouses and partners and our adult children. Our geographical and denominational mobility and the decreasing role of the pastor as a friend of the family are among the reasons why pastors today play a less significant relational role in the lives of their parishioners. Where supportive relationships do develop, it is increasingly difficult for these to survive over the years.

On the other hand, pastors can exemplify these life-attitudes of trust, patience, and modesty in their personal and professional lives and thereby represent them to the congregation as not only worthy of being cultivated for their own sakes but also as necessary to the maintenance of a hopeful orientation to life. The church as a community may represent these life-attitudes as well: by striving to be a community in which these attitudes are valued and prized, a community in which despair, apathy, and shaming are recognized as inevitable facts of life but not allowed to dominate and control the church's life.

I am primarily concerned in this book, however, with the pastor's role in assisting *individuals* to hope. This focus is implied in the first chapter of the book, where I presented three pastoral care cases, all concerned with individuals who were in danger of losing hope. The first case of the young high school woman who was pregnant outside of marriage posed the threat of despair, the danger that her long-term goals would never be realized. The second case of the woman who was hospitalized for infections posed the threat of apathy, the danger that she would not devote herself to short-range objectives because she felt that she had no control over what would ultimately happen to her. The third case of the young man who was sexually active and despised himself for it posed the threat of shame, the danger that he would become so negative about himself that he would not be able to break the self-destructive cycle in which he presently found himself. All three were in danger of becoming hopeless, and in all three cases the danger was real. The pastors involved discerned that the threat of hopelessness was the central issue, and they directed their efforts toward helping the individual maintain hope in the face of adversity and pain.

In chapter five, where I discussed the three major threats to hope, I made suggestions for how pastors might make use of their sensitivity to the matter of hope in their pastoral care of individuals. In this final chapter, I want to make a more substantive proposal along these lines, focusing on the fact that hope and time have an intimate relationship to each other. Specifically, I want to relate the roles of the pastor as agent of hope and as one who helps other persons reframe the problems and difficulties in their lives. In my book *Reframing: A New Method in Pastoral Care,*[1] I recommended that pastors make more self-conscious use of the reframing method, a method that is regularly used by psychotherapists and by trained pastoral counselors, but has not been available, for the most part, to pastors. I also pointed to the fact that contemporary reframing methods are nothing new, as reframing occurs with considerable frequency in the Bible. I cited especially Jesus' own parables and healings and the reframing that God achieved in the story of Job.

Reframing essentially involves placing a problem or difficulty within a new perceptual framework and thereby changing its meaning. To illustrate, I cited the ancient Chinese Taoist story reported in Richard Bandler and John Grinder's book on reframing:[2]

> There was a farmer in a poor country village. He was considered very well-to-do because he owned a horse that he used for plowing and transportation. One day his horse ran away. All his neighbors exclaimed how terrible this was, but the farmer simply replied, "Maybe."

1. Donald Capps, *Reframing: A New Method in Pastoral Care* (Minneapolis: Fortress Press, 1990).
2. Richard Bandler and John Grinder, *Reframing: Neuro-Linguistic Programming and the Transformation of Meaning* (Moab, Utah: Real People Press, 1982), 1.

A few days later the horse returned and brought two wild horses with it. The neighbors all rejoiced at his good fortune, but the farmer simply replied, "Maybe."

The next day the farmer's son tried to ride one of the wild horses, but the horse threw him and broke the son's leg. The neighbors all offered their sympathy for his misfortune, but the farmer again replied, "Maybe."

The next week conscription officers came to the village to take young men for the army. They rejected the farmer's son because of his broken leg. When the neighbors told him how lucky he was, the farmer replied, "Maybe."

Bandler and Grinder use this story to show that the meaning any event has for us depends upon the *frame* in which we perceive it. When we change the frame, we change the meaning. Having two wild horses is a good thing until it is seen in the context of the son's broken leg. Then, the broken leg seems to be bad in the context of peaceful village life; but in the context of conscription and war, it suddenly appears good. "This is called reframing: changing the frame in which a person perceives events in order to change the meaning. When the meaning changes, the person's responses and behaviors also change."[3]

In this chapter, I want to suggest ways in which pastors may use reframing methods to encourage hopefulness. While every reframing method of which I am aware (and I discuss several in *Reframing*) has potential for creating conditions for hope, I will focus on two such methods here, as I believe they have particular relevance to our preceding discussions of hope. One is the method of envisioning the future, and the other is the method of revising the past. These two methods have particular value for creating and sustaining hope because both involve the reframing of time. As we have seen throughout our study of hope, but especially in our discussion of the major threats and allies of hope, time plays a critical role in determining our sense of hope or of hopelessness. The first method encourages us to take a future perspective on the present, thereby enabling us to escape the captivity of a controlling present. The second invites us to locate our past within a new frame, thereby revising the meaning it has held for us, and thus "changing" the past from a basis for hopelessness into a basis and resource for hopefulness.

3. Ibid.

FUTURE VISIONS

Two Finnish psychotherapists, Ben Furman and Tapani Ahola, devote a chapter of their book *Solution Talk* to "future visions."[4] They note the effect of our past on our view of the future and the effect of our vision of the future on our lives today: "Since the future is often connected to the past, people with a stressful past are prone to have a hopeless view of their future. In its turn a negative vision of the future exacerbates current problems by casting a pessimistic shadow over both past and present" (p. 91). (This negative view of the future is nicely expressed in Yogi Berra's observation that "the future ain't what it used to be.") Yet, if a negative view of the future exacerbates current problems, "the converse is also true; a positive view of the future invites hope, and hope in its turn helps to cope with current hardships, to recognize signs indicating the possibility of change, to view the past as an ordeal rather than a misery, and to provide the inspiration for generating solutions" (p. 91).

The authors provide several case illustrations in which they challenged their clients to fantasize about the future in such a way that the fantasizing helped them to set goals for change and to recognize the resources that were already available to them. In a case entitled "When the Problem Is Over," Tapani Ahola tells about a woman who phoned to say that her husband was on another drinking binge and they needed urgent help. She informed Ahola that every few weeks her husband would go straight from work to a bar and begin drinking with strangers. On these occasions he would stay away from home for days, sometimes for weeks. During his drinking binges he usually kept in touch with his wife by phone.

Ahola asked the woman if her husband was aware that she was calling him. She said that he was, but that he was not interested in therapy. Ahola said that he would meet with her alone if her husband preferred that, and then suggested that just in case he changed his mind they should take a little time before the meeting and entertain the fantasy that their life could be in order. Then, when he met with them, they would continue with the idea that they were in the future and he would ask questions such as, "How is your life these days?" and "What do you think made the change possible?"

When Ahola arrived at their house as planned (itself a kind of reframing as it is customary for psychotherapists to expect clients to

4. Ben Furman and Tapani Ahola, *Solution Talk: Healing Therapeutic Conversations* (New York: W. W. Norton, 1992), 91–106.

come to their offices, a reframing that improved the chances of the husband being involved), both Riina and her husband Heikki were home. Heikki was suffering from withdrawal symptoms, trembling and perspiring heavily. Ahola asked him if he knew what he had asked them to do before he came. Heikki said that he knew and that he found the suggestion interesting since he had been thinking a lot about the future recently. Ahola asked him, "Well, then, how are things now that the problem is over?" Heikki responded, "What do you mean, the problem is over?" He had not yet grasped Ahola's idea of future visioning.

So Ahola continued, "Do you remember that we met two years ago? If I remember right, you had some problems with alcohol or something like that. I get the impression that things are O.K. nowadays, am I right?"

Riina was the first to respond, "Yes, Heikki doesn't drink any longer." Then Heikki corrected her, "She means that I've reduced the amount I drink, that I only drink a glass or two of wine every now and then." The three of them developed this imaginary future world for quite some time, and then, as the end of the session drew near, Ahola addressed the question of how they explained the change. Heikki said that much of it had to do with the fact that Riina had begun to share the responsibility for family economics. He explained that previously Riina had merely thrown all the bills into a drawer, leaving him to take care of her tax declaration at the end of each year: "For two years now, she's gathered her bills neatly into piles and completed her declaration all by herself, only asking me for occasional advice." Another explanation that emerged was that Heikki had effected a major change in his working career.

As Ahola left the house, he had the sense that Heikki and Riina seemed more hopeful, "as if some of the things in the fantasy had actually come true." Later, he learned that Heikki had made a career change and that he had drastically reduced his drinking.

The method of "future visioning" is revealing for what it precludes. By focusing on a time in the future when the problem has been overcome, rather than upon the past where the problem is assumed to have originated, neither Riina or Heikki engage in the blaming of one another which usually occurs in marriage counseling. By locating the solution in the future, Heikki is able to say that Riina has contributed to his drinking problem, but he does so in a way that says that he believes her behavior is readily changeable. He also accepts her view that he can do something about his drinking. They are not, therefore, condemned to repeat the past, but are already acting on the presumption that a new and different future has already begun to be realized. They are hopeful because they believe they have the personal autonomy necessary to make a different future for themselves. As Furman and Ahola point out, "Positive visions of the future enable people to see their current predicaments as phases in a continuing narrative, where hardships are steps on the path to a better tomorrow. From this viewpoint problems can be perceived as valuable learning experiences and the people involved can be seen as helpers rather than obstacles" (p. 93).

In another case, Ahola invites the patient to view her current circumstances from the far distant future. Siru was a fifteen-year-old girl who had been a patient in the adolescent inpatient unit of a psychiatric hospital for several months. During a consultation session with Siru, Ahola asked her how she came to be in the hospital in the first place. Siru replied in a matter-of-fact way, "I'm here because I went crazy." "And what made you go crazy?" "My father killed himself and I couldn't take it." One of the nurses present explained that Siru's father had been an alcoholic for many years and one day when he had been very drunk he took his life. Ahola and the girl talked for some time about what had happened and how, with the help of the hospital, she had begun to cope with the tragedy. Then, toward the end of the session, he said to her,

> You have gone through a very rough period in your life and what has happened has undoubtedly had a great impact on you. It may be impossible to foresee what the effects will be in the long run, but let's imagine that some time in the far distant future you are a grandmother with an adult daughter and a teenage granddaughter. You have told your daughter about your father's suicide and about the time you spent in a mental hospital. Your daughter, in turn, has told your story to her daughter. Your story will serve as a teaching story. It will be wisdom that is of value not only to your daughter but also to your granddaughter. What do you imagine that wisdom might be? (p. 147)

After a moment of silence Siru said, "First, I've realized that it is possible to survive even the most terrible things." She paused and then continued, "Second, I used to be the kind of person who kept my thoughts to myself. That wasn't good. Here at the hospital I've learned that talking helps" (p. 147).

In this case, the patient is encouraged to project herself far into the future and to view her current situation from that perspective. While she has already begun to make progress in getting over the tragedy of her father's death, the response she gives to Ahola's question about the wisdom she would give to her daughter and granddaughter reinforces the progress she has already made and extends it further. Placing her tragedy in the context of a long and rewarding life (including becoming the mother of a daughter and a grandmother as well) gives her greater hope in the present.

Furman and Ahola conclude their discussion of the method of future visioning with this observation:

> The future is perhaps one of the most gratifying subjects for therapeutic conversations. It is a country which no one can own and which is therefore open to all possible ideas and imaginings. People have different ideas about what lies in the future, and they may disagree about what it should bring, but since people know deep down that no one can ultimately know what the future will bring, it is a wonderful place for constructive conversations. (p. 106)

Thus, key to their future visioning method is the assumption that we can have a different future from the one our present difficulties and problems would predict, and that we can take personal responsibility for effecting this alternative outcome. In this way, the method engenders hope, and grounds this hope in our personal autonomy, in our capacity to take the future into our own hands and shape it according to our desires.

Theologically informed readers of Furman and Ahola's book are often quick to note that what underlies their future visioning method is a kind of realized eschatology. The future is already here, in the present, so that what we have been hoping for—our heartfelt desires—is already being met. Ahola's cases show that clients are quite willing to engage in the imaginative act of future visioning, and that, when they do, they have a lively perception of having made the future present. The therapist's skill is required in establishing the future time frame: Will it be two years, as in the case of Heikki and Riina, will it be in the far distant future, as in the case of Siru, or might it be in six months, or three months, or weeks from now? As our discussion of the threats to hope revealed, much of the reason why it is difficult to maintain an attitude of hopefulness is that we seem to have so little control over the future, as the future appears like a vast wasteland with no discernible markers. By setting such markers and giving the future a recognizable structure in terms of days, weeks, months, or even years, it no longer seems so overwhelming, and we begin to feel that we can exercise some personal autonomy in relation to it. Despair and apathy are especially relevant here for they are the companions of a controlling future. Furman and Ahola's therapeutic skill involves establishing the future time frame that will enable the counselee to visualize the resolution of the problem and the steps required to get there. On the other hand, not all of our problems relate to a controlling future. Some result from a controlling past, and this is especially the case when the past has been one in which we experienced shame, shame that we carry with us in the present and project into our future. Furman and Ahola address this situation as well.

REVISING THE PAST

Placed at the beginning of Furman and Ahola's chapter entitled "The Role of the Past" is the epigram: "It's never too late to have a happy childhood." In this chapter, they discuss the fact that we tend to view our past as the source of our problems. They argue that as long as we view the past this way, we set up an adversarial relationship with ourselves because our history is an integral part of us. This adversarial relationship with ourselves can be reduced, if not overcome, by viewing our past as "a resource, a store of memories, good and bad, and a source of wisdom emanating from life experience" (p. 18).

This re-visioning of our past is a reframing, as our past is placed in a new frame of meaning. It is no longer "the source of our problems" but "resource for solutions." As they put it:

> Even if solution talk tends to be focused on the future rather than the past, this does not mean that the talking about the past should become a forbidden or even an undesirable topic. The past does not need to be discussed in terms of the source of troubles but as a resource. One can learn to see one's past misfortunes as ordeals that, in addition to having caused suffering, have also brought about something valuable and worthwhile. (p. 36)

They emphasize that "the view that adverse life events—even being victimized—can later, in hindsight, be seen as valuable learning experiences does not in any way justify violence, abuse, or neglect" (p. 37). In making this point to their clients, they have often used the metaphor of healing bones: "Even if fractured bones may sometimes become stronger after healing, if does not justify fracturing bones. However strong a bone may become from recovering from an accidental fracture we do all in our power to protect ourselves and others from such injury" (p. 37). After all, we cannot know in advance whether the bone will heal stronger or weaker than before, or whether it will heal at all.

An illustration of this reframing of the past from source of problems to resource for solutions is Ben Furman's case entitled "Imagination in the Cupboard," involving a woman who was referred for therapy because of depression and constant weeping. Flora was struggling with a number of problems, all related to her two sons and her ex-husband. In contrast to her personal life, she was successful in her professional life. In her work with children she was respected for her creativity and her talent for establishing rapport with children.

In therapy, it came out that Flora's mother had a serious drinking problem, which caused Flora to be ashamed of her mother throughout her childhood. Until now, Flora had not shared with anyone her childhood experience of her mother. With tears running down her cheeks, she revealed that when her mother was drunk she used to shut Flora in a dark cupboard for long periods of time. Furman asked, "What did you do there in that dark cupboard? How did you pass the time?" With a miserable look on her face she explained that she used to make up all kinds of imaginary creatures to play with. To Furman's suggestion that what she used to do in the cupboard was responsible for the skills she now has with the children, Flora laughed heartily through her tears "as she suddenly became able to see her past in this tragicomic light" (p. 24).

Note here that Furman does not minimize the abuse that Flora suffered. There is no attempt to excuse Flora's mother for what she did. But he asks Flora a question that she did not anticipate, and one that you and I, in our concern to be truly sympathetic toward Flora, might not have been inspired to ask: "What did you do there in that dark cupboard? How did you pass the time?" The presumption is that Flora developed survival skills in the closet. She dissociated herself from her predicament, but did so in an unusually creative manner for so threatened a child. She "made up" imaginary creatures to play with. The fact that he knew that Flora was in fact a creative person today may well have been the source of his own insight that perhaps her creativity could be traced to her experience of victimization, and thus this may have prompted the question in the first place. In any event, through this insight the awful experience in the cupboard is reframed and is now seen as the occasion in which she put her autonomy to work. The one thing that her mother could not forbid her to do in the cupboard was to use her imagination, and this she did, creating imaginary creatures to play with there so that she would not be so utterly alone.

In his article entitled "The 'Midrash' and Biographic Rehabilitation," Mordechai Rotenberg, a professor of social work at The Hebrew University at Jerusalem, addresses the rehabilitative value of the statement, "I hope to have a good past."[5] This assertion, like Furman and Ahola's "It's never too late to have a happy childhood," seems nonsensical. As Rotenberg points out:

> Being reared to think in Western historically-based terms, we would probably dismiss such a declaration as senseless because we were taught to believe that our past is a closed book. Accordingly, we train our ex-criminals or ex-mental patients to redeem themselves either in a present based "here and now" existential salvation, or in a "not yet here and not yet now" futurist "clean leaf" rehabilitation by asking them to erase or accept their unchangeable failing past. (p. 41)

By advocating such rehabilitative formulas, however, "we rarely come to full terms with the problem of whether and how people are really capable of trading or integrating their old, failing, 'Mr. Hyde' self with a new, reborn, 'clean leaf,' 'Dr. Jekyll' self" (p. 41).

For Rotenberg, the question is why individuals must reject or hide their guilty or shameful pasts. Why aren't they enabled instead to "correct" their past so that it becomes integral to their new identity, both as a resource sustaining this identity and as the object of the rehabilitation that the new identity itself effects? In this way, one's subsequent rehabilitation "grants a new rereading of one's past . . . which retrospectively presents a relatively positive and harmonious image of one's total personality (including one's past) in one's own and one's society's eyes" (p. 42).

While Rotenberg, as a professor of social work, is especially concerned with the sociopathic personality, he recognizes that the method of "biographic rehabilitation" has universal application, as all of us, as Furman and Ahola point out, have some sort of adversarial relationship to our past and thus to ourselves.

Rotenberg's article traces this method of revising the past in the light of present intentions and future possibilities to the Midrash (i.e., the expositions and commentaries on biblical texts carried out by

---

5. Mordechai Rotenberg, "The 'Midrash' and Biographical Rehabilitation," *Journal for the Scientific Study of Religion* 25 (1986): 41–55.

teachers and rabbis), together with accompanying legends, stories, and parables that were developed in response to Judaism's need to apply the written law (Torah) to new conditions and circumstances of life. He suggests that the best way to understand how the possibility of biographic rehabilitation follows from the Midrash is to examine midrashic cases of rebiographing in the light of the concept of repentance (or *teshuva*).

One possible meaning of repentance is that one's sinful past is blotted out. It is forgiven or erased like a debt. Another is that one's sinful past is rectified. It is "cognitively and emotionally elevated and transformed into personal assets via the process of reinterpretation" (p. 44). Rotenberg says that the first possibility is problematic because it requires a kind of schizophrenic or amnesic disconnection from the past. The second possibility is more constructive because it maintains a relationship between present and past. But how can it be achieved? According to the midrashic interpretation of the Talmud, "the Talmud seeks to institutionalize a socio-cultural norm by which repenters will not merely be given a 'from now on' 'new leaf' chance, but be granted full 'biographic rehabilitation' by being permitted to correct, reinterpret or assign new meaning to their past failing history" (p. 44).

Rotenberg discusses several biblical examples of rebiographing, such as the reinterpreting of Rachel's theft of her father Laban's graven images by asserting that she took them in order to prevent her father from idol worship, or the absolving of King Solomon of sin for building places of worship for his Gentile wives. But perhaps the most interesting biblical instance of biographical rehabilitation is the story of Joseph, because here the method is not employed by a rabbi interpreting the story *ex post facto,* but is used by a major character in the story itself. Thus, with Joseph,

> we have the reconsideration of a seemingly detrimental callous act as an eventual useful event for humanity. What first appeared as the "sinful" selling of Joseph is reinterpreted by Joseph himself, when he assures his brother retroactively: "Ye thought evil against me, but God meant it for good . . . to save much people alive" (Genesis 50:20). (pp. 44–45)

This story provides, as it were, biblical warrant for the method of biographical rehabilitation itself.

Rotenberg argues, however, that for the rabbis to offer such reinterpretations, there must be evidence that the individual repented in a specific present. This, too, is reflected in the story of Joseph and his brothers because Joseph did not offer his brothers the above assurance until they had passed the test he set for them (that is, the chance to save themselves by allowing their youngest brother Benjamin to be made a scapegoat in their stead, an opportunity which they to their credit rejected out of hand).[6] Without such repentance and resolve to conduct oneself differently in the future, the reinterpretation of the sinful past makes no sense, as then there is no "new" present with which the "old" past needs to be reconciled. Thus, according to Rotenberg, "the Midrash use David's subsequent full repentance as a pivotal beginning point to reverse the meaning of David's earlier sins, in order to make possible the retrospective presentation of a positive and harmonious role-model image to encourage prospective repenters" (p. 47). Also, the fact that biographic rehabilitation was accorded to King Menase, who committed every possible sin under the sun, illustrates how far the rabbis were willing to go to rehabilitate an individual's past. This was a reflection of their own belief in the mercy of God and their conviction that "*prospective* self-renewal . . . is infinitely possible through the retrospective attribution of repentance . . ." (p. 49).

Rotenberg recognizes that the midrashic method of revising the past to fit with a repentant present may appear to be a major distortion of life, that "it is unrelated to the historical objectivity that underlies most psychodynamic rehabilitation formulas which must maintain a 'closed book' conception of the past" (p. 50). But he contends that the claim of historical objectivity is itself false, that when we tell the story of our past it can be told in alternative ways. It all depends upon the frame in which we situate these past experiences. On the other hand, to minimize the potential uses of biographical rehabilitation for purposes of denial (either one's own sins or the sins of others against us),[7] Rotenberg suggests that it is usually necessary "to first teach individuals to read their past from the angle of failure and delinquency and only after the repenting change has occurred, to help them reread the same past event from a broader and more constructive perspective" (p. 53). The same procedure would apply to individuals whose past requires rehabilitation because, like Joseph, they were victims of abuse; though,

6. On this point, see Sandor Goodhart, " 'I am Joseph': René Girard and the Prophetic Law," in Paul Dumouchel, ed., *Violence and Truth: On the Work of René Girard* (Stanford, Conn.: Stanford Univ. Press, 1985), 53–74.

7. Alice Miller, for example, claims that a major reason child abuse remains hidden is that we have great investment in sparing our parents, often out of the deep need to justify our propensity to live a trustful existence. See her *Thou Shalt Not Be Aware,* trans. Hildegaarde and Hunter Hannum (New York: A Meridian Book, 1986), 321ff; also, *For Your Own Good,* trans. Hildegaard and Hunter Hannum (New York: Farrar, Straus & Giroux, 1983), 251ff. See also Leonard Shengold, *Soul Murder: The Effects of Childhood Abuse and Deprivation* (New York: Fawcett Columbine, 1989), 115–17.

as in the case of Flora, the recognition that the abuser had no right whatsoever to do what she did would precede the recognition that something valuable occurred in the cupboard as Flora imagined that she was not really alone there.

Rotenberg also emphasizes the importance of "rebiographing" in the presence of others, for the "dialogical *intra*personal process by which one may freely contract or expand one's failing past may have minimal rehabilitative effects if it is not legitimized, i.e., socially re-inforced through a concomitant 'social contraction' process of *inter*personal dialogue" (p. 53). This is similar to Michael Lewis's discussion of the rehabilitative effects of confessing one's shame to another person who, because he or she has a certain social status or authority, is perceived to be able to extend forgiveness (cf. our discussion of shame in chapter five).

In short, Rotenberg's discussion of biographic rehabilitation in the Midrash tradition provides a religious rationale for Furman and Ahola's practice of encouraging individuals to view their past not as a source of problems but as a resource for solutions. This rationale, which involves the conviction both that God's mercy is boundless and that prospective self-renewal is infinitely possible, also provides a basis for hope. Rotenberg makes an explicit link between rebiographing and hope when he says that rebiographing addresses the "hope" to have a good past, suggesting that hopes can be entertained for the past as well as for the future.

Thus, the important contribution that rebiographing makes to pastoral care is its claim that the past is as open and possibility-filled as the future. To say this is to seem to speak nonsensically, for only a fool believes that the past can be other than what it was. Yet there is also wisdom—a kind of foolish wisdom—in this affirmation of the openness of the past, as it says that what is always open about the past is the meaning or significance we assign to it. In support of this view, we have Joseph's contention that the turning of his brothers' act of betrayal into a "useful event for humanity" is a viable method of reframing because it is grounded in the boundless mercy of God, who is able to take sinful actions that we or others committed in the past and make of them something better than we would ever have imagined.

To see God in this way is to recognize that God is the original and eternally Hopeful Self, who uses the autonomy that is God's own to hold both past and future open for ever new possibilities. That we exist at all, and that we may contemplate a future for ourselves, is due ultimately to the fact that it is God's very nature to be hopeful. We live because God, in response to God's own felt deprivation, was fueled by desire and perceived that something new could come into being. As James Weldon Johnson, author of the poem "Creation," expresses this: "And God stepped out on space, and he looked around and said: I'm lonely—I'll make me a world."[8] This world that God made is a *self-*projection, one into which God's very own self has been invested from the beginning until now and forever after.

Yet, this was a self-projection that carried great risk for God, as hopes, once realized, may take on a life of their own, having effects not originally intended. Hopes are wonderful things, but they are also dangerous, a fact to which the world, and especially the history of humankind, is tragic testimony. Thus, it is essential that we know that God remains a reliable Other who has not abandoned us, and that some of us be pastors, ones who, like Hopeful in *The Pilgrim's Progress,* assist others in keeping their heads above water, and who testify to, and carry in their very being, the risks inherent in hope itself.

Since I began by expressing doubt that I would have written this book if Erik Erikson had not placed hope—and religion—in the beginning stage of life, I will conclude with a poem by Joan M. Erikson, written only weeks before her husband's death.[9]

> *Hope*
> The word "Hope" the learned say
> is derived from the shorter one "Hop"
> and leads one into "Leap."
> Plato, in his turn, says that the leaping
> of young creatures is the essence of play—
> So be it!
>
> To hope, then, means to take a playful leap
> into the future—to dare to spring from firm ground—
> to play trustingly—invest energy, laughter;
> And one good leap encourages another—
> On then with the dance.

We cannot fall out of this world, so let hope spring eternal!

8. James Weldon Johnson, "The Creation," in *God's Trombones: Seven Negro Sermons in Verse* (New York: Penguin Books), 17.

9. Joan M. Erikson, unpublished poem. The poem appears on the back of the printed program for the service of "remembrance and celebration" of the life of her husband, Erik H. Erikson (1902–1994).

INDEX

Acedia, 107–12, 153
  See also Apathy
Acedic selves, 107, 112, 116–17, 120–22, 151
Adversaries of hope, 5, 26–27, 98–99, 135–38, 164
  See also Apathy, Despair, Shame
Agents of hope. *See* Pastors
Ahola, Tapani, 166–72
Allies of hope, 5, 27, 138, 161, 163
  See also Modesty, Patience, Trust
Angelus Silesius, 36
Anticipation, 34–36, 38–40, 43
Apathy
  and the acedic self, 107–17, 121–22
  and the sociopathic personality, 117–22
  as adversary of hope, 27, 98–99, 131, 135–38, 153–54, 164, 170
  See also Patience
Augustine, 49, 121
Autonomy, 46–51, 96

Bandler, Richard, 164–65
Beckett, Samuel, 110, 149–50
Benedek, Therese, 30, 140
Berger, Peter, 139–40, 142
Berra, Yogi, 166
Bipolar self, 126–30, 157–58
Blackwell, Albert, 141 n.6
Bradford, Gerald, 107 n.7
Bunyan, John, 3–4, 146–47, 176

Cabot, Richard C., 57 n.3
Capps, Donald, 5 n.3, 6 nn.6–8, 71 n.16, 107 n.7, 115 nn.13–14, 121 n.20, 131 n.33, 133 n.35, 134 n.37, 141 n.6, 164 n.1
Capps, Walter, 5–6, 43, 67 n.13, 99 n.1, 107 n.7
Caretakers, 31–32, 141–42
Chaucer, Geoffrey, 112–14, 116, 121–22, 153
Churchill, Winston, 154
Confession, 133–35
Constancy, 113, 117, 120–21, 153
Courage, 113, 117, 120–21, 153

David, 174
Depression, 101–5
Deprivation, 60–64, 77, 79, 83–86, 94
Desire
  and apathy, 108–11, 116
  educated, 111–12, 114, 121–22
  elevated, 111–12, 114, 120–22
  energized, 114–15, 121–22
  and hoping, 26, 35–36, 58–60, 63–64, 83–84, 105
  psychoanalytic approach, 111–14
Despair
  as adversary of hope, 27, 98–99, 105–7, 112–13, 135–38, 144, 146, 163, 170
  and depression, 101–5
  and disgust, 100, 105
  See also Trust

Dicks, Russell L., 57 n.3
Diligence, 113, 117, 120–21, 153
Dittes, James, 121 n.20
Dworkin, Gerald, 50, 147

Elkind, David, 149, 153
Erikson, Erik
    on autonomy, 48–50
    on despair, 100
    on hope's development, 6, 28–33,
        46–48, 176
    on hope's projection, 70, 76
    on the infant-mother relationship,
        31–33, 37, 44, 46–50, 140, 151
    on trust, 138
    on virtues, 29, 113–14
Erikson, Joan, 29, 176
Exodus, 67

Failure, 157–59, 161
Farley, Margaret, 95–96
Fear
    and religion, 142–44, 147
    v. trust, 142–44, 151, 161–62
Fortitude, 113, 117, 120–21, 153
Fowler, Gene, 57 n.3
Frankl, Viktor, 99
Freud, Sigmund, 66–67, 73, 140, 158
Frustration, 151–53, 161
Furman, Ben, 166, 168–72

Gilligan, Carol, 48–49
God, 58, 67–68, 141–44, 147, 161–
    62, 175–76
Goodhart, Sandor, 174 n.6
Grandiose self, 126–30, 157–58
Grinder, John, 164–65
Guilt, 123–25, 131
    See also Shame

Habel, Norman C., 150 n.11
Hammarskjöld, Dag, 153–54
Hope
    and autonomy, 28, 46–51, 96
    and the capacity to be alone, 45–
        46, 51
    as catalyst for change, 69–71
    as a creative illusion, 65–67
    defined, 52–53

development in life-cycle, 29–33,
    47–49
as envisioning the realizable, 71–
    75, 77, 79, 84–86, 94, 105
and God, 28, 36, 43, 46, 50–51,
    67–68, 144, 147, 161–62, 175–
    76
images of, 37–46, 51
and the imaging of God, 67–68
and love, 76, 94–95, 122
and the perception of the future,
    41, 51
as projection, 54, 64–71, 77, 79,
    85, 105, 123, 136
and reframing, 164–65, 175
and risk, 75–77, 85–89, 120, 131,
    157
and the role of pastors, 1–9, 13–
    15, 19–21, 25–28
and the self, 6–7, 28, 59–60, 73–
    75, 77–78, 135–36, 175–76
as self-projection, 68–69, 123,
    136, 176
and transitional experiences, 41–
    45, 47, 51
    See also Adversaries of hope,
        Allies of hope
Hoping
    contrasted with wishing, 33–43,
        46, 59–60
    defined, 52–53
    and desire, 26, 35–36, 59–60, 63–
        64, 83–84, 105, 108
    as perception, 53–58, 63, 71, 77,
        83–86, 105
    as a response to felt deprivation,
        60–64, 77, 79, 83–86, 94
    as a solitary act, 56–58
    as unexplainable, 54–56
Humor, 158–59

Ibsen, Henrik, 90–96, 130
Idealizing self, 126–30, 157–58
Images of hope. See Hope
Impermanence, 158–59

Jacob, 59, 104–5
James, 5, 150–52
James, William, 49, 142–44, 146–47

Jesus, 37, 50–51, 96–97, 133, 164
Job, 5, 60, 73, 150–52, 164
Johnson, James Weldon, 176
Jonah, 153
Jones, Ernest, 37
Joseph, 173–75
Judas, 113

Kaplan, Bert, 107–15, 121
Kasdorf, Julia, 97
Kaufman, Gershen, 129–33
Keats, John, 65–66, 74
Kierkegaard, Søren, 99
Kohut, Heinz, 126–28, 158–59
Kovel, Joel, 59
Kristeva, Julia, 58–59
Kübler-Ross, Elizabeth, 154

Lacan, Jacques, 58
Levertov, Denise, 162
Lewis, Michael, 133–35
Lifton, Robert Jay, 78 n.19
Long-term goals, 102–7, 118–19
Loss, 61–62, 72–73, 103
    See also Deprivation
Love, 30, 76, 94–95, 122
Loyalty, 102–7, 118–19
Luke, 51, 133
Lynch, William, 5
Lynd, Helen Merrell, 124–26

Marcel, Gabriel, 155–56
"Mary," 15–21, 26–27, 149, 153, 164
Matthew, 97
Meissner, W. W., 42–43
Meister Eckhart, 37
Melges, Frederick Townes, 63, 101–7, 117–19
Metz, Johannes, 6
Miller, Arthur, 75
Miller, Alice, 174 n.7
Modesty
    as ally of hope, 7, 27, 138, 154–61, 163
    v. failure, 157–60
Moltmann, Jürgen, 5–6, 67, 78, 99
Moral counseling
    limits of, 89–92

Norton, David L., 93–94, 96
Noyce, Gaylord, 92 n.2

Pasten, Linda, 154
Pastors
    as agents of hope, 1–6, 8–9, 13–15, 19–21, 25–28, 89–90, 98–99, 106–7, 115, 117, 163
    as moralists, 89–92
Patience
    as ally of hope, 5, 7, 27, 138, 148–54, 161, 163
    v. frustration, 151–53
Paul, 30, 38, 49, 73
Piers, Gerhart, 124
Pining, 34–36, 38–40, 43, 46, 51
Pride, 131–33
Projection, 64–65
    See also Hope
Proverbs, 104
Pruyser, Paul
    on hope, 5, 28, 33–36, 40, 43–47, 55, 60, 155–57
    on hope and religion, 36–38, 41–42
    on the role of pastors, 2–3
Psalms, 43, 45, 159–60

Rachel, 59, 104–5, 173
"Ramon," 21–27, 92, 164
Reframing, 5, 164–65
    as envisioning the future, 165–70
    as revising the past, 165, 170–75
Reik, Theodor, 40
Repentance, 173–74
Revelation, 45
"Rhoda," 80–82
    as illustration of hope, 79, 83–85
    moral implications, 89–92
    self-obligations, 92–96
    taking risks, 85–89
Rich, Adrienne, 148–49, 153
Rilke, Rainer Maria, 36, 67–68
Risk, 75–77, 85–89, 120, 131, 157
Ritual, 42–43, 45
Romans, 73
Rotenberg, Mordechai, 172–75

Sartre, Jean-Paul, 108

Schleiermacher, Friederich, 141–42
Scott, W. C. M., 33–38
Self-obligations, 92–97
Sellars, James, 83
Shame
    as adversary of hope, 27, 98–99,
        123–26, 135–38, 154–55, 164,
        170
    and the bipolar self, 126–29
    and confession, 133–35
    and pride, 131–33
    and striving for perfection, 130–31
    and striving for power, 129–31
    v. guilt, 123–25
    See also Modesty
Shengold, Leonard, 174 n.7
Singer, Milton, 124 n.21
Skill, 102–7, 118–19
Sociopathic personalities, 107, 117–
    122, 151, 172
    See also Apathy
Solomon, 173

Solzhenitsyn, Alexander, 53
Styron, William, 44

TeSelle, Eugene, 121 n.20
Tolstoy, Leo, 146–47
Transitional objects, 41–45, 47, 145,
    152
Trust
    as ally of hope, 7, 27, 138–47,
        154, 161, 163
    in a caretaker, 141–42, 145
    in a reliable other, 138–41, 145
    v. fear, 142–44, 151, 161–62

Virtues, 29, 113–14, 153

Waiting, 34, 36, 38–40, 43
"Wanda," 9–15, 26–27, 92, 163–64
Wimberly, Edward, 26 n.1
Winnicott, D. W., 41, 45, 145, 151–
    52
Wishing. *See* Hoping